T0355155

Propositional Content

Peter Hanks defends a new theory about the nature of propositional content. According to this theory, the basic bearers of representational properties are particular mental or spoken actions. Propositions are types of these actions, which we use to classify and individuate our attitudes and speech acts. Hanks abandons several key features of the traditional Fregean conception of propositional content, including the idea that propositions are the primary bearers of truth-conditions, the distinction between content and force, and the concept of entertainment. The main difficulty for this traditional conception is the problem of the unity of the proposition, the problem of explaining how propositions have truth conditions and other representational properties. The new theory developed here, in its place, explains the unity of propositions and provides new solutions to a long list of puzzles and problems in philosophy of language.

Peter Hanks is a Professor in the Department of Philosophy at the University of Minnesota. His research is in philosophy of language and the history of analytic philosophy.

CONTEXT AND CONTENT

Series editor: François Recanati, Institut Nicod

Other titles in the series:

The Inessential Indexical
On the Philosophical Insignificance of Perspective and the First Person
Herman Cappelen and Josh Dever

Fixing Reference
Imogen Dickie

Propositional Content
Peter Hanks

The Mirror of the World
Subjects, Consciousness, and Self-Consciousness
Christopher Peacocke

Assessment Sensitivity
Relative Truth and its Applications
John MacFarlane

Context
Robert C. Stalnaker

Conjoining Meanings
Semantics Without Truth-Values
Paul M. Pietroski

Propositional Content

Peter Hanks

OXFORD
UNIVERSITY PRESS

OXFORD
UNIVERSITY PRESS

Great Clarendon Street, Oxford, OX2 6DP,
United Kingdom

Oxford University Press is a department of the University of Oxford.
It furthers the University's objective of excellence in research, scholarship,
and education by publishing worldwide. Oxford is a registered trade mark of
Oxford University Press in the UK and in certain other countries

Published in the United States of America by Oxford University Press
198 Madison Avenue, New York, NY 10016, United States of America

British Library Cataloguing in Publication Data
Data available

Library of Congress Cataloging in Publication Data
Data available

ISBN 978-0-19-968489-2 (Hbk.)
ISBN 978-0-19-882271-4 (Pbk.)

Links to third party websites are provided by Oxford in good faith and
for information only. Oxford disclaims any responsibility for the materials
contained in any third party website referenced in this work.

For Francisca

Acknowledgments

This book started life as my 2002 UC Berkeley dissertation. Thanks first of all to my dissertation advisor, John Searle, whose wisdom and honesty have been crucial for me. He has been unflaggingly supportive, even though he disagrees with virtually everything I have to say.

In Spring 2012 I gave four lectures on this material at the Institut Jean-Nicod. Thanks to François Recanati for the invitation and for all of the conversations we've had about the content–force distinction. That whole experience in Paris gave me a huge boost of confidence and really made this book possible.

I owe an equally great debt to anonymous referees for *Mind* and *Philosophy and Phenomenological Research*, whoever you are. My view about propositional content took major steps forward in the course of revising (Hanks 2011) and (Hanks 2013a) for publication. Portions of these papers, and (Hanks 2013b), are reprinted here with kind permission from the publishers, Oxford University Press, John Wiley and Sons, and Taylor and Francis (www.tandfonline.com), respectively. Thanks also to three anonymous readers for Oxford University Press, who provided extremely useful and challenging comments on the manuscript. The same goes for Bjørn Jesperson and Indrek Reiland, who generously read and commented on an earlier draft.

In Fall 2011 Matt McGrath invited me out to Missouri to give a talk on propositions, and then he organized a symposium on propositions at the 2014 Chicago APA, with me, Scott Soames, Friederike Moltmann, and Jeff Speaks. Both experiences were incredibly helpful. Thanks again Matt.

David Taylor attended my seminar on propositions in Spring 2013 and saved me from a number of wrong turns. My conversations with David have continued and have been great. Sometimes I think he understands my view better than I do. Thanks also to the graduate students in that seminar, especially Melanie Bowman, Justin Kuster, and Patrick Laine.

Ben Caplan and his seminar at Ohio State read part of the book manuscript in Spring 2014. Thanks to Ben and the other members of the seminar, in particular Jenn Asselin and Scott Brown, for lots of great objections and constructive criticism.

Over the past decade or so I have given talks about propositional content at Indiana, St. Andrews, Bates College, Harvard, Minnesota, UC Davis, Minnesota-Duluth, UC Santa Cruz, Chapel Hill, St. Cloud State, Minnesota State Mankato, Missouri, Glasgow, Stirling, CSMN in Oslo, Columbia, Ohio State, Manitoba, and Texas Tech. I learned something at every single one of these events. Thanks to all of the audiences and to the people who put the time and effort into bringing me out to their institutions or conferences. Special thanks to Alexandra Arapinis, Gregory Bochner, Jason Bridges, Ray Buchanan, Matthew Chrisman, John Collins, Roy Cook, Jonathan Ginzburg, Alex Grzankowski, Marie Guillot, Bill Hanson, Daniel Harris, Geoffrey Hellman, Tom Hodgson, Thomas Hofweber, Christopher Hom, Graham Hubbs, David Hunter, Jeff King, Ernie Lepore, John MacFarlane, Doug Marshall, Michelle Mason, Marc Moffett, Friederike Moltmann, Michael Murez, Stephen Neale, Steve Nelson, Gary Ostertag, Brendan O'Sullivan, Chris Pincock, Gurpreet Rattan, Mark Richard, Jeremy Schwartz, Ori Simchen, Scott Soames, Isidora Stojanovic, Barry Stroud, Chris Tillman, Jack Woods, Nick Zangwill, and Dan Zeman. I'm sure I'm forgetting someone.

Since 2009 I have been the Director of Graduate Studies for the Department of Philosophy at Minnesota. This book would not be finished were it not for the tireless and cheerful effort of my assistant, Anita Wallace. In Fall 2014 I had the honor of being named the John Dolan Professor of Philosophy at the University of Minnesota, which freed up valuable time for me in the late stages of finishing the manuscript.

Most of all, thanks to my mother, father, and brother, my kids, Abraham, Mary Jane, and Theodore, and my wife, Francisca Reines. I saved the best for last.

Contents

Introduction   1

1. Three Pictures of Content   12
  1.1. The Fregean Picture   12
  1.2. An Alternative to the Fregean Picture   20
  1.3. Soames's Picture   33

2. The Problem of the Unity of the Proposition   42
  2.1. Going Primitive   43
  2.2. Frege on the Composition of Thoughts   47
  2.3. Russell on True and False Propositions   51
  2.4. King on Propositional Unity   55

3. Predication and Unity   64
  3.1. Acts of Predication   64
  3.2. Tokens, Types, and Truth Conditions   73
  3.3. Relational Propositions   80
  3.4. Quantified Propositions   87

4. Cancellation and the Content–Force Distinction   90
  4.1. Cancellation Contexts   90
  4.2. Truth, Negation, Target-shifting, and Anti-predication   98
  4.3. Conjunction and Disjunction   103
  4.4. Supposition and Hypothesis   108

5. Proper Names and Types of Reference Acts   113
  5.1. Rigidity   113
  5.2. Semantic Reference Types   116
  5.3. Paderewski and Ideal Conditions   120
  5.4. Semantic Competence with Names   122
  5.5. Frege's Puzzle About Identity   125
  5.6. Names and Translation   128

6. Empty Names   131
  6.1. Empty Names and Semantic Reference Types   131
  6.2. Existence and Target-shifting   135
  6.3. Problems and Objections   142

7. Propositional Attitude Reports   149
  7.1. That-clauses and Target-shifting   149
  7.2. Standard and Super-standard Contexts   152
  7.3. Extra Super-standard Contexts and Designation Types   155

7.4.	Sub-standard Contexts and the Paderewski Puzzle	156
7.5.	Propositional Attitude Relations	161
7.6.	Denial	166
8. First-person Propositions		**170**
8.1.	Context Sensitive Reference Acts	171
8.2.	*De Se* Reference	175
8.3.	First-person Propositions and Communication	179
8.4.	*De Se* Reports	182
9. Asking and Ordering		**186**
9.1.	Asking	186
9.2.	Wh-questions	189
9.3.	Ordering	194
9.4.	Non-declaratives in Attitude Reports	197
9.5.	Declarations and Other Non-propositional Speech Acts	199
Conclusion		**205**
References		213
Index		223

Introduction

We use propositional contents, and contents more generally, to identify, classify, and individuate our mental states and speech acts. In the attitude report 'Obama believes that Clinton is eloquent' we attribute a certain belief to Obama. Which belief? The belief that Clinton is eloquent. The attitude report tells us not just that Obama has some belief or other, but that he has this particular belief. It does this by relating Obama to a certain entity, the proposition that Clinton is eloquent. This is how we single out and attribute beliefs—by relating ourselves to these entities.

Suppose Obama also believes that Clinton is persistent. We take this to be a different belief than the belief that Clinton is eloquent. Why is this a different belief? Because it has a different propositional content, and propositional contents individuate beliefs. In reporting these beliefs we relate Obama to different propositions. The fact that these propositions are different shows that we regard the attributed beliefs as different. When we want to distinguish between different beliefs we do so by relating ourselves to different propositions. Propositions are the entities we use for individuating our beliefs.

The fact that this is how we individuate our mental states and speech acts is an instance of a wider strategy in natural language for describing and classifying objects. In a large range of cases we attribute properties to objects by relating those objects to abstract objects that fit together into structured systems. This is how we talk about height, weight, temperature, and age:

Obama is 6 feet 1 inches tall.
Obama weighs 180 pounds
Obama has a temperature of 98.6 °F.
Obama is 51 years old.

In each case the property attributed to Obama occupies a position in a range of similar properties. Instead of assigning a unique predicate to each property in the range, as we do with colors, we graft a numerical scale onto the range of properties and then relate objects to nodes on the scale. Of course, we do not use a numerical scale for attributing mental states and speech acts. Rather, the "scale" we use consists of a multidimensional space of propositions.

What lesson should we draw from this analogy between attitude reports and sentences about properties like height and weight? One might try to use it to gain insight into the nature of our mental states and speech acts. But this won't get us very far, for reasons that Wittgenstein nicely articulates in a remark about subject–predicate sentences:

Imagine two planes, with figures on plane *I* that we wish to map on to plane *II* by some method of projection. It is then open to us to fix on a method of projection (such as orthogonal projection) and then to interpret the images on plane *II* according to this method of mapping. But we could also adopt a quite different procedure: we might for some reason lay down that the images on plane *II* should all be circles no matter what the figures on plane *I* may be. That is, different figures on *I* are mapped on to *II* by different methods of projection. In order in this case to construe the circles in *II* as images, I shall have to say for each circle what method of projection belongs to it. But the mere fact that a figure is represented on *II* as a circle will say nothing. —It is like this with reality if we map it onto subject-predicate sentences. The fact that we use subject-predicate sentences is only a matter of our notation. (Wittgenstein 1975, 118–19)

Wittgenstein is surely right about this. The fact that a sentence is in subject-predicate form tells us next to nothing about the nature of the state of affairs that it represents. We gain no insight into what it is for an object to be green by observing that 'o is green' is in subject–predicate form. The subject–predicate form is an all-purpose linguistic tool we use for representing all sorts of disparate states of affairs.

There may be a little more to be gained from observing the relational form of attitude reports, but not much. The states of affairs we represent with attitude reports must be such as to allow us to represent them by relating people to propositions. This tells us something about the structure of our attitudes. Whatever beliefs really are, the totality of all possible belief-states must have a structure that lends itself to individuation by the multidimensional space of propositions (Matthews 2007). This is like saying: whatever the metaphysical or empirical nature of weight, the totality of weight properties must have a structure that corresponds somehow to the numerical scales we use to measure weight. That may be true, but we do not learn much from this about what it is for Obama to weigh 180 pounds.

Are there any other lessons to be learned from the analogy between attitude reports and sentences about height and weight? I think there are. We put the analogy to better philosophical use by applying it to questions about the nature of propositions. The point of the analogy is to highlight the fact that we classify and individuate mental states and speech acts by relating people to propositions, in much the same way that we classify people according to height and weight by relating them to nodes on height and weight scales. How should we think about these entities that we use to classify and individuate our attitudes and speech acts? This is the guiding question of this book.

In posing the question this way I am putting one of the traditional roles for propositions on center stage, namely their role as the objects of the attitudes. Another traditional role for propositions is to be the original or primary bearers of truth conditions. To accept this role for propositions is to take on an explanatory commitment: the possession of truth conditions by anything other than a proposition, e.g. a belief, assertion, or sentence, is to be explained by its relation to a proposition with those truth conditions. Propositions are supposed to be the original or primary bearers of truth conditions in the sense that they have their truth conditions in an explanatorily basic way. Now, I think that propositions have truth conditions. (Or, at least, I think that one kind of proposition has truth conditions, the assertive kind. As we will see, I am going to argue that there are three different varieties of propositions, only one of which has truth conditions.) But I reject the idea that propositions are the *primary* bearers of truth conditions. This idea is a relic of a Fregean picture of content and thought that I think we must abandon. On this Fregean picture, propositions are out there, with their truth conditions intact, waiting to be judged and asserted. A subject latches onto one of these propositions—Frege calls this "grasping a thought"— and then goes on to endorse it in thought (judgment) and put it forward as true in speech (assertion). The truth conditions of the judgment and assertion then come from the proposition grasped by the subject. I believe we need to reverse the explanatory order. Propositions get their truth conditions from particular acts of judgment and assertion, which are themselves the original or primary bearers of truth and falsity. The source of truth conditions is to be found in the acts of representation we perform when we make judgments and assertions, not in the propositional contents we use to classify and individuate these actions. More precisely, the source is to be found in acts of *predication* through which, in the simplest cases, people attribute properties and relations to objects. The explanation for why propositions have truth conditions must appeal to these acts of predication.

In broad strokes, this is how I propose to solve the problem of the unity of the proposition, which is best understood as the problem of explaining how propositions have truth conditions. The Fregean picture makes this problem intractable. This is not because of Frege's commitment to senses as the constituents of propositions. Russell's conception of propositions founders on the unity problem just as much as Frege's does. The source of the problem for both Frege and Russell was their acceptance of a picture of the relation between content and thought on which the contents of judgments have their representational features in a way that is explanatorily prior to the representational features of particular acts of judgment. This is what I am calling the Fregean picture of content and thought, and Russell (for a time, at least) accepted this picture as much as Frege. The picture bars us from appealing to the actions that people perform in thinking and speaking about the world when we want to understand how propositions have their truth conditions. This is hopeless. Representation and truth conditions begin with acts of predication, and propositions inherit their representational features from these acts. Expanding on this alternative to the Fregean picture, and using it to solve the problem of the unity of the proposition, is the primary aim of chapters 1–4.

The third traditional role for propositions is to be the contents of sentences. We characterize and classify our sentences by relating them to propositions in much the same way we do with mental states and speech acts. To say that 'Clinton is eloquent' and 'Clinton est éloquent' express the same proposition is to classify these sentences together according to a semantic scheme of classification. We divide up sentences along semantic lines by relating them to propositions. This allows us to pose an analog of the question I raised earlier. How should we think about these entities that we use to classify and individuate our sentences? I won't have much to say directly about this question in this book, although I will have a lot to say about the contents of subsentential expressions, including proper names, indexicals, demonstratives, predicates, connectives, quantifiers, and wh-expressions. I am going to propose accounts of the semantic contents of all of these expressions, although I won't have anything directly to say about the semantic contents of sentences. Still, my aim is to indirectly answer this question about the contents of sentences by answering the corresponding question about the contents of mental states and speech acts. It should be clear that we use the same system of entities to classify our beliefs as we do our sentences. If this weren't the case then it would be mysterious how understanding the sentence someone uttered can tell us what she believes, or how we use sentences in the complement clauses of attitude reports to attribute beliefs. Beliefs and sentences must share the same contents, for otherwise we couldn't use sentences to express and attribute beliefs. A theory of the propositional contents of beliefs and assertions will therefore also be a theory of the propositional contents of sentences.

The central question of this book concerns the nature of the entities we use to classify and individuate our mental states and speech acts. This is how I would like to approach the issue of the nature of propositional content. But let's first ask a more general question. What sorts of entities in general do we use for classifying things? There is a tightly connected family of entities that serve this purpose: properties, relations, types, concepts, characteristic functions, sets. Each item on this list bears a special relationship to things that "fall under it". Objects instantiate properties and relations. Types have tokens. Concepts apply to things. Characteristic functions map some of their arguments to 1. Sets have members. These special relationships make these entities classificatory by nature. The property of being green, by its nature, classifies things into two groups, the things that instantiate it and those that don't.

Propositions have their own special relationship to the things they classify. Beliefs and assertions have propositions as their contents. This is the sense in which beliefs and assertions "fall under" a proposition. The proposition that Clinton is eloquent, by its nature, sorts things into two groups, those things that have it as content and those that don't. Obama's belief that Clinton is eloquent falls into the first group, his belief that Clinton is persistent falls into the other (along with lots of other things that don't have content at all, like my desk). In the case of sentences we have a term for this special relationship to propositions. We say that a sentence *expresses* a proposition. Propositions sort sentences into those that express them and those that don't.

My point here is that propositions fit neatly into this family of classificatory entities. This raises a question about whether we can profitably think about propositions by assimilating them to another member of this family. I think we can. We make headway in understanding our practices of identifying and reporting attitudes and speech acts by identifying propositions with types. More precisely, types of actions—the types of actions we engage in when we form mental states or perform speech acts. The tokens of these types are the mental and spoken actions that we classify with propositions, as well as the states that result from these actions. Propositions identify, classify, and individuate our mental states and speech acts in the same way that types identify, classify, and individuate their tokens. A judgment or assertion has a propositional content in the sense that it is a token of the type that is that propositional content.

Let's return for a moment to the analogy between propositional content and attributes like height and weight. How should we think about the entities that we use to classify height and weight? Philosophers who have noticed the analogy tend to hold that measurement sentences report relations between people and numbers. According to Stalnaker, for example, "height in inches, weight in pounds, age in years, are all nonintentional relations between persons, or other physical objects, and numbers" (Stalnaker 1987, 8).[1] On this view, when we say that Obama is 73 inches tall we relate Obama to the number 73. For this to make sense, the relation involved must be something like the two-place relation x-has-height-in-inches-y. This builds the units into the relations, not into the entities to which we are relating Obama. The sentence 'Obama is 73 inches tall' would be written semi-formally as 'Height-in-inches (Obama, 73)'. 'Obama is 185.42 cm tall' would be 'Height-in-centimeters (Obama, 185.42)'. Weight and temperature reports will also have to fit this model. On this way of viewing measurement sentences, we use these relations to report heights, weights, temperatures, and ages by attributing them to objects and nodes on a single, all-purpose scale—the number line.

---

[1] See also (Matthews 2007, 124) and (Davidson 1989, 59; 1997, 83).

This departs in substantial ways from how we intuitively think about measurement. Inches and centimeters give us different scales for measuring height. Switching from Imperial/American to Metric is to change from one system of entities for measurement to another. This should be obvious for temperatures. It is a truism to say that Fahrenheit and Celsius are different temperature scales. Philosophers who think that measurement reports relate objects to numbers have to deny this. These philosophers hold that there is a single numerical scale used for all measurement sentences, and the differences between these sentences are just a matter of the different relations attributed to objects and numbers on the single all-purpose scale. The obvious alternative is to take the varieties of measurement reports to involve different scales. This amounts to building the units into the entities to which we relate objects in making measurement reports. When we say that Obama has a temperature of 98.6 °F we relate Obama to a temperature, 98.6 °F, which is a node on the Fahrenheit temperature scale. When we say that he has a temperature of 37 °C we relate him to 37 °C, a different node on a different scale. Measurement sentences report relations between objects and things like lengths, weights, and temperatures, not between objects and numbers.

But what are entities like 98.6 °F or 37 °C? What is a temperature or a length or a weight? It makes intuitive sense to identify these entities with types. 180 pounds is a type whose tokens all have the same weight. To say that Obama weighs 180 pounds is to say that he is a token of this type. The relation expressed by 'weighs' is a tokening relation, and similarly for the other measurement relations. To say that Obama is 51 years old is to say that he is a token of the type 51 years old.

The same goes for the relations we bear to propositions. Judgment and assertion are tokening relations. To say that Obama judged that Clinton is eloquent is to relate Obama to a certain type of action, the proposition that Clinton is eloquent. Obama bears the judgment relation to this type in the sense that he performed a judgment that is a token of this type. Propositions are types of actions, and propositional attitude relations are tokening relations. I develop this idea further in chapter 7, where I explain how this view applies to mental states like belief, as well as some obvious problem cases, such as the attitude of denial.

Here then are some of the central theses of this book. Propositions are types of actions we use to identify, classify, and individuate our mental states and speech acts. Judgments and assertions have propositional contents in the sense that they are tokens of these types. The relations we bear to propositions, such as judgment and assertion, are tokening relations. In performing tokens of these types we perform acts of predication that are the explanatorily basic bearers of truth conditions. Propositions have truth conditions because they are types of these actions, which inherit representational features from their tokens.

One of the ways I will build a case for these claims is by showing how the identification of propositions with types solves a long list of problems in philosophy of language. I am going to use this account to give solutions to Frege's puzzles about substitution in identity sentences (chapter 5) and attitude reports (chapter 7), Kripke's puzzles about belief, both the London/Londres version and the Paderewski version (chapter 7), the problem of empty names and true negative existentials (chapter 6), and the problem of *de se* belief (chapter 8). These solutions will make heavy use of what I call *semantic reference types*. These are certain types of reference acts, for example, a type of reference act Obama performs when he uses the name 'Clinton'. Very roughly, and putting aside lots of complications, two acts of reference fall under the same semantic reference type just in case anyone who is semantically competent with the terms used in those acts will know that those two acts co-refer. I work through all the complications in chapter 5.

The key to all of these solutions will be the identification of the semantic contents of names, indexicals, and demonstratives with semantic reference types. This is neither a Millian nor a Fregean descriptivist approach to the contents of referential terms. The content of the name 'Clinton' is not Clinton herself, nor is it a Fregean mode of presentation of Clinton. It is a certain way of referring to Clinton. Although this is not a descriptivist approach to proper names, it is closer in spirit to the Fregean view than the Millian. The identification of the contents of names with semantic reference types implies that most syntactically distinct co-referential names have different semantic contents. On my account 'Hesperus' and 'Phosphorus', 'Cicero' and 'Tully', 'Mark Twain' and 'Sam Clemens', will all be assigned different contents. I have already hinted at the reason for this. It is possible to be semantically competent with the names 'Hesperus' and 'Phosphorus' and yet fail to realize that uses of these names co-refer. That is why uses of these names fall under different semantic reference types, and why the names themselves have different contents. Our semantic scheme of classification puts these names into different categories.

Despite the fact that this account of names is more Fregean than Millian, the larger theoretical framework for the account is decidedly un-Fregean. As I mentioned above, my aim is to provide an alternative to the Fregean picture of content and thought. A central component of this Fregean picture is the distinction between content and force. On one way of understanding this distinction it is the idea that speech acts with different forces all share the same propositional contents. Frege held, for example, that the contents of assertions are the same as the contents of yes–no questions.[2] Let's call this the taxonomic version of the content–force distinction. This is the view that there is a single kind of propositional content, with truth conditions, running through all the different kinds of attitudes and speech acts. On another way of understanding the content–force distinction, it is the view that there is nothing distinctively assertive about propositional contents. Frege, of course, also believed this. He held that "two things must be distinguished in an assertoric sentence: the content, which it has in common with the corresponding propositional question; and assertion" (Frege 1918a, 329). Let's call this the constitutive version of the content–force distinction.

I think we should reject both the taxonomic and constitutive versions of the content–force distinction. Assertive, interrogative, and imperative speech acts have different kinds of propositions as contents, and these propositions are individuated using concepts of force. I think there are assertive, interrogative, and imperative propositions. This three-way distinction between propositions lines up with the three-way distinction in English between declarative, interrogative, and imperative sentences.

---

[2] This is Frege's mature view, the view he expressed in "Thought" (Frege 1918a). In "On Sense and Reference" (Frege 1892a) he distinguishes between the contents of declarative, interrogative, imperative and optative sentences, calling these thoughts, questions, commands, and wishes respectively. Even in the later work he continued to distinguish between thoughts, on the one hand, and commands and wishes on the other:

> We should not wish to deny sense to a command, but this sense is not such that the question of truth could arise for it. Therefore I shall not call the sense of a command a thought. Sentences expressing wishes or requests are ruled out in the same way. (Frege 1918a, 329)

This means that Frege himself never accepted the taxonomic content–force distinction in full generality.

The distinction between kinds of propositions is marked in our language by the differences in sentential mood.

This means, of course, that I have to confront Frege's arguments for the content–force distinction. His most powerful argument begins with the undeniable fact that it is possible to utter a declarative sentence, without any change in content, without asserting it. This happens when we use declarative sentences inside conditionals or disjunctions, or when an actor utters a sentence onstage as a line in a play, or when a poet writes down a sentence while composing a poem. Generations of philosophers have followed Frege in concluding from these phenomena that assertion is wholly separate from the propositional contents of declarative sentences.

This conclusion is too hasty. Another way to look at this is to hold that the content of a declarative sentence does have a distinctively assertive element, but this element is cancelled when the sentence is used in certain linguistic or practical contexts. These contexts include the use of a sentence after the word 'if', or on stage, or in poetry. An assertoric element is built into the proposition, but it is cancelled under certain conditions and in certain contexts. Explaining and defending this notion of cancellation is a major task of this book (chapter 4).

The content–force distinction is part of a package of views that I am calling the Fregean picture of propositional content. Earlier I mentioned another important part of this package—the concept of grasping or entertaining a proposition. (Here I am using the terms 'grasping' and 'entertaining' interchangeably, but this will change when we get to chapter 8.) There is no such thing as entertainment, as Frege understood it. Fregean entertainment is supposed to be a kind of neutral cognitive contact between a person and a proposition, which serves as necessary precursor to, or ingredient in, judgment and assertion. This is an illusion bred of unquestioning acceptance of the Fregean picture. In most cases, when we make a judgment we just predicate a property of something. There does not have to be any bare contemplation of a proposition prior to this act of predication, and there is no compelling reason to think that somehow contained inside the act of predication there is something neutral and non-committal.

Here is the plan for the book. In chapters 1–4 I will set out and defend my alternative to the Fregean picture of propositional content. In doing so, I will solve the problem of the unity of the proposition, explain my notion of cancellation, and argue against Fregean entertainment. In chapters 5 and 6 I turn to proper names and semantic reference types. This is where I solve Frege's puzzle about identity statements, as well as the problem of empty names and negative existentials. In chapter 7 I will give a detailed semantic analysis of propositional attitude reports, which will solve Frege's and Kripke's puzzles about belief. In chapter 8 I will use semantic reference types to give accounts of the semantic contents of indexicals and demonstratives. A solution to the problem of *de se* belief will fall directly out of these accounts. Finally, in chapter 9 I extend my theory of propositions to interrogatives and imperatives, propose a semantic account of wh-expressions, and suggest an alternative to Searle's taxonomy of speech acts.

Finally, in the conclusion I will make some brief remarks about three areas for future work. The first has to do with the connection between the theory of propositional content in this book and Wittgenstein's rule-following considerations, the second concerns the relationship between mental and spoken acts of predication, and the third bears on the debate about whether perceptual experiences are representational.

1

Three Pictures of Content

The purpose of this chapter is to give preliminary characterizations of three different views about content and its relation to judgment and assertion. One of these is the Fregean picture I mentioned in the introduction, the second is the one I will defend, and the third is due to Scott Soames (Soames 2010, 2012, forthcoming; King, et al. 2014). Soames's picture is a halfway point between my picture and Frege's, which makes it useful for clarifying the contrasts between the three positions. I won't try to argue for my view or against the Fregean view in this chapter. That is what the rest of the book is for. I will, however, try to convince you that Soames's picture is an uncomfortable compromise.

1.1 The Fregean Picture

The following is a familiar and widely held picture of the relation between content, judgment, and assertion. The picture is rarely argued for or even made explicit. It operates largely in the background of much contemporary philosophy of language and mind. In setting out this picture I am going to rely heavily on Frege's writings, but my aim is not Frege interpretation. It may be that this Fregean picture is one that Frege never really held (Ricketts 1986; Kremer 2000). The picture could with equal justice be attributed to Russell, for a time at least, and there are parts of it, especially in connection with truth and judgment, that are definitely more Russellian than Fregean. Nevertheless, it remains true that the picture has its hold on contemporary philosophers because of Frege's clear, powerful, and oft-repeated exposition.

There are mind-independent, objective propositional contents. These contents are not ideas or mental images or conscious episodes of any kind. They are not the products of mental processes or inner acts. A propositional content does not belong to any one particular person, it is not created by anyone, and it does not vary from one person to another. Propositional contents are sharable, in the sense that many people can think or entertain the very same content. They are repeatable, in the sense that one person can entertain the same content on many different occasions. But propositional contents do not depend on being thought or entertained for their existence. They were there before anyone ever thought about them, "just as a desolate island in the Arctic Ocean was there long before anyone had set eyes on it" (Frege 1979, 133).

Truth and falsity are, in the first instance, properties of these mind-independent propositional contents. Their possession of these properties is independent of our recognition of them as true or false. It is independent of our thinking of them at all. There are true propositions that no one has ever recognized as true, and there are true propositions that no one has ever entertained. We cannot make propositions true, or change their truth-values, by entertaining or judging them. Judgment does not generate entities with the properties of being true and false. Propositional contents are already there, with their truth-values, waiting to be entertained and judged.

There are other things that have the properties of truth and falsity, but they have these properties in a way that is secondary or derivative from the truth and falsity of propositions. Sentences, judgments, beliefs, and assertions are true and false, but only because they express propositions, or have propositions as their contents. The truth conditions and truth-values of these other things are just the truth conditions and truth-values of the propositions they have as contents. A proposition is true or false in itself. Sentences, judgments, beliefs, and assertions are true or false because of the relations they bear to propositions.

The Fregean picture has a top-down structure for the explanation of truth conditions. At the top are propositions (in Frege's third realm). Underneath are sentences, judgments, beliefs, and assertions. In explaining why a judgment has its truth conditions we must first make reference to a proposition and then explain how the judgment bears a special relationship to this proposition. The judgment takes on the truth conditions of the proposition to which it bears this relationship. The direction of explanation is from propositions to anything else that bears truth conditions. This is to view propositions as a source of truth conditions. Propositions are treated as a repository of truth conditions and representation, which we make use of in thought and language.

In order to judge or assert a proposition you must entertain it, or "grasp" it. Frege has a number of related metaphors he uses for this:

> The metaphors that underlie the expressions we use when we speak of grasping a thought, of conceiving, laying hold of, seizing, understanding, of *capere, percipere, comprehendere, intelligere*, put the matter in essentially the right perspective. What is grasped, taken hold of, is already there and all we do is take possession of it. Likewise, what we see or single out from amongst other things is already there and does not come into existence as a result of these activities. (Frege 1979, 137)

To grasp or entertain a proposition is to take hold of it, but not in a literal sense. We do not literally reach out and grab propositions. Propositions are not spatial or material things, and we cannot touch them or see them. Frege also says that to grasp a proposition is to "take possession of it". But again, he cannot mean this literally. A proposition does not become mine when I grasp it. Propositions do not literally belong to anyone.

What is he trying to get at with these metaphors? The least metaphorical, and hence the most helpful, is the idea that to entertain a proposition is to "single out" that proposition. A myriad of propositions are out there, prior to anyone's ever thinking about them. To make a judgment or assertion one must first identify which proposition in this myriad is to be judged or asserted. This is what entertainment does for us. We grasp, seize, and lay hold of a proposition in the sense that we single out and identify that proposition. Dummett says that grasping a proposition is "fixing one's attention on it" (Dummett 1981, 298). This makes it clear why entertainment is a necessary element in judgment. You must first identify the proposition you are going to judge before you can judge it. On the Fregean picture, judgment is a two-part process: first you identify a proposition and then you affirm it, endorse it, or acknowledge its truth. Affirmation cannot happen without entertainment, although it does not have to happen *after* entertainment. You can grasp a proposition and then affirm it, or you can do both at once. In the latter case we can still distinguish between a neutral identificatory component of the act and a non-neutral affirmative component.

But the idea that we single out propositions cannot be all there is to the notion of entertainment. You can identify a proposition in an oblique way without entertaining it, for example with an expression like 'the proposition Obama asserted'. In addition to the "laying hold of" metaphors, Frege also explains grasping by saying that we comprehend and understand propositions. Propositional contents are essentially *thinkable* entities (Frege chose to call them 'thoughts'). To entertain a proposition is to single it out *by* thinking, comprehending, or understanding it.

What is it to think, comprehend, or understand a proposition? Most philosophers would decline to answer. These notions are regarded as primitive. Better to ask for examples of entertainment that occur in the absence of judgment and assertion.

For Frege, pure cases of grasping propositions occur when we ask yes–no questions.

An advance in science usually takes place in this way: first a thought is grasped, and thus may perhaps be expressed in a propositional question; after appropriate investigations, this thought is finally recognized to be true. (Frege 1918a, 330)

When a scientist asks 'Is oxygen condensable?' she grasps a propositional content, the same one she could go on to assert by uttering 'Oxygen is condensable'. In fact, in asking the question she grasps two propositions, the proposition that oxygen is condensable and the proposition that oxygen is not condensable. Frege says that "we grasp the content of a truth before we recognize it as true, but we grasp not only this; we grasp the opposite as well" (Frege 1979, 7). In asking questions we grasp propositions in pairs.

Pure cases of entertainment also occur when we understand sentences and linguistic utterances. Frege wrote that "the thought, in itself imperceptible by the senses, gets clothed in the perceptible garb of a sentence, and thereby we are enabled to grasp it" (Frege 1918a, 328). Understanding a sentence involves entertaining the proposition that is the content of the sentence. You are doing that right now as you read this sentence. The same thing occurs when you understand an assertion. To understand someone's assertion is at least in part to grasp the proposition she has asserted. It is not enough for this merely to single out the proposition she asserted. I can identify the proposition someone asserted without understanding her assertion. Suppose I happen to know that Obama and Clinton asserted the same thing at separate news conferences. Then I can identify the proposition Clinton asserted—it's the same one Obama asserted at his news conference—but I don't know what Clinton asserted. To know that I have to comprehend the content of her assertion.

Yes–no questions and linguistic understanding are examples of pure entertainment—entertainment in the absence of judgment or assertion. In Frege's writings, however, entertainment is introduced and most often discussed as a necessary preliminary to judgment. First and foremost, entertainment is something you have to do in order to make a judgment. This brings us to the Fregean conception of judgment. In his early work Frege says that judgment is "inwardly to recognize something as true" (Frege 1979, 7). In later work he changes this to "the acknowledgement of the truth of a thought" (Frege 1918a, 329). Frege scholars have recently begun trying to understand what these claims mean (Heck and May 2006; Textor 2010). There is agreement that he did not mean that to judge a proposition is to attribute the property of truth to it, since that leads to a dilemma. The act of attributing a property to an object is either to judge that the object has that property, or it is a neutral, non-committal form of property attribution. The first horn leads to a regress. To attribute the property of truth to a proposition is to judge that the proposition is true. To judge that p is then judging that p is true, which is judging that <that p is true> is true, which is judging that <<that p is true> is true> is true, and so on. On the second horn, attributing the property of truth to a proposition p is not sufficient for judging that p. It is tantamount to entertaining the proposition that p is true. Furthermore, for Frege, there is no difference between the proposition that p is true and the proposition that p (Frege 1892a, 158). If attribution is non-committal, then attributing the property of truth to the proposition that p is nothing more than entertaining the proposition that p. On either of these horns, then, judgment cannot be a matter of attributing the property of truth to a proposition.

What, then, does Frege mean when he says that judgment is the acknowledgment of the truth of a thought? Perhaps it is best to view judgment as a primitive in Frege's system, in which case there is no informative answer to be found. As Frege put it, "judgment is something quite peculiar and incomparable" (Frege 1892a, 159). Our primary concern, however, is not with the interpretation of Frege. Our concern is with the contemporary manifestation of the Fregean picture, as it operates in current philosophy of language and mind. On this contemporary version of the picture, judgment is an attitude toward a proposition (this is a point at which Russell's influence is felt). It is a matter of taking a certain stance toward a proposition. To judge that p is to endorse it in thought, to accept it, to undertake a commitment to it. The propositional content is there with its truth-value. To judge the proposition you take hold of it by entertaining it, and then you make an additional move. You ratify it, approve it, sanction it, assent to it. Note that we cannot say that to judge the proposition is to take it to be true. That would generate the same sort of regress that came up just now in the discussion of Frege's account of judgment. To take a proposition to be true is just to judge it to be true, which rules out an explanation of judgment as taking a proposition to be true. It may be that as a matter of necessity whenever you judge that p you also judge that p is true. Whether this is so raises difficult issues about whether it is possible to make judgments at all without having the concept of truth (Davidson 1975, 1982). We can bypass these issues by restricting the generalization in the following way: for anyone who possesses the concept of truth, judging that p is necessarily conjoined with judging that p is true. Even so, these are two distinct judgments, and the former cannot be analyzed as the latter on pain of regress.

Entertainment and judgment are both inner, mental acts. When we turn to outer, spoken acts we find an analogous pair of actions. This is the distinction between expression and assertion. Just as entertainment is a necessary, neutral kernel inside judgment, expression is a necessary, neutral kernel inside assertion. You cannot assert a proposition without expressing it, although you can express it without asserting it. To express a proposition is to present a proposition in such a way that it can be grasped by an audience, and it is possible to do that without asserting the proposition. According to Frege, pure cases of expression occur in acting and poetry:

If a man says something with assertoric force which he knows to be false, then he is lying. This is not so with an actor on stage, when he says something false. He is not lying, because assertoric force is lacking. (Frege 1979, 234)

In poetry we have the case of thoughts being expressed without being actually put forward as true, in spite of the assertoric form of the sentence. (Frege 1918a, 330)

The actor and poet are verbally presenting propositions to their audiences, although they are not asserting these propositions. Like entertainment, to express a proposition is not merely to identify or single out that proposition for someone else's benefit. I can single out a proposition without enabling you to grasp it. To express a proposition requires performing an utterance that makes the proposition available to be entertained by a hearer who understands that utterance. Expression is a way of singling out a proposition for an audience by way of getting the audience to entertain that proposition.

Expression is necessary for assertion, but not sufficient. To assert a proposition is to express it and thereby put the proposition forward as true. For Frege, assertion is the manifestation of a judgment (Frege 1918a, 329). In an assertion you manifest the fact that you have made a judgment with a certain propositional content. For this to have any chance of being correct the concept of manifestation has to be understood in such a way that one can manifest a mental state that one does not have. We can obviously assert things we do not believe. If assertion is the manifestation of a judgment, then it must be possible to manifest a judgment that has not been made. Manifesting a judgment is something like exhibiting yourself as having made a judgment, where that is possible without having actually made the judgment. The trouble now is understanding why the actor and poet do not meet this condition. In any case, Frege's basic thought is clear. An assertion is an outward, verbal display of an inner state, a judgment or belief. To make an assertion is to give voice to this inner state.

Frege's idea that assertion is essentially the expression of an attitude is now one of several approaches to assertion. Some other recent approaches hold that assertion is a move in a language game defined by certain constitutive rules (Williamson 1996), or that assertion is an attempt to add information to the conversational common ground (Stalnaker 1999), or that assertion is the undertaking of certain commitments (Brandom 1983, 1994; Macfarlane 2005).[1] There are interesting differences between these views, but these differences do not matter for our purposes. The point I want to draw out is that each of these views about assertion incorporates, or is at least consistent with, Frege's distinction between merely expressing a proposition and asserting it. Each allows us to factor an act of assertion into a neutral act of expressing a proposition and some non-neutral, assertive addition.

These approaches to assertion are also amenable to another Fregean distinction—the distinction between content and force. There are two

---

[1] Here I follow the taxonomies of approaches to assertion in (Macfarlane 2011) and (Cappelen 2011).

ways of understanding the content–force distinction, one taxonomic and the other constitutive. I mentioned these in the introduction. On the taxonomic understanding, the content–force distinction is the view that speech acts with different forces all share the same truth-conditional contents. To accept the taxonomic version of the distinction is to hold that an assertion that Clinton will be eloquent, a question whether Clinton will be eloquent, and a command to Clinton to be eloquent all have the proposition that Clinton will be eloquent as their shared content. The idea is that there is a truth-conditional core in each of these speech acts, in the form of a shared propositional content, which is put forward in different ways in the different speech acts. In the assertion the speaker puts the proposition forward as true, in the question the speaker asks whether it is true, and in the command the speaker tries to bring it about that it is true. As I noted earlier, Frege never fully endorsed this idea. In "On Sense and Reference" (Frege 1892a), he distinguishes between thoughts, questions, and commands, where these are the contents of declarative, interrogative, and imperative sentences, respectively. He reverses himself in later work, but only for declaratives and yes–no interrogatives. All along he recognized a separate category of propositional contents for imperatives, which he called commands. Even this attenuated form of the distinction is abandoned in the current semantic literature on interrogatives. It is now commonplace to distinguish questions, the contents of interrogatives, from propositions (Groenendijk and Stokhof 1997).

The constitutive version of the content–force distinction, which is really the heart of the distinction and central to the Fregean picture of content, is the idea that there is nothing inherently assertive about the propositional contents of assertions. Similarly, there is nothing interrogative about the contents of interrogative speech acts, nor anything imperative about the contents of orders. On this view, propositional contents are devoid of any feature that has to be characterized using concepts of force. Concepts of force characterize our actions. Propositional contents are prior to these actions and do not depend on them for their natures or representational features. This view is upheld even by those philosophers who reject the taxonomic version of the content–force distinction.

It is important to see how deeply embedded the constitutive version of the content–force distinction is in the Fregean picture of content. The

Fregean picture starts by positing a realm of mind-independent, objective propositions. These propositions are utterly independent of our mental and spoken actions. In making judgments and assertions we latch onto these propositions and do various things with them, but the propositions themselves are ontologically and constitutively independent of these actions. Propositions are not artifacts. They are not created by us and do not owe their intrinsic or essential properties to us. We put propositions to various uses in thought and communication, but the propositions themselves are not defined by these uses. Consider a stone that can be used as a tool, for example for cutting. The stone itself is not something that is constituted by its being put to this use. A scientific or metaphysical account of the stone need not mention the fact that it can be used for cutting. This is unlike a knife, which has its purpose built into its nature or essence or definition. The concept of cutting has to figure in a theory or analysis of the nature of the knife. Accepting the constitutive version of the content–force distinction involves viewing propositions as more like stones than knives. They are entities that we put to various uses in thought and talk, but these uses are just as incidental to the natures of these entities as its use as a cutting instrument is to the stone. Concepts of judging, asserting, asking, and ordering have no place in a theory of what propositions are. This is the conception of propositional content given to us by the constitutive version of the content–force distinction, and it is crucial for the larger Fregean picture of content, judgment, and assertion.

1.2 An Alternative to the Fregean Picture

The Fregean picture of content swings as far away as one can get from a psychologistic conception of content on which the meanings of words and the contents of thoughts are ideas or mental images. Framing an alternative does not require a lurch back to psychologism. The view I am going to present in this section shares a great deal with the Fregean picture. It holds that propositional contents are sharable and repeatable. It holds that propositions were there before anyone judged or asserted them, and rejects the idea that propositions depend for their existence on being judged or asserted. Propositional contents will be just as mind-independent and objective on this alternative picture as they are on Frege's. The difference is where we start. Whereas the Fregean picture starts with propositional contents, this alternative starts with the actions we perform in thinking and speaking about the world.

We make judgments and assertions. In simple cases, performing these actions consists in predicating properties of objects. When Obama judges that Clinton is eloquent he predicates the property of being eloquent of Clinton. This is an inner act of predication. When he asserts that Clinton is eloquent he performs an outer, spoken act of predication. In both cases Obama characterizes Clinton as being a certain way, thereby positively affirming that she is that way. Both actions commit Obama to Clinton's being eloquent. These acts of predication are not preliminaries to judgment and assertion. Predicating a property of an object is a matter of applying or attributing the property to the object in a non-neutral, fully committal sort of way.

Predication is a type of action that can have mental and linguistic (spoken or written) tokens. Predication resides at a level of generality high enough to encompass both kinds of tokens. There are lots of differences between mental and linguistic tokens of predication, but these differences do not prevent these actions from all counting as acts of predication. Furthermore, mental and linguistic acts of predication are independent of one another. It is possible to mentally predicate elo-quence of Clinton without doing so in an assertion, and vice versa. Someone who asserts that Clinton is eloquent but does not believe it has performed a spoken act of predication without the corresponding mental act.

Predicating a property of an object does not require any sort of neutral, non-committal preliminary. Suppose Obama enters a room, sees Clinton sitting in a chair and judges that Clinton is sitting. There is no neutral act of entertainment that precedes this judgment, whether conscious or unconscious. He just spontaneously makes the judgment and in so doing predicates the property of sitting of Clinton. He does not first contemplate the possibility that she is sitting and then decide to judge it to be the case. Nothing like that has to happen consciously or unconsciously. He could do something like that, of course. He could reflectively consider whether Clinton is sitting before judging that she is. But he does not have to do that in order to predicate the property of sitting of Clinton. All of this holds for assertions too. In the flow of conversation Obama might assert that Clinton is sitting without any kind of non-assertive preparatory act. Someone asks him what Clinton is doing and without hesitating he asserts that Clinton is sitting. His answer does not have to be preceded by him wondering whether Clinton is sitting or hypothesizing that she is sitting or anything of the sort. He just asserts that Clinton is sitting and thereby performs an act of predication.

Similarly, we cannot factor an act of predication into two components, one neutral and the other not. To judge that Clinton is eloquent is not to make a non-committal attribution of eloquence to her and then accept or endorse that attribution. (This is how Soames conceives of judgment. More on this in the next section). The act of predication does not have a neutral core with a superimposed layer of commitment. Predication is inherently judgmental and assertive, but not because a component of it is judgmental or assertive.

In predicating a property of an object the subject characterizes the object as being a certain way and thereby does something that can be evaluated for truth and falsity. Acts of predication are true or false. An act of predicating eloquence of Clinton is true if and only if Clinton is eloquent. The act has these truth conditions by its nature, by virtue of the kind of act it is.

Here is an analogy that I find helpful in thinking about predication. Imagine we are sorting a pile of marbles. As a first step we have to choose a principle for sorting, for example we could choose to sort out the green marbles from the rest. The property of being green would then serve as our principle for sorting. As we sort the marbles we put the green ones in one pile and the others in another pile. Predicating a property of an object is analogous to picking up a marble and putting it in the green pile. To predicate is to sort an object with other objects according to a property or principle of organization. Now, it is obvious that we can make mistakes when sorting the marbles. If I pick up a red marble and put in it the green pile then I have done something incorrect. Given a principle of sorting, acts of putting the marbles into one pile or the other can be evaluated for correctness or incorrectness. The same goes for predication. If you predicate the property of being green of a marble in a judgment or in an assertion then you have done something that is just as correct (true) or incorrect (false) as an act of physically sorting the marble with other green marbles.

If we randomly and arbitrarily divide the marbles into two groups without any principle of sorting then it would not make sense to say that putting a marble in one group is correct or incorrect. The existence of the correctness conditions requires that we sort the marbles according to a property. The possibility of truth or falsity for acts of predication carries a similar requirement. Unlike actual sorting, however, acts of predication cannot exist in the absence of a predicated property. We can randomly divide the marbles into two groups, but we cannot randomly predicate. There are no bare acts of predication. As a matter of necessity, an act of predication must involve a property. It must also involve an object, or some other kind of target for the act of predication, or at least an attempt to identify such a target. It makes no sense to predicate a property with no intended target for your act of predication.

This draws out the fact that acts of predication have a certain structure. In the simplest cases, to engage in an act of predication requires referring to an object, identifying a property, and predicating that property of the object.[2] Suppose Obama asserts that Clinton is eloquent. In doing so, he *refers* to Clinton, he *expresses* the property of being eloquent, and he *predicates* this property of Clinton. These three sub-acts make up Obama's act of asserting that Clinton is eloquent. The same holds when Obama judges that Clinton is eloquent. To do so, he has to think of Clinton, think of the property of eloquence, and predicate this property of her. In this case, his acts of reference, expression, and predication occur in thought. Reference to objects and expression of properties are types of actions that one must perform in order to perform an act of predication.

Why have I separated the act of expressing a property from the act of predicating that property? Why not bundle these two acts together into a single act of expressing/predicating? This would be to hold that the act of identifying a property is inherently predicative: we identify properties by applying them to objects. But this is a mistake. We can do things with properties other than predicate them of objects. Suppose Obama *asks* whether Clinton is eloquent. In asking this question Obama does not

---

[2] I don't want this talk of "identifying a property" to be taken in an overly Platonistic way. It should not automatically be understood as a matter of picking out an abstract object in Plato's heaven. To express a property in an act of predication is to give yourself a rule or principle for sorting objects, where this rule determines the conditions under which your act of predication is correct or incorrect. My talk of expressing or identifying a property in an act of predication should be taken as a convenient *façon de parler* for whatever it is that we do to give ourselves these rules. How do we do that? That is the problem of rule-following (see Wright 2001). I won't attempt to solve that problem in this book.

predicate the property of eloquence of Clinton. He asks whether this property applies to her. Similarly, suppose Obama orders Clinton to be eloquent. Again, he hasn't predicated eloquence of Clinton in his order. He told her to have this property.

Predication, asking, and ordering are three ways in which a subject can combine a property with an object in thought or speech. None is more basic or ontologically prior, and each can be performed independently of the others. On the other hand, like predication, each kind of combinatory act requires that the subject refer to an object and express a property. The structure of an act of asking or ordering is similar to the structure of an act of predicating. In simple atomic cases, each involves an act of referring to an object, an act of expressing a property, and a combinatory act. The differences are found in the different combinatory acts: predicating, asking, or ordering.

These different combinatory acts generate different kinds of satisfaction conditions. Acts of predication have truth conditions. Acts of asking determine their answers; they have answer-hood conditions. Acts of ordering determine conditions under which they are fulfilled; they have fulfillment conditions. The latter two kinds of actions do not surreptitiously have truth conditions. There is no shared truth-conditional core running through all of these actions. Asking whether Clinton is eloquent is not to predicate eloquence of Clinton and then ask whether this predication is true. Ordering Clinton to be eloquent is not predicating eloquence of Clinton and then ordering that this become true. Acts of asking and ordering do not have acts of predication inside them. These are wholly distinct, independent ways of combining objects with properties with different kinds of satisfaction conditions.

Like predication, asking and ordering are types of actions that reside at a level of generality high enough to cover tokens in thought and speech. An inner act of wondering whether Clinton is eloquent counts as a token of the interrogative mode of combination. Wondering is to asking as judging is to asserting. Similarly, an inner act of wanting Clinton to be eloquent counts as token of the imperative mode of combination. If this is surprising then it is due to terminology. It is hard to come up with a good term for what I have been calling ordering, or the imperative mode of combination. 'Ordering' is misleading. The type of act I intend by the term 'ordering' is supposed to be general enough to cover a family of mental states and speech acts that includes desires, wishes, intentions, requests, promises, and orders.[3] All of these have fulfillment conditions. They all have world-to-mind or world-to-word direction of fit. They are all reported using infinitive clauses, e.g. 'Obama wants Clinton to be eloquent', 'Obama ordered Clinton to be eloquent', and 'Clinton intends to be eloquent'. They are all species of a certain way of combining a property with an object, which for lack of a better term I will call ordering, or the imperative mode of combination. ('Imperative/optative' is somewhat better but also not perfect, since it leaves out intentions and promises. I will stick with the shorter 'imperative'.) The imperative mode of combination is a type of action general enough to encompass any actions that have fulfillment conditions and world-to-mind/word direction of fit.

On this alternative to the Fregean picture, acts of predicating, asking, and ordering are basic. Propositions are abstractions from these actions. More precisely, propositions are types of these actions. Consider Obama's assertion that Clinton is eloquent. In making this assertion Obama performs a token of a type of action, which we can symbolize as follows:

1.   ⊢ <**Clinton,** ELOQUENT>

This is a type of action that Obama performs when he asserts that Clinton is eloquent. The single turnstile, '⊢' stands for predication. **Clinton** is a type of reference act, and ELOQUENT is a type of expression act. (I am going to use this notational convention throughout the book.

---

[3] To form an intention, on this view, is to perform a token of the type of action I call ordering. One might think that this leads to a regress in my account of predication. (This concern was raised by an anonymous referee, and I have heard it several times in conversation.) Let's assume that predicating a property of an object is an intentional action, which requires having a certain intention. If so, then performing this act of predication requires having an intention to do so. Having this intention involves performing an act of ordering, which we can assume is also an intentional action, which requires a further intention, and so on. There are two things to note about this regress. The first is that essentially the same regress arises for the Fregean picture. Let's assume that entertaining the proposition that p is an intentional action requiring a certain intention. Intention is a propositional attitude, and so requires entertaining another proposition, which requires a further intention, and so on. So the Fregean picture faces a version of the same regress. Second, as is hopefully now clear, the regress is perfectly general and arises for any intentional action whatsoever. If intentionally doing A requires having an intention to do A and having this intention requires an intentional act of intention-formation, then the regress is off and running. If there is a problem here at all, which I doubt, then it is a very general problem in the philosophy of action, which I think I can safely refer to philosophers with more expertise in that area.

Bold will always be used for types of reference acts, and SMALL CAPS for types of expression acts.) This type, (1), is the proposition that Clinton is eloquent. Its tokens are particular actions in which subjects refer to Clinton, express the property of being eloquent, and predicate this property of Clinton. Because these particular actions are true if and only if Clinton is eloquent, the type (1) is true if and only if Clinton is eloquent. The order of explanation for truth conditions goes from particular judgments and assertions to propositions. This holds in general for all kinds of satisfaction conditions, not just truth conditions. Particular acts of judging, asserting, wondering, asking, wanting, intending, requesting, promising, and ordering are the explanatorily basic bearers of satisfaction conditions. Propositions inherit their satisfaction conditions from these actions.

Suppose Obama asks whether Clinton is eloquent. The type of action he performs in this case can be represented as follows:

2.   ? <**Clinton**, ELOQUENT>

The question mark, '?', stands for the interrogative mode of combination. As before, **Clinton** is a type of reference act, and ELOQUENT is a type of expression act. Let's call this type an interrogative proposition. (We could also call them 'questions', but I prefer 'interrogative proposition'. The term 'question' has an act/content ambiguity that 'interrogative proposition' does not.) Similarly, suppose Obama orders Clinton to be eloquent. The type of which this is a token can be represented as:

3.   ! <**Clinton**, ELOQUENT>

The exclamation mark, '!', stands for the imperative mode of combination. Let's call this type, with the caveats I expressed earlier, an imperative proposition.

This conception of propositional content abandons both the taxonomic and constitutive versions of the content–force distinction. An assertion that Clinton is eloquent, a question whether she is eloquent, and an order to Clinton to be eloquent have different propositions as contents. These are (1), (2), and (3), respectively. Furthermore, each of these contents has an element of force. Assertoric propositions like (1) have a distinctively assertive component, in the form of predication, ⊦. Interrogative propositions have an interrogative component, ?, and imperative propositions have an imperative component, !. These different propositions are certain types of actions, which have to be understood using concepts that pertain to the actions we perform in representing the world. Propositions are abstractions from these actions and are therefore conceptually dependent on them.

This is not to say that we create or invent propositions. As types, propositions are mind-independent and objective. Suppose that no one has ever judged or asserted that Clinton is eloquent and never will judge or assert this. Suppose that throughout the whole history of the universe there are no token actions in which a subject predicates the property of being eloquent of Clinton. This does not mean that the type (1) does not exist. It just means that it doesn't have any tokens. The type is there, waiting to be tokened in particular actions, but it doesn't depend for its existence on having any tokens. Consider, by analogy, a complicated and difficult type of dive that no one has or will ever execute. The fact that no one has ever pulled off a token of that type doesn't mean that the dive itself, the type, doesn't exist as a mind-independent, objective entity. All of Frege's warnings about treating the dive as a mental entity apply. When two divers have a discussion about the dive they are not talking about their own ideas or mental images. Someone who deduces that the dive could only be performed from a platform of such-and-such a height has not made a discovery about her own state of consciousness. Types like (1)–(3) are just as mind-independent and objective, and just as existentially independent of their tokens. Propositions are types of mental or spoken actions, but we do not create them by performing tokens of them.

In addition, as types, propositions are sharable and repeatable.[4] They are sharable because many people can perform tokens of these types. Suppose Obama and Biden each assert that Clinton is eloquent. Then each has performed a token of (1). Obama and Biden asserted the same proposition. Propositions are repeatable because a single subject can perform multiple tokens of the same proposition. Suppose Obama asserts on two separate occasions that Clinton is eloquent. On each occasion he performed a token of (1); he asserted the same proposition twice.

---

[4] An exception occurs in the case of the propositions we assert using indexicals and demonstratives. It will turn out that these types are neither sharable nor repeatable. This is important for the solution to the problem of *de se* belief in chapter 8.

As we have seen, by incorporating an assertive element into truth-conditional propositions, in the form of predication, this approach abandons the constitutive version of Frege's distinction between content and force. Predication is inherently assertive in the sense that it is not a neutral component inside an act of assertion. In simple, normal cases, to perform an act of assertion is just to perform an act of predication. It is important to see, however, that the concept of predication is not the same as the concept of assertion. There are two reasons for this. The first is that there can be acts of predication that are not acts of assertion. This happens in cases of *cancelled* predication, which I begin to discuss in the next paragraph. The second is that the relations of assertion and predication have different relata and different adicities. Assertion is a two-place relation between a person and a proposition.[5] On my account, attitude relations like assertion and judgment are tokening relations between people and propositions. Predication, by contrast, is not a relation to a proposition. It is a multi-grade relation between a person and various objects, properties, or relations. Acts of assertion are grounded in acts of predication, but the two kinds of acts have different analyses and must be kept distinct.

An important element of this approach to assertion is the idea that in certain contexts one can perform an act of predication without thereby asserting anything. Words like 'if' and 'or' generate these sorts of contexts. When you say 'If Clinton is eloquent then she will win the election' you predicate eloquence of Clinton in uttering the antecedent, but you do not assert that Clinton is eloquent. This is because your use of 'if' creates a context in which acts of predication do not count as assertions. I call these 'cancellation contexts'. If an act of predication is cancelled then it is not an assertion. An act of cancelled predication is an act of predication that takes place in a cancellation context. More on this notion of cancellation below, and in chapter 4.

On the Fregean picture, propositional contents are analogous to natural objects that we take hold of and put to various uses. This might lead one to think that on my alternative propositions are like artifacts that we create in order to serve some purpose or function. That is not quite right. We do not create propositions. Nevertheless, there is a

---

[5] This is one of the lessons of Wittgenstein's objection to Russell's multiple relation theory of judgment, which I return to in chapter 7 (section 7.5).

conceptual connection between the nature of propositions and the uses to which we put them. Propositions are types, and types are essentially classificatory. Propositions, by their natures, are classificatory entities. This captures the role that propositions play in our thought and talk about our mental states and speech acts. We are constantly making judgments and assertions, asking and wondering about things, wanting various things, giving each other orders, and so on. We need some way to keep track of all of these mental states and speech acts. We need some way to tell them apart and link them together. To do this we abstract away from our particular states and actions and arrive at types of these states and actions. We then use these types to identify, attribute, classify, and individuate our mental and spoken actions and states. To say that someone has judged or asserted that p is to classify her judgment or assertion under the type p. We don't literally create the types that we use for this purpose, but the types themselves are essentially suited to play this role.

Types are abundant. Any act of judgment or assertion falls under an indefinitely large array of types of varying levels of fineness of grain. At one end of the array are very finely grained types that include lots of details about the action. At the other end are very coarsely grained types that abstract away from these details. Suppose Obama asserts that Clinton is eloquent. When he performs this action Obama is located at a certain place at a certain time, he speaks with a certain volume, he is dressed in a certain way, and so on and so forth. By including these sorts of details we can formulate a very specific type: the type of act of predicating eloquence of Clinton while standing behind the desk in the Oval Office and speaking with such-and-such volume while wearing a blue suit, holding a classified document, looking out the window, etc. Obama's action also falls under very coarsely grained types, e.g. the type of act of saying something about Clinton, or the type of act of predicating the property of eloquence, or the type of act of predicating, or the type of act of uttering the sentence 'Clinton is eloquent', or the type of act of uttering an English sentence, or the type of act of making an utterance, or the type of act of making noises with your mouth, etc.

Amidst this vast array, types like (1)–(3) are the ones we use to classify and individuate our mental states and speech acts in making attitude reports. This is revealed by the forms of these reports. Compare the complement clauses in these pairs:

4a. Obama asserted that Clinton is eloquent.
  b. Biden judged that Clinton is eloquent.
5a. Obama asked whether Clinton is eloquent.
  b. Biden wondered whether Clinton is eloquent.
6a. Obama ordered Clinton to be eloquent.
  b. Biden wants Clinton to be eloquent.

We report these different actions and states in different ways, using different kinds of complement clauses: a that-clause in (4a–b), a whether-clause in (5a–b), and a non-finite clause in (6a–b). This shows that we classify the actions and states in each pair under the same types, and the actions and states in the different pairs under different types. These types are propositions.

The larger point here is that we should look to the kinds of sentences we use to report mental states and speech acts to provide insight into the propositions we use to classify those states and speech acts. This is the best way to identify the types that serve as propositions. Taking this seriously means that we should take different complement clauses, like the ones in (4)–(6), to designate different propositions.

Intuitions about sameness or difference of content are not as helpful in identifying propositions. Many philosophers think that someone can ask the very same thing that someone else asserted, for example when Obama asserts that Clinton is eloquent and Biden asks whether Clinton is eloquent. Many find it intuitive to say that something can be shared across speech acts with different forces, and that what is shared is propositional content. I suspect that this intuition is less pre-theoretical and more a symptom of the influence of the Fregean picture. In any case, I agree that there is something shared between Biden's question and Obama's assertion, I just deny that it is a proposition. There is nothing wrong with saying that Biden asked the same thing that Obama asserted. To say this is to classify Biden's question and Obama's assertion under a certain type, and there are lots of types under which they both fall. For example, they both referred to Clinton and expressed the property of being eloquent. They both performed a combinatory act of one kind or another ($\vdash$ or ?) with eloquence and Clinton. They both uttered the words 'Clinton', 'is', and 'eloquent' (although not in the same order). The question is whether any of these types is a proposition. The fact that we report these actions using different complement clauses provides a good reason to say that they are not. Propositions are the types we use to classify mental states and speech acts when we use complement clauses in attitude reports. The only guaranteed way of keying in to these types is through these complement clauses. Unvarnished intuitions about sameness or difference in what two people have judged, asserted, asked, wondered, wanted, intended, or ordered are not reliable guides to sameness or difference of propositional content.

The complement clauses in (4)–(6) are the embedded forms of the following stand-alone sentences:

4c. Clinton is eloquent.
5c. Is Clinton eloquent?
6c. Clinton, be eloquent!

Embedded under attitude verbs, these sentences show up as a that-clause, a whether-clause, and a non-finite clause. (4c)–(6c) are examples of the three major sentential moods, declarative, interrogative, and imperative. These different types of sentences are, of course, designed for the performance of acts of predication, asking, and ordering, respectively. The kinds of sentences we use to perform actions of the types (1)–(3) are the very sentences, in their embedded forms, which we use to report actions of these types.

On this picture, sentential moods are semantically significant. The combinatory types found in propositions—⊢, ?, and !—are the contents of the declarative, interrogative, and imperative moods, respectively. The declarative mood is semantically associated with acts of predication, the interrogative mood with acts of asking, and the imperative mood with acts of ordering. Embedding a sentence inside another sentence does not dissolve these associations. The propositional content of a declarative sentence contains predication, ⊢, whether it occurs as a free-standing sentence (4c), or embedded inside another sentence, (4a–b). The propositional content of 'Clinton is eloquent' does not lose its predicative element when it occurs inside a conditional or disjunction or that-clause.

Why then aren't we asserting that Clinton is eloquent when we utter 'Clinton is eloquent' inside a conditional or disjunction or that-clause? Because the act of predication has been cancelled. Words like 'if', 'or', and 'believes' create cancellation contexts. These are contexts in which acts of predication do not count as assertions. Assertion is not predication plus something else (e.g. endorsement). It is predication in the absence of cancellation. Here's an analogy. Suppose two people, A and B, are playing a game of chess. B is new to the game and does not know how the knight moves. A says 'Allow me to demonstrate', and moves her knight in the usual way. This obviously does not count as A's turn in the game, and she does not have to leave her knight where she placed it. A moves her knight in the standard way, but this act does not have the usual consequences or commitments of a move in the game. This is what cancelled predication is like. To perform an act of predication in a cancellation context is to do exactly the same sort of thing you do in an ordinary, uncancelled context. The difference is that the cancelled act of predication does not count as an assertion and does not carry the usual consequences and normative requirements. We use words like 'if', 'or', and 'believes' to create cancellation contexts for our acts of predication, in much the same way that A created a cancellation context by saying 'Allow me to demonstrate'. I will say a bit more about cancellation in the next section, and much more in chapter 4.

To this point I have only discussed how this approach to content handles very simple atomic propositions. To get the view off the ground I need to show how it applies to more complicated kinds of propositions, including relational, compound, and quantified propositions, along with the propositions expressed by attitude reports and wh-interrogatives. I will do all of this in subsequent chapters.

Another area of detail I need to fill in concerns the nature of the reference type **Clinton** and the expression type ELOQUENT. There are indefinitely many ways of referring to Clinton and indefinitely many ways of expressing the property of eloquence. Exactly which reference and expression types figure in propositions? Although I will focus on reference types, the answer I give in chapter 5 can be extended in obvious ways to expression types.

My aim in this section has been to set out in a preliminary way the view of propositional content that I will defend over the course of this book. Before I begin to argue for my view and against the Fregean picture, it will be useful to consider an approach to propositional content that falls in between the Fregean conception and the one I am defending.

1.3 Soames's Picture

At first blush, Soames's approach to propositional content seems to be a vigorous rejection of what I have been calling the Fregean picture of content. He says that "if by 'propositions' one means what Frege and Russell did, then there are no such things" (Soames 2010, 32). He talks disparagingly about "the familiar story of propositions as denizens of a 'third realm' (beyond mind and matter), which are 'grasped' by a mysterious intellectual faculty of platonic extrasensory perception" (Soames 2010, 7). He charges the "Frege-Russell" account of propositions with taking "the mysterious, unexplained, and supposedly intrinsic representational properties of propositions to be the source from which the cognitive states of agents, and the sentences they employ, inherit their representational properties" (Soames 2010, 107). For Soames, this explanatory strategy is hopeless.

In addition, Soames's positive view about the nature of propositional content looks strikingly similar to the one I introduced in the previous section. One of his key recommendations is that we need to "reverse our explanatory priorities" by holding that "propositions are representational *because* of their intrinsic connection to the inherently representational cognitive events in which agents predicate some things of other things" (Soames 2010, 107). To do this, he proposes identifying propositions with types of acts in which, in simple atomic cases, subjects predicate properties of objects. For Soames, the proposition that o is red is the minimal act type in which an arbitrary subject predicates redness of o. Tokens of this type are the primary bearers of truth conditions and other representational properties. The act type derives its truth conditions and representational properties from its tokens. All of this sounds very close to the view that I am defending. Like my approach, Soames's picture starts with the actions we perform in predicating properties of objects and then identifies propositions with types of these actions. The explanatory order for truth conditions goes from particular acts of predication to the propositions that are types of these actions.

On closer inspection, however, it is clear that Soames's view retains many of the central features of the Fregean picture and departs in significant ways from my own. The key is the way Soames understands predication. For Soames, the act of predicating a property of an object is neutral and non-committal. Like Fregean entertainment, Soamesian predication is a necessary neutral kernel inside judgment. Judgments have a two-part structure: to judge that *o* is red is to neutrally predicate redness of *o* and endorse this act of predication. Instead of eliminating Fregean entertainment, Soames analyzes it in terms of his notion of predication.

> Since to entertain the proposition *that o is red* is simply to predicate redness of o, and since this predication is included in every attitude with that content, entertaining the proposition is one component of any propositional attitude we bear to it. To *judge* that o is red is to predicate redness of o, while endorsing that predication. (Soames 2010, 82)[6]

Furthermore, since predication is neutral and non-assertoric, Soames's view preserves the constitutive version of the content–force distinction.[7] The type of act of predicating redness of *o* is inherently predicative, but the sort of predication involved is not judgmental or assertive in character.

The only essential difference between the Fregean and Soamesian pictures is the order of explanation for truth conditions. Soames reverses this explanatory order while keeping everything else in the Fregean picture intact. This fails to appreciate the fact that the elements of the Fregean picture, in particular the Fregean notion of entertainment, get their *raison d'être* from its top-down explanatory structure. Reversing this structure removes the motivation we might have had for positing Fregean entertainment.

On the Fregean picture, judgments and assertions derive their truth conditions from propositions. Propositions are already there, and to judge one is a matter of endorsing it in thought. You cannot do this unless you have identified which proposition you are going to endorse. This is why entertainment is required for judgment. A judgment has truth conditions because is appropriately related to a proposition, and this relation cannot obtain unless the subject singles out a particular

---

[6] More recently Soames trades in talk of endorsing an act of predication with talk of forming or activating dispositions. He says that "to *judge* that B is red is for one's predicating redness of B to coincide with one's forming or activating certain dispositions" (Soames forthcoming, 26). The important point for our purposes is the two-part structure of judgment: judgment contains a neutral act of predication and some additional non-neutral act or event.

[7] In a symposium session at the Central Division APA meeting in February 2014 Soames indicated that he does not accept the taxonomic version of the content–force distinction.

proposition. Entertainment is therefore a necessary precondition on a judgment's deriving its truth conditions from a proposition. If judgments do not derive their truth conditions from propositions then there is no longer any compelling reason to hold onto the notion of entertainment or the two-part conception of judgment. The idea that there is a neutral core contained inside every judgment owes its plausibility to the Fregean picture of content in which it is embedded.

One might object that there is another reason to recognize acts of neutral predication inside judgments: doing so allows us to retain the constitutive version of the content–force distinction. If predication is neutral and non-committal, then including predication in propositional contents does not entail that there is anything judgmental or assertive about those contents, and so there is then no problem about the fact that we do not assert the antecedents or consequents of conditionals. In uttering the antecedent of 'If Clinton is eloquent then she will win the election' you neutrally predicate eloquence of Clinton, but this does not mean that you have asserted that Clinton is eloquent. The propositional content of 'Clinton is eloquent' retains its predicative component when it occurs inside a conditional, and in uttering the conditional you perform a token of this propositional content. Given that this token act of predication is neutral, it does not follow that you have judged or asserted that Clinton is eloquent.

This is a compelling reason to accept neutral predication only if there is no other way of explaining the fact that we do not assert the antecedents or consequents of conditionals. My notion of cancellation is supposed to provide us with such an alternative explanation. We are *not* forced to recognize neutral predication by the sorts of facts that motivate the constitutive version of the content–force distinction.

However, a stronger point can be made. Soames's notion of neutral predication is incoherent. It cannot account for the facts about conditionals because it does not make sense. It cannot account for anything.

If it weren't for the comfort philosophers already felt with the Fregean concept of entertainment then I think Soames's notion of neutral predication would strike us as strange and dubious. I do not believe in Fregean entertainment, understood as a necessary preliminary or ingredient inside judgments, but I can see what Frege was getting at. Sometimes, prior to judging that p, we do things like ask whether p, or hypothesize that p, or suppose that p, or contemplate the possibility of judging p.

These are the kinds of actions that Frege points to when he wants to illustrate entertainment. The error comes in making these actions pre-conditions for judgments. In some cases acts of judgment are preceded by entertainment-like preliminaries, but they do not have to be. Entertainment has some intuitive appeal, but only because sometimes we do things that look like Fregean entertainment.

On the other hand, I do not understand Soames's notion of neutral predication. I do not understand what it would be to attribute a property to an object while remaining completely neutral about whether the object has that property. To attribute a property to an object is to characterize the object as being a certain way. How is it possible to do that and yet not take any stand at all about whether the object is that way? That seems incoherent.

The incoherence stems from two features of Soamesian predication: truth-evaluability and neutrality. It is crucial for Soames that token acts of predication can be true or false, since this is required for his bottom-up explanation of how propositions have truth conditions. In addition, he regards token acts of predication as neutral, in the sense that in predicating a property of an object the subject takes no position about whether the object has that property. Now, consider what we might call a *pure* act of predicating the property of being F of an object *a*, that is, a simple, stand-alone, ordinary act of predication. The idea here is to isolate the act of predication as much as possible in order to focus on the nature of this action. A pure act of predication would not take place in what I am calling a cancellation context—more on this in a moment. In addition, in Soames's case, a pure act of predicating F of *a* is not a judgment that *a* is F, since judgment requires an additional non-neutral element of endorsement or affirmation. For Soames, such pure acts of predication occur when we think of *a* as F, or see, visualize, or imagine *a* as F.[8] Now, suppose that *a* is not F. If so, then this act of predication is false and hence the agent did something incorrect. The agent made a mistake. But how could the agent

---

[8]   See, for example, (Soames forthcoming, chapter 2). It is important to distinguish what I am calling "pure" acts of predication from what Soames calls "bare" acts of predication. According to Soames, any act of predicating F of *a* has to be performed in a particular way, e.g. by thinking of *a* as F, or seeing *a* as F, or imagining *a* as F. Considered as bare, we abstract away from the particular way in which an act of predication is performed. Soames rightly denies the existence of bare acts of predication that are not identical to acts of predication performed in some particular way (King, et al. 2014, 229–30).

have made a mistake if she took no stand one way or the other about whether *a* is F? It is incoherent to suppose that an agent can make a mistake by predicating F of *a* while taking no position at all about whether *a* is F.

The senses of 'correct' and 'mistake' here are not normative. I am not relying on rules or norms for acts of predication, e.g. a norm that says 'If *a* is not F then do not predicate F-ness of *a*'. There may be such norms of predication, but I do not need them in order to raise this problem for Soames. I am relying on the fact that acts of predication have correctness conditions, in the form of truth conditions. An act of predicating F of *a* is correct, that is, true, iff *a* is F. If you perform an act of predicating F of *a* and *a* is not F, then your act is incorrect. If the act is pure then you made a mistake, but not in the sense that you violated a norm of predication. You made a mistake in the sense that you did something incorrect.

Incoherence sets in when Soames also regards acts of predication as neutral and non-committal. If it is possible to make a mistake in predicating a property of an object, then in performing that act you cannot remain neutral about whether the object has the property. Here, then, are the steps in this argument against Soames. Begin by supposing that S performs a pure act of predicating F of *a* and that *a* is not F. It follows that:

1. S's act of predication is false.
2. S's act of predication is incorrect.
3. S made a mistake.
4. S must have taken a position about whether *a* is F.
5. S's act of predication was not neutral.

Each move in this argument is based on a triviality. The step from (1) to (2) is based on the fact that truth conditions are correctness conditions. The step from (2) to (3) comes from the fact if you did something incorrect then you made a mistake. The step from (3) to (4) relies on the fact that you cannot make a mistake about whether *a* is F without taking a position one way or the other about whether *a* is F. Finally, the move from (4) to (5) is based on the idea that if you take a position about some issue then you have not remained neutral about that issue.

One potential response available to Soames would be to reject (1).[9] This amounts to denying that token acts of predication are true or false.

---

[9] This is in fact how Soames responded during a symposium session at the February 2014 Central Division APA.

In his most recent work, (King, et al. 2014) and (Soames forthcoming), Soames gives a fairly subtle explanation of how types of acts of predication acquire their truth conditions.[10] The explanation is silent about whether token acts of predication have truth conditions.

> The explanation begins with agents. First, we observe that when an agent sees or thinks of o as red, the agent represents o as red. Next, we consider *what the agent does*—namely *represent o as red*, which I call "predicating redness of o". At this point, we appeal to a derivative sense of "represent" in which this act itself *represents o as red*. Though distinct from the primary sense in which *an agent* represents o as red, this extended sense is related to that primary sense in a way analogous to the way in which . . . some acts are intelligent, stupid, thoughtful, or kind is related to the primary sense in which *agents who perform those acts* are intelligent, stupid, thoughtful, or kind. (King, et al. 2014, 239–40).

By "act" here, Soames means act types. The type of act of predicating F of *a* represents *a* as F, and is true if and only if *a* is F, because in performing a token of this type the agent represents *a* as F. This explanation moves from agents representing *a* as F to the possession of representational features and truth conditions by that type of action. The possession of truth conditions by the agent's token act of predication seems to play no role in this explanation, which may open up room for Soames to deny that token acts of predication are representational or have truth conditions.

This doesn't mean that it is plausible for him to make this denial. Soames's account of how types of acts of predication are representational carries over straightforwardly to token acts. A token act of predicating F of *a* represents *a* as F, and is true if and only if *a* is F, because in performing that token the agent represented *a* as F. This is analogous to the way in which token acts are intelligent, stupid, thoughtful, or kind. A token act has one of these features because in performing it an agent was intelligent, stupid, thoughtful, or kind. Even if he is not explicit about it, Soames is committed to the view that token acts of predication are true or false.

In any case, it is easy to reformulate the argument against Soames without mentioning token acts of predication at all. By predicating F of *a*, an agent accurately or inaccurately represents *a* as being a certain way. If *a* is not that way, then the agent made a mistake, and hence must have

---

[10] I give my own explanation in chapter 3.

taken a position about whether a is F. This allows for a different and simpler argument against Soames. Suppose again that S performs a pure act of predicating F of a, and that a is not F:

1'. S inaccurately represented a as F.
2'. S made a mistake.
3'. S must have taken a position about whether a is F.
4'. S's act of predication was not neutral.

As before, each step in this argument is based on a triviality.

Another potential response for Soames would be to block the argument at the very beginning, before step (1), by denying that pure acts of predication ever occur. This is not a view he in fact holds, but perhaps he could say that acts of predication never occur in isolation; they are always abstractions from more complex acts of judgment or assertion etc. But that does nothing to eliminate the incoherence in his *concept* of predication. The point of focusing on pure acts of predication is to concentrate attention on the concept of predication, considered as a type of action. The problem for Soames is that his concept of predication, insofar as it combines truth-evaluability and neutrality, is incoherent. The incoherence remains even if Soames says that pure acts of predication never occur.

Why doesn't the same incoherence apply to my concept of cancelled predication? On my account, cancelled acts of predication are both truth-evaluable and neutral. Why isn't my notion of cancelled predication incoherent for just the same reason as Soames's notion of predication?

The key is that cancelled predication is not pure predication. Acts of cancelled predication are not pure because they take place in cancellation contexts—contexts in which an act of predication does not have its usual status or consequences. In a cancellation context we do not hold an agent responsible for her act of predication. This makes the concept of a mistake inapplicable, which blocks the move from (2) to (3) in the argument against Soames ((1') to (2') in the revised argument). For example, when someone says 'a is F or b is G' her use of 'or' creates a cancellation context for her acts of predicating F of a and G of b. In evaluating this assertion we do not charge her with a mistake if a is not F. Of course, if both disjuncts are false then the speaker made a mistake, but that stems from an uncancelled act of predicating a disjunctive relation of two propositions (see section 4.3), not from either of the two cancelled acts of predicating F of *a* and G of *b*.

A pure act of predication is an isolated act of predication in an ordinary context. No *pure* act can be both truth-evaluable and neutral, but that doesn't mean that the act cannot become neutral when it occurs in a wider, impure environment. Compare: a substance that is poisonous in its pure form becomes benign when dissolved in the right sort of solution. Similarly, an act of predication, which is fully committal when it occurs in isolation, becomes non-committal when it occurs in the right sort of context. The concept of cancelled predication is no more incoherent than the concept of neutralized poison.

How could Soames have missed the incoherence in his concept of neutral predication? It is probably because, in Soames's theory, predication replaces the Fregean concept of entertainment, and there is no similar incoherence in the Fregean concept. On the Fregean picture, *acts* of entertaining propositions are *not* truth-evaluable. The propositions entertained are true or false, but the acts of entertaining them are not. You cannot falsely entertain a proposition. There is no mistake involved in entertaining a false proposition. The mistake occurs when you judge the proposition, not when you entertain it. Because acts of entertainment are not truth-evaluable there is no problem about also regarding them as neutral and non-committal. But one cannot have it both ways. Predication is either neutral and non-truth-evaluable, like entertainment, or it is truth-evaluable and non-neutral, like judgment. The problem for Soamesian predication is that it incoherently combines the neutrality of entertainment with the truth-evaluability of judgment. The lesson is that if acts of predication are to be true or false, which they have to be in order to ground the truth conditions of propositions, then they cannot be neutral and non-committal. The only option for those who want to pursue this explanatory strategy is to regard predication as judgmental or assertive in character. This means that we need a correlated concept of cancellation in order to handle assertions of disjunctions and conditionals and the like. It also means that we can discard the Fregean concept of entertainment, understood as a necessary, neutral kernel inside judgments. Entertainment gets its raison d'être from the Fregean idea that propositions are there waiting to be judged, and that in order to make a judgment you must single out one of these propositions. If we give up this conception of content then we no longer need to suppose that judgments are constituted in part by a neutral, entertainment-like core.

Despite his rhetoric, Soames's account of propositional content is really a conservative attempt at retaining as much as possible about the Fregean picture of content while reversing its explanatory order. This is misguided. The various elements of the Fregean picture hang together in a mutually supporting whole. It is a mistake to think that we can change one part of the picture without undermining the motivation for the other parts, and it is incoherent to suppose that we can replace the Fregean notion of entertainment with something both neutral and truth-evaluable. Soames is right that we need to reverse the explanatory order contained in the Fregean picture. He is wrong in thinking that it is possible to do so without a more radical shift away from that picture.

2

The Problem of the Unity of the Proposition

In this chapter I am going to present the main problem for the Fregean picture of propositional content. This is the problem of the unity of the proposition. Properly understood, this is the problem of making sense of how propositions have truth conditions. On the Fregean picture, our judgments and assertions derive their truth conditions from propositions. Propositions must therefore have their truth conditions prior to and independently of these acts of judgment and assertion. This naturally leads to questions about whether it is possible to explain how propositions themselves have truth conditions. In giving such an explanation the Fregean is barred from appealing to anything that subjects do or think or say—that is why the problem is so hard. But perhaps there is no need for the Fregean to provide an explanation for how propositions have truth conditions. Perhaps it is simply primitive that propositions are bearers of truth conditions, not explainable in terms of other facts. I will start by considering this idea. Then I will turn to Frege's and Russell's attempts at solving the unity problem, and finally a more recent attempt due to Jeffrey King.[1]

---

[1] The unity problem, as I will approach it, is a problem about propositions, the non-linguistic contents of beliefs. There is a closely related problem about the unity of sentences. How are the parts of sentences combined into meaningful wholes? What distinguishes a sentence from a mere list of words? Several recent discussions of the unity problem put the linguistic form of the problem at the forefront, including (Collins 2011), (Davidson 2005), and (Gibson 2004). (Gaskin 2008) is a wide-ranging and historically informed discussion of the unity problem in both its linguistic and non-linguistic forms. (Searle 2008a) is a neglected discussion of both forms of the unity problem, which draws an interesting contrast between the unity of sentences and the unity of perceptual experiences. In order to keep the focus on the non-linguistic form of the unity problem and to keep the discussion manageable, I won't discuss these works in this book.

2.1 Going Primitive

The problem of the unity of the proposition is easiest to motivate under the assumption that propositions have constituents that correspond to the meaningful constituents of sentences. For example, it is very natural (but not mandatory) to think that the proposition that Clinton is eloquent has constituents corresponding to the subject and predicate in the sentence 'Clinton is eloquent'. Let's call this proposition's subject part C and its predicate part E. C could be Clinton herself, or a mode of presentation of Clinton, or something else (on my view it is a type of act of referring to Clinton). E could be the property of eloquence, or a mode of presentation of this property, or something else (a type of act of expressing the property of eloquence). These differences do not matter at this point.

Since the proposition is one thing, and the constituents C and E are two things, there must be something about the proposition that joins C and E together into a single thing. The constituents must bear a relation to one another that unifies them into a proposition. In addition, on the Fregean picture, the fact that the proposition has truth conditions looks like it has to fall out of the fact that it has these constituents joined together by this unifying relation. For the Fregean, propositions have their truth conditions independently of what subjects do in performing judgments or assertions. Given this commitment, in giving an explanation for how a proposition has truth conditions the obvious first place to start is by looking to the constituents of the proposition and their relation to one another. We cannot appeal to what a subject does in forming a judgment or making an assertion. In fact, we are barred from appealing to anything that subjects do or think or say. This is the problem of the unity of the proposition for the Fregean picture. It is the problem of explaining how the constituents of a proposition are bound together into a single, unified entity with truth conditions.

Certain attempted solutions are non-starters. The proposition that Clinton is eloquent cannot be the set consisting of C and E, or the ordered pair of C and E, since neither the set nor the ordered pair has truth conditions. The ordered pair <C, E> doesn't say anything about how the world is. It is just there, like a pair of objects sitting on a table. We could assign truth conditions to the ordered pair, but then it would not have its truth conditions in the intrinsic sort of way demanded by the Fregean picture.

At this point, instead of casting around for a different solution, the Fregean could insist that the relation between C and E is primitive. She could call it the "propositional relation"—a primitive relation that joins constituents like C and E together into propositions and explains how those propositions have truth conditions.

The Fregean might be able to get away with this were it not for the fact that she uses propositions to explain how our judgments and assertions have truth conditions. The unity problem, considered as a metaphysical exercise in explaining how a certain variety of abstract object has truth conditions, should interest us only insofar as a solution helps us understand how we represent the world in thought and speech. Treating the propositional relation as primitive does not advance this understanding. We want to know how it is that our judgments have truth conditions. The Fregean explains this by positing a realm of composite entities whose constituents are bound together by a primitive and unanalyzable relation that has the power to endow its products with truth conditions. These truth conditions are then inherited by our judgments. This sheds very little light on the fact that our acts of judgment have truth conditions. At the very least it should invite us to look for other ways of explaining how we represent the world in making judgments.

Instead of holding that the propositional relation is primitive, many philosophers have found it more attractive to say that propositions themselves are primitive and sui generis (Bealer 1993, 1998; Schiffer 2003; McGlone 2012; Merricks 2015). This involves giving up the assumption with which we began, namely that propositions have constituents. One might think that this dissolves the unity problem. If propositions do not have parts then there is no need to identify a relation that binds these parts together into truth-conditional wholes. But we can still ask about how a part-less proposition has truth conditions. This is not a unity problem per se, but it is the same question that motivates the unity problem and gives it its interest. The reason to look for a propositional relation is the hope that finding such a relation will explain how propositions have truth conditions, which will in turn explain how our thoughts and speech acts have truth conditions. Giving up the assumption that propositions have constituents does not eliminate the demand for such an explanation.

Philosophers who treat propositions as primitive entities reject this demand. The explanation for truth conditions has to end somewhere.

The primitivist about propositions thinks it ends with simple, sui generis entities that have their truth conditions by nature. But the Fregean probably cannot stop there. If propositions do not have constituents then we cannot analyze entertainment as some kind of mental operation on those constituents, e.g. a neutral act of predicating or ascribing or composing. What could it be, then, to grasp one of these part-less, *sui generis* entities? It is hard to see what the primitivist could say about this, other than repeating the Fregean metaphors of grasping, latching onto, seizing, laying hold of.[2] If we go primitive about propositions, it looks as though we will also have to go primitive about entertainment.

The same goes for the act of judgment. Judgment, on the Fregean view, is an act of endorsing or accepting a proposition. Again, though, if propositions are simple and unstructured, we cannot take this act of endorsement to consist in a mental operation performed on the constituents of a proposition. Furthermore, as we saw in the previous chapter, we cannot say that to endorse a proposition is to accept it as true. To accept a proposition p as true is either to judge that p is true or it is a neutral, non-committal act of attributing truth to p. If accepting p as true is to judge that p is true then we've analyzed one judgment, judging that p, in terms of another, judging that p is true. This leads to a regress. The alternative is to treat accepting p as true as a neutral act of attributing truth to p. But this is not sufficient for judging that p. So, the act of endorsing a proposition cannot be analyzed as accepting a proposition as true. What is it then, to endorse a proposition? Like entertainment, it looks as though the Fregean is going to have to view judgment as a primitive attitude one can bear to a proposition.

Here, then, is the explanation we get from the Fregean primitivist for the fact that a judgment has truth conditions. There are sui generis entities that have truth conditions by their natures. A subject enters into a primitive entertainment relation with one of these entities, and then performs a primitive act of judging it. The resulting judgment takes on the truth conditions of the proposition that is entertained and endorsed.

---

[2] Bealer's algebraic approach to propositions (1993, 1998) may be able to avoid treating entertainment as primitive. On Bealer's view, the proposition that Clinton is eloquent is the value of a function, the singular predication function $pred_S$, applied to Clinton and the property of being eloquent. Bealer could say that to entertain this proposition is to think of the value of $pred_S$ for these two arguments. This trades in a primitive propositional relation for a primitive function, $pred_S$, which generates sui generis propositions with truth conditions. I do not think that this advances the issue in any substantial way.

This is even less satisfying than the appeal to a primitive propositional relation. It is hardly even worth calling it an explanation.

It is worth pausing here to ask about the kind of explanation we are looking for when we ask why our judgments have truth conditions. What kind of question are we asking when we ask why a judgment has truth conditions? Here is an analogy. Consider a volume of gas with a certain temperature. There are (at least) two kinds of explanations we can give for why the gas has this temperature. The first cites a cause, for example the fact that a heat source was applied to the gas at a certain time. The second provides a fact that grounds or constitutes the fact that the volume of gas has this temperature. In this case it is the fact that the gas molecules have such-and-such kinetic energy. The kinetic energy of the gas molecules does not cause them to have a certain temperature. It is what their having this temperature consists in.

When we ask why a judgment has truth conditions we are asking for the second sort of explanation. We are asking for the facts that ground or constitute the fact that a judgment has certain truth conditions. On the Fregean picture, the answer is that there is a proposition with these truth conditions, and the judgment bears a special relationship to this proposition (it is the one the subject entertained and endorsed in making the judgment). But this is totally unhelpful if the Fregean goes on to say that it is primitive that the proposition has these truth conditions, or if she appeals to a primitive propositional relation to explain how the proposition has its truth conditions. This is like trying to explain why the volume of gas has a certain temperature by appealing to primitive facts about the temperatures of the individual gas molecules. If we are puzzled about what it is for the volume of gas to have a certain temperature then we will be equally puzzled about what it is for an individual gas molecule to have a certain temperature. It is no help at all to be told the latter is primitive and unexplainable.

The lesson is that going primitive about the propositional relation, or about propositions themselves, will not allow the Fregean to provide a satisfying explanation of how our judgments and assertions have truth conditions. The explanation cannot stop with a primitive propositional relation or with sui generis propositions.[3] We need an informative solution

---

[3] In the Q&A after a paper I gave at a conference on speech acts in New York in September 2013, Robert Stalnaker asked how properties get their satisfaction conditions. At

to the unity problem—an explanation of how propositions are truth-conditional representations—if the Fregean picture is to provide philosophical illumination into how it is that our thoughts and speech acts have truth conditions.

Frege and Russell both saw this clearly. Both felt the need to answer questions about how the constituents of propositions are joined together into truth-conditional wholes. Unfortunately for the Fregean picture, both of their answers face serious problems.

2.2 Frege on the Composition of Thoughts

There is an interpretive issue for Frege about whether thoughts have senses as constituents. One approach understands the composition of thoughts in terms of composition at the level of sentences. On this model senses combine in thoughts in a way that is analogous to the way in which words and phrases combine to form sentences. Just as 'Clinton' and 'is eloquent' are constituents of 'Clinton is eloquent', the sense of 'Clinton' and the sense of 'is eloquent' are constituents of the thought that Clinton is eloquent. Another approach understands the composition of thoughts in terms of composition at the level of reference. The sense of 'Clinton' combines with the sense of 'is eloquent' in the way that Clinton combines with the Fregean concept of eloquence. Since the values of

the time I didn't understand his question—thanks to Gary Ostertag for helping me see what he meant (cf. Ostertag 2013, 519). It is tempting to answer Stalnaker by saying: it's just primitive that properties have satisfaction conditions—this isn't something we need to explain. But if that attitude is justified for properties then why isn't a similar attitude justified for propositions? That, I think, was the drift of Stalnaker's question. One quick response is that propositions are representations and properties are not, and it is representation that calls out for philosophical explanation. I think this response is right as far as it goes but it misses something interesting about Stalnaker's question. The role for properties in acts of predication is to determine the correctness conditions for those acts. An act of predicating greenness of an object o is correct just in case o is green. In explaining how our acts of predication get their correctness conditions it is tempting to say that we latch onto Platonic properties, which have their satisfaction conditions primitively and essentially, and these satisfaction conditions fix the correctness conditions of our acts of predication. But this Platonistic story is of a piece with locating the source of truth-conditions in sui generis propositions, and it raises a host of metaphysical and epistemological problems of its own (see Wright 2001). If we put this story to one side then we are left with the problem of explaining where the correctness conditions for acts of predication come from. That is the problem of rule-following. This is the deep problem raised by Stalnaker's question, and there is no easy solution.

concepts are simple, non-composite objects (the True or the False), this view takes thoughts themselves to be unstructured and non-composite.

The texts do not settle this issue, and I do not want to take a stand on it.[4] We have already considered the view that propositions are part-less and unstructured. For our purposes, we can therefore assume the linguistic model on which thoughts have senses as constituents. The question before us now is whether, given that propositions are structured and have constituents, there is an explanation to be found in Frege's writings for how these constituents are bound together into representational wholes.

Frege's explanation appeals, of course, to his distinction between saturated and unsaturated entities. Thoughts are unified through the saturation of unsaturated senses.

> But the question now arises how a thought comes to be constructed, and how the parts are so combined together that the whole amounts to something more than the parts taken separately.... The unity of the whole comes about through the fact that the thought saturates the unsaturated part or, as we can also say, completes the part needing completion. And it is natural to suppose that, for logic in general, combination into a whole always comes about by the saturation of something unsaturated. (Frege 1918c, 390)

In the thought that Clinton is eloquent the sense of 'Clinton' saturates the sense of 'is eloquent'. The resulting thought retains these senses as parts, but now they are unified because the name-sense completes the predicate-sense.

Frege knew that this is metaphorical. In "On Concept and Object" he says that "'complete' and 'unsaturated' are of course only figures of speech; but all that I wish or am able to do here is to give hints" (Frege 1892b, 193). Is there a way to cash the metaphor? What is the literal truth behind the saturated/unsaturated distinction?

Frege's saturated/unsaturated distinction runs through all three levels of language, sense, and reference. At the level of language the distinction is between unsaturated predicates and saturated names. What difference between predicates and names could this metaphor be aimed at capturing?

---

[4] In a letter to Russell from 1904, Frege remarks that "the sense of the word 'moon' is a component part of the thought that the moon is smaller than the earth" (Frege 1980, 163). On the other hand, in "Compound Thoughts" Frege says that "to be sure, we really talk figuratively when we transfer the relation of whole and part to thoughts" (Frege 1918c, 390). See (Heck and May 2006) for discussion.

One obvious answer is found in the concept of adicity. There are one-place predicates, two-place predicates, three-place predicates, and so on. We cannot make the same distinctions for names. It does not make sense to talk about a one-place or two-place or three-place name. At the level of language, the unsaturated/saturated distinction looks like the distinction between expressions that have adicity and those that do not. Something similar holds at the level of reference. There are one-place functions, two-place functions, three-place functions, and so on. There are no such distinctions for objects. At the level of sense, then, the literal truth behind the metaphor of unsaturatedness is that predicate-senses have adicity. There are one-place predicate-senses, two-place predicate-senses, three-place predicate-senses, and so on, but there are no similar distinctions for name-senses.

The problem is that this difference between predicate-senses and name-senses cannot explain how senses combine to form thoughts with truth conditions. Adicity cannot bear this burden. At the level of language, the adicity of a predicate tells us how many names a predicate needs in order to form a complete sentence. This does not explain how a sentence is more than a mere list of words. At the level of reference the adicity of a function tells us how many objects a function needs in order to determine a value. It does not shed light on the notion of functional application. For thoughts, then, the adicity of a predicate-sense determines how many name-senses a predicate-sense needs in order to form a complete thought. This clarifies what it is for the predicate-sense to be unsaturated. But it does not explain the unity of thoughts. It does not explain how name-senses join with a predicate-sense to generate something with truth conditions. In fact, it does not explain how the components of a thought are united at all, much less united into something with truth conditions. The fact that a predicate-sense has adicity and a name-sense does not tells us nothing about how the name-sense joins with the predicate-sense to form a single, unified entity.

At this point Frege could appeal to the relation of saturation by which a saturated name-sense joins with an unsaturated predicate-sense. And this is where Frege's theory becomes mysterious and unhelpful. The concept of adicity gives us a grip on the distinction between saturated and unsaturated entities, but adicity cannot explain how these senses are joined together into a thought. To fill this gap, Frege appeals to the relation of saturation, but he is incapable of giving anything more than a metaphorical account of what this relation amounts to.

On the other hand, we do understand saturation at the level of language and at the level of reference. At the level of language, saturation consists in syntactic relations that bind words into sentences. At the level of reference, saturation consists in the relation of functional application by which a function maps an argument to a value. We thus have two models of saturation, and perhaps saturation at the level of sense can be understand by analogy with one or the other of these models.[5] But here is the problem. Neither of these varieties of saturation can explain how something has truth conditions. The mere fact that words bear syntactic relations to one another cannot explain how a sentence has truth conditions. The words themselves must also have meanings—they have to bear semantic relations to things in the world. Remember that the kind of explanation we are looking for is constitutive. We want to explain how a sentence has truth conditions by finding a fact that constitutes its having truth conditions. It may be that syntactic relations can only obtain between meaningful expressions. Even so, the fact that a sentence has truth conditions has to be constituted in part by the semantic properties and relations that attach to its words—it cannot be constituted solely by the obtaining of syntactic relations between these words. The point is even easier to make for the level of reference. There is nothing at the level

---

[5] In a recent paper, Heck and May argue that saturation at the levels of language and reference provide everything we need for understanding composition at the level of sense:

> We can now see why there is no need for any 'sense-glue' to bind the parts of a thought together—or, less metaphorically, why we do not need an independent account of how senses compose. On Frege's view, the parts of a thought are bound together by the interaction of two more fundamental forces: The determination of reference by sense, and the composition of references. The parts of thoughts 'stick together' because words that express senses combine in ways determined by their formal properties, to form sentences that have truth conditions, as determined by the composition of the references that the senses determine. Thoughts are coherently organized not because there is some organizing principle that binds senses themselves together, but because senses are related to references that compose *via* function-application. (Heck and May 2011, 153)

This is intriguing. The thought is that there is no special relation at the level of sense that binds senses together into thoughts. Rather, senses are "coherently organized" because of their relations to items at the level of language and the level of reference. But Frege needs a single entity, a thought, at the level of sense that is capable of being true or false. Unless there is a unifying relation between senses, it is hard to see how we have a unified, truth-evaluable thought, as opposed to a disconnected collection of senses. These senses may bear various relations to words, and to objects and concepts, but without unifying glue for the senses themselves we do not seem to have a single entity at the level of sense that is capable of being true or false.

of reference that has truth conditions. The level of reference is not a representational level—it is the level of what is represented. Functional application can account for combination at the level of reference, but it cannot explain how anything at the level of reference has truth conditions, since nothing has truth conditions at that level. To the extent, then, that we have models for saturation at the levels of language and reference, these models are no help in clarifying how saturation at the level of sense could generate something with truth conditions.

These considerations lead to a more general pessimism about the prospects for a Fregean solution to the unity problem. The relations of saturation at the levels of language and reference explain composition at these levels. But as we have seen, they do not account for how the results of composition have truth conditions. Syntactic relations explain how words are united into sentences, and functional application explains how concepts unite with objects to determine truth-values. But neither kind of saturation explains how the results of saturation have truth conditions. By contrast, an account of saturation at the level of sense has to accomplish both of these tasks. It has to explain how the constituents of a thought are united into a single entity *and* explain how this entity is capable of being true or false. The relations of saturation at the levels of language and reference fail to accomplish this second task. This naturally leads to doubts about whether any relation of saturation at the level of sense is up to the task of explaining truth conditions. Saturation does not play this role at the level of language or at the level of reference. Why should it be asked to play this role at the level of thoughts? This is where the top-down explanatory structure of the Fregean picture makes itself felt. Given this structure, we cannot go outside the thought to explain how it has truth conditions. We cannot appeal to what subjects do with thoughts, or to what they think or say, in order to account for the truth conditions of thoughts. The Fregean is forced to look to the internal constituents of the thought and their relations to one another to account for its representational properties. It is natural to wonder whether this is simply asking too much of these relations.

2.3 Russell on True and False Propositions

The problem for Russell's *Principles of Mathematics* (1903) account of propositions is well known: there are no false propositions. Or rather, on Russell's theory, false propositions do not *exist*. They merely subsist, like non-existent golden mountains or the present King of France. Russell held that propositions contain objects, properties, and relations, which are unified by the fact that the objects instantiate the properties or relations:

Consider, for example, the proposition "*A* differs from *B*". The constituents of this proposition, if we analyze it, appear to be only *A*, difference, *B*. Yet these constituents, thus placed side by side, do not reconstitute the proposition. The difference which occurs in the proposition actually relates *A* and *B*, whereas the difference after analysis is a notion which has no connection with *A* and *B*. (Russell 1903, 49)

The proposition that Clinton is eloquent contains Clinton and the property of eloquence and is unified because Clinton bears this property. The proposition that Obama admires Clinton contains Obama, Clinton, and the relation of admiration and is unified by the fact that the admiration relation relates Obama and Clinton. But if Clinton is not eloquent, or if Obama does not admire Clinton, then these constituents are not unified and the propositions do not exist.

Russell was aware of the problem. At least until 1904 he accepted false propositions in his ontology as shadowy, Meinongian entities, which he variously called "false Objectives", "objective non-facts", "objective falsehoods", and "fictions". False propositions are unified in the same way as true ones. The difference is that false propositions merely subsist, whereas true ones exist. By 1906 he had lost confidence in this position (Russell 1906), and by 1910 he had abandoned propositions altogether in favor of his multiple relation theory of judgment (Russell 1910).[6] In doing so he gave up the Fregean picture of propositional content. This is one of the reasons why I call it the Fregean picture, as opposed to the Frege-Russell picture.

This problem about false propositions is sufficient on its own to discount Russell's 1903 theory of propositions. We could, at this point, simply move on. Instead, I would like to draw out another problem for Russell's theory, which arises even if we accept non-existent false propositions in our ontology. The problem is that the states of affairs that Russell identifies with propositions are not bearers of truth and falsity. The state of affairs in which Obama admires Clinton is not a

---

[6] See (Hanks 2007) for more of the historical details.

representation. It does not say anything about the way the world is. Consider two rocks, A and B, one sitting on top of the other. On Russell's theory this arrangement of rocks is the proposition that A is on top of B. It's quite clear, though, that a pile of rocks is not true or false. A pile of rocks seems even less suited to being true or false than an ordered pair.

Russell didn't seem to be bothered by this problem, but he did recognize that his account of propositions forced him to change his view about truth and falsity. In particular, Russell saw that he had to give up the correspondence theory of truth. If the proposition that Obama admires Clinton is the state of affairs in which Obama admires Clinton, then we cannot say that the truth of this proposition consists in its correspondence with this state of affairs. Correspondence requires two things to correspond to one another, and here we have only one thing—the proposition/state of affairs in which Obama admires Clinton. (And correspondence cannot be identity, since false propositions are identical with themselves.) Identifying a proposition with the state of affairs it represents rules out analyzing truth as a relation between propositions and corresponding states of affairs.

In the light of this, Russell was forced to say that truth and falsity are simple, unanalyzable, monadic properties of propositions:

> It may be said—and this is, I believe, the correct view—that there is no problem at all about truth and falsehood; that some propositions are true and some false, just as some roses are red and some white; that belief is a certain attitude towards propositions, which is called knowledge when they are true, error when they are false.... Thus the analogy with red and white roses seems, in the end, to express the matter as nearly as possible. What is truth, and what falsehood, we must merely apprehend, for both seem incapable of analysis. (Russell 1904, 523–4)

> If we accept the view that there are objective falsehoods, we shall oppose them to facts, and make *truth* the quality of facts, *falsehood* the quality of their opposites, which we may call fictions. Then facts and fictions together may be called *propositions*. A belief always has a proposition for its object, and is knowledge when the object is true, error when its object is false. Truth and falsehood, in this view, are ultimate, and no account can be given of what makes a proposition true or false. (Russell 1906, 48)[7]

---

[7] In *Principles of Mathematics* Russell uses the obscure notion of *logical assertion* to distinguish true and false propositions:

> But there is another sense of assertion, very difficult to bring clearly before the mind, and yet quite undeniable, in which only true propositions are asserted. True and false propositions alike are in some sense entities, and are in some

The truth of a proposition, on this account, is the fact that it exists, and the falsity of a proposition is the fact that it merely subsists. The difference between truth and falsity is the difference, for states of affairs, between existence and mere subsistence. The fact that a proposition is capable of being true or false, then, is the fact that it is capable of existing or merely subsisting.

This sort of move trivializes the unity problem. The same strategy could be used to show that virtually anything is capable of being true or false. Suppose we identify the proposition that Clinton is eloquent with the ordered pair <Clinton, eloquence>. It is easy enough to define properties that ordered pairs can have, and then identify these properties with truth and falsity. Let's say that the ordered pair <Clinton, eloquence> has the property of being T iff Clinton bears the property of being eloquent. More generally, $<o_1, \ldots o_n, R^n>$ is T if and only if $<o_1, \ldots o_n>$ instantiates R^n. Then we can identify truth with the property of being T and falsity with not being T. We can then "explain" how ordered sets are capable of being true or false by pointing to the fact that they can be T or not T. But this strategy is trivial, and does not change the fact that ordered sets are not true or false.[8] The basic problem here is that ordered sets are not representational, and being representational is necessary for being true or false. The same goes for Russell's propositions.

Like Frege, then, Russell also fails to provide a satisfactory account of how propositions have truth conditions. However, the failure of these accounts is suggestive. Both Frege and Russell attempted to explain how

> sense capable of being logical subjects; but when a proposition happens to be true, it has a further quality, over and above that which it shares with false propositions, and it is this further quality which is what I mean by assertion in a logical as opposed to a psychological sense. (Russell 1903, 49)

I think this is best read as an early attempt by Russell to capture the difference between what he later called facts and fictions. True propositions (facts) are logically asserted in the sense that they exist, while false propositions (fictions) are not logically asserted in the sense that they do not exist but only subsist.

[8]   This line of argument applies to Jeff Speaks's theory of propositions (King, et al. 2014, chapter 5). On Speaks's account, the proposition that Amelia talks is the property of being such that Amelia talks. This property is instantiated if and only if everything is such that Amelia talks. Speaks then identifies truth with instantiation: the proposition that Amelia talks is true iff it is instantiated. This is like "explaining" how ordered sets can be true or false by identifying truth with the property of being T. Like Russell's propositions and ordered sets, Speaks's properties are not representational, which disqualifies them from being true or false.

propositions have truth conditions solely by appeal to their internal constitutions. The structure of the Fregean picture barred them from appealing to anything that subjects do or think or say in explaining how propositions have truth conditions. For something to have truth conditions, however, it has to say that the world is a certain way, and it is natural to think that the only way for something to do that is for us to take it to do that. No entity on its own is a representation. We turn things into representations through the way we interpret them.

2.4 King on Propositional Unity

Here is a natural line of thought to take if one is a Fregean inclined to give an informative solution to the unity problem. It won't work to try to explain how propositions have truth conditions intrinsically, that is, without appeal to contributions from thinking subjects. This is what Frege and Russell tried and failed to do. The explanation for how propositions have truth conditions has to involve something that people do or think. On the Fregean picture, propositions are there, waiting to be entertained and judged. Since these entities cannot have their truth conditions on their own they must get their truth conditions from us. We give them their truth conditions. We interpret them in certain ways and thus endow them with truth conditions.

In very broad strokes, this is King's strategy for explaining how propositions have truth conditions.[9] For King, propositions are certain facts in which objects, properties, and relations bear structural relations to one another. We endow these facts with truth conditions by interpreting them to have these truth conditions. More specifically, we interpret the structural relations in propositions in such a way that the facts they bind together have truth conditions. Without these acts of interpretation the facts in question would not be true or false. The fact that my computer is on top of my desk is not true or false, but it could be if we all decided to take it to represent some other state of affairs. Suppose we decided to interpret the fact that my computer is on top of my desk to mean that the President is in the White House. Through this

---

[9] King's view has evolved since its first appearance in the mid-nineties (King 1994, 1995, 1996). I am going to base my remarks on the most recent published presentation of King's views in (King 2007, 2009, 2013; King, et al. 2014).

act of interpretation we could endow the fact that my computer is on my desk with truth conditions: it would be true true just in case the President is in the White House. The fact that my computer is on my desk does not have these truth conditions intrinsically, but only in virtue of our interpreting it in the way we do. On King's view, this is more or less how propositions come to have their truth conditions.

To fill in the details King needs to tell us which facts are propositions, and he needs to explain how it is that we interpret them. His account starts with the observation that sentences have their truth conditions because of the ways in which we interpret the syntactic relations that bind them together. We can think of sentences as facts in which words are bound together by syntactic relations. These facts get their truth conditions through our acts of interpretation.

For ease of exposition I will borrow one of the examples from (King 2009). Consider the English sentence 'Dara swims', which can be represented as in figure 1:

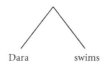

Dara   swims

Figure 1

The branching lines represent the syntactic relation between the words 'Dara' and 'swims' in the sentence 'Dara swims'. Call this relation R. According to King, the sentence 'Dara swims' is true iff Dara swims because of the way we interpret R. He says that we "take the syntactic concatentation in the sentence to ascribe the semantic value of 'swims' to the semantic value of 'Dara'" (King 2009, 262). For King, the semantic value of 'swims' is the property of swimming and the semantic value of 'Dara' is Dara. His claim, then, is that in this case we take the syntactic relation R to ascribe the property of swimming to Dara. That is why the sentence is true iff Dara swims—because we interpret its syntactic relation to be ascribing this property to Dara.

On the face of it, this is an odd thing to claim. Ascription is a kind of action. People ascribe properties to objects, not syntactic relations. We would be guilty of a bad category mistake if we literally took R to ascribe the property of swimming to Dara. But that is not what King means. The sense in which we take R to ascribe the property of swimming to Dara is that when we (competent speakers of English) hear or read 'Dara swims' *we* ascribe the property of swimming to Dara. It is we who perform this act of ascription, not the relation R itself. This is in the sense in which, for King, we interpret R as ascribing the property of swimming of Dara. Here is how he puts it:

> Competent English speakers, when they encounter the sentence 'Dara swims', spontaneously and without thinking take the sentence to be true iff Dara swims. They thereby take the syntactic concatentation in the sentence to ascribe the semantic value of 'swims' to the semantic value of 'Dara'. In other constructions, speakers spontaneously and without thinking take syntactic concatenation differently; for example, when they encounter 'red house' they do something like conjoin properties, and when they encounter 'Everyone swims' something altogether different. In all these cases, competent speakers, when encountering concatenated expressions, compose the semantic values of the concatenated expressions in characteristic ways. This is what their *interpreting* the syntactic concatenation comes to. (King 2009, 262)

In general, sentences have truth conditions because we compose semantic values in the ways we do when we encounter these sentences. Our composing semantic values in these ways amounts to our interpreting syntactic relations as composing semantic values in the same ways. Because of these acts of interpretation, sentences have truth conditions.

King's account of how propositions have truth conditions builds on this account of how sentences have truth conditions. Whatever propositions are, we will interpret them in the same way that we interpret the sentences that express them. If we interpret 'Dara swims' to be true iff Dara swims, then we interpret the proposition that Dara swims to be true iff Dara swims. Furthermore, the way we interpret the proposition will be the same as the way we interpret the sentence: by taking its unifying relation to ascribe a property to an object.

> Now consider all the facts that consist of Dara and the property of swimming bound together by some relation and that would have been candidates to be the proposition that Dara swims. My thought is that *whichever* of these had been 'chosen' to be the proposition that Dara swims, the relation binding together Dara and the property of swimming in the proposition inevitably would be interpreted as ascribing the property of swimming to Dara in virtue of the fact that speakers implicitly and without thinking took the proposition to be true iff Dara possesses the property of swimming. Interpreting the relation in question as ascribing the property of swimming to Dara is required for the proposition to have these truth conditions. Speakers implicitly taking the proposition to have the same truth conditions as the sentence 'Dara swims' results in their so interpreting the propositional relation. (King 2009, 267)

The only remaining question, then, is which facts are propositions. King thinks that, whichever facts these are, it is guaranteed that we will interpret their unifying relations in the same ways that we interpret the syntactic relations in sentences. It has to work like this, since, as King believes, this is the only way for propositions to get their truth conditions.

The facts that King settles on as the most likely candidates for being propositions are built in part out of the very same syntactic relations that occur in sentences. Figure 2 is a picture of the fact that is the proposition that Dara swims:

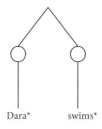

Figure 2

Following King, Dara* is Dara and swims* is the property of swimming. This object and property are the only two constituents of this fact. The branching line represents R, the syntactic relation in the sentence 'Dara swims'. The circles represent the relation between properties of joint instantiation (see King 2007, 30–1). Intuitively, the idea is that the words 'Dara' and 'swims' have been "existentially generalized" out of the fact, leaving only Dara and the property of swimming as constituents. The vertical lines represent the semantic relations that 'Dara' bears to Dara and 'swims' bears to the property of swimming. Putting all of this together, figure 2 depicts the fact in which Dara and the property of swimming are joined together by the following two-place relation: *there is a language L, a context c, and lexical items a and b of L such that a and b occur at the left and right terminal nodes (respectively) of the syntactic relation R that in L encodes ascription and ___ is the semantic value of a in c and ___ is the semantic value of b in c.* (The idea that R in L "encodes ascription" is King's shorthand for the fact that we interpret R as ascribing the property of swimming to Dara.) If King is right, we interpret this relation, the one expressed in italics, as ascribing the property of swimming to Dara. As in the case of R, we interpret this propositional relation as ascribing swimming to Dara just in the sense that we ascribe this property to Dara when we entertain the proposition that Dara swims.[10] Because of this, the fact depicted in figure 2, which is the proposition that Dara swims, is true iff Dara swims.

This is ingenious. In my view it is the best hope for solving the unity problem on the Fregean picture of content, even if it means giving up the idea that propositions have their truth conditions completely independently of what subjects do or think or say. The basic thought is very intuitive. If, on the Fregean picture, the entities that are propositions cannot have their truth conditions independently of us, then they must get their truth conditions from us through the way we interpret them.

But what are these acts of ascription that speakers are supposed to perform when they are interpreting sentences? King's notion of ascription looks very similar to Soames's notion of predication. I do not have to judge or assert that Dara swims when interpreting the sentence 'Dara swims', and interpreting this sentence does not commit me to her possessing the property of swimming. Ascription for King must be neutral and non-committal in the same way that Soamesian predication is neutral and non-committal. Furthermore, acts of ascription must have truth conditions. How else could they explain how sentences and propositions have truth conditions? King's idea is that when we encounter the sentence 'Dara swims' we spontaneously and unreflectively ascribe the property of swimming to Dara, and the fact that this happens explains why the sentence 'Dara swims' has its truth conditions. He must think that the sentence gets its truth conditions from these acts of ascription, which of course requires that acts of ascription themselves have truth conditions. Therefore, King's acts of ascription are actions in which speakers ascribe properties to objects, thereby doing something that can be evaluated for truth and falsity, while remaining completely neutral about whether the objects have those properties. As I argued in

---

[10] In recent work King explicitly claims that we ascribe properties to objects when entertaining propositions:

> When we entertain a proposition, we work our way up the propositional relation, combining semantic values to yield new semantic values for further combining. Obviously we must combine or compose those semantic values in some way. In the case of [the proposition that Michael swims], were we to do anything other than ascribe the property of swimming to Michael, we would not be combining semantic values in a manner that is consistent with the way we interpret the syntax of ['Michael swims']. (King 2013, 80)

chapter 1, this is incoherent. Take any pure, isolated act of ascribing a property to an object, which for King occurs whenever we engage in a pure, isolated act of interpreting a subject–predicate sentence. This act of ascription is true iff the object has the property ascribed to it. These truth conditions are correctness conditions, and if an act has correctness conditions then it is possible to make a mistake in performing that act. If Dara does not swim, then I make a mistake if I ascribe the property of swimming to her. My act of ascription is incorrect (false) because Dara does not have this property, and if my act is incorrect then I made a mistake. But I cannot make a mistake if I take no stand either way about whether Dara swims. Like Soames's notion of neutral predication, King's notion of ascription does not make sense. There are no acts of ascription in King's sense.

I am not denying that "competent English speakers, when they encounter the sentence 'Dara swims', spontaneously and without thinking take the sentence to be true iff Dara swims," (King 2009, 262). That seems unobjectionable.[11] What I am denying is that our interpreting this sentence in this way should be understood in terms of an act of ascribing the property of swimming to Dara. I know what the sentence 'Dara swims' means, and when I see it I interpret it to mean that Dara swims. What I do not do is ascribe or predicate the property of swimming of Dara when I see or hear this sentence. That cannot be what I am doing, since if it were then I would be guilty of an error if Dara does not possess this property, and I cannot be guilty of an error by correctly interpreting the sentence 'Dara swims' to mean that Dara swims. If King is right, we make mistakes every time we correctly interpret false sentences to mean what they mean.

As with Soames, I suspect that King misses these problems because he takes the traditional notion of entertainment to consist in acts of ascription. For King, entertaining the proposition that Dara swims is a matter of ascribing the property of swimming to Dara. Since there is nothing incoherent about entertaining this proposition, there must not be anything incoherent about ascribing this property to Dara. But as we

---

[11] Although maybe not. If King is right, then whenever we read or hear sentences we spontaneously form meta-linguistic beliefs about the truth conditions of those sentences. The only way for this to be plausible is if these beliefs are largely unconscious. Whether we really do form these unconscious meta-linguistic beliefs seems like an empirical question for psycholinguists.

THE UNITY OF THE PROPOSITION 61

have seen, this overlooks the fact that acts of entertainment, unlike acts of ascription, are not truth-evaluable, and cannot be truth-evaluable if they are to be neutral. Soames and King make the same mistake of trying to combine the neutrality of entertainment with the truth-evaluability of judgment, with incoherent results.

But let's bracket this problem. Let's grant to King that speakers perform acts of ascribing or predicating properties of objects (neutral or otherwise), and that these acts can be evaluated for truth and falsity. If we are capable of performing truth-evaluable actions, then why go through this elaborate explanatory detour in explaining how our judgments and assertions have truth conditions? King's solution to the problem of propositional unity is grafted onto the top-down explanatory structure of the Fregean picture. On King's account speakers perform acts of ascription, which explains why sentences have truth conditions, which explains why propositions have truth conditions, which explains why judgments and assertions have truth conditions. The whole thing looks needlessly baroque. If we can perform actions that have truth conditions then we might as well locate those actions directly in the actions we perform when we make judgments and assertions.

Another problem for King's explanatory strategy is that it is unavoidably incomplete. King's basic strategy is to explain how propositions have truth conditions by appealing to the ways in which we interpret propositions. On this approach, propositions do not have truth conditions until we engage in these acts of interpretation. Surely, though, performing these acts of interpretation requires making judgments, forming intentions, and having various propositional attitudes. How are we to account for the truth or satisfaction conditions of these attitudes that we must have prior to performing the acts of interpretation that endow propositions with truth conditions? If propositions do not have truth conditions until we perform such acts, then they cannot be used to explain how these prior attitudes have their truth and satisfaction conditions. We need some other explanation for how these attitudes get their representational features.

King could try to give a bottom-up explanation for the representational features of these prior attitudes, e.g. by appealing to acts of predication that subjects perform in forming judgments and other attitudes. But if a bottom-up explanation works for these attitudes then it should work across the board for all attitudes. Alternatively, he could repeat his theory all over again for these prior attitudes. Let's call the propositions in King's original theory A-propositions. For King, A-propositions are certain facts that have truth conditions because of the way we interpret them. For us to interpret them in this way we need to have attitudes of various kinds, and the contents of these attitudes cannot be A-propositions. We therefore need another kind of proposition, B-propositions, which are the contents of the attitudes we form in interpreting A-propositions. Like A-propositions, B-propositions can only get their truth conditions from our acts of interpretation, which will in turn require further judgments and other attitudes. Now we need C-propositions to account for the contents of these additional attitudes. And so on.

This regress arises for any interpretivist explanation of how propositions have truth conditions. An interpretivist approach identifies certain structures or entities that are to play the role of propositions, and then explains how these structures have truth conditions by appealing to the way in which we interpret them. Pursuing that strategy consistently will require the existence of a continually expanding list of different kinds of propositions and attitudes with these propositions as contents. The regress is clearly vicious, since in order to endow any proposition with truth conditions we would have to perform an infinite sequence of prior acts of interpretation for other kinds of propositions.

King could try to halt the regress by appealing to "proto-intentional states" to explain how we perform the acts of interpretation required for endowing propositions with truth conditions (King 2007, 66–7; King, et al. 2014, 60). These proto-intentional states would be capable of conferring truth conditions on propositions, but they themselves would not have truth or satisfaction conditions and so would not require their own propositional contents. But this is like appealing to proto-beliefs to solve the regress of epistemic justification, or proto-causes to solve the regress of causes, or proto-explanations to solve the regress of explanations. Laurence Bonjour describes this general strategy for solving philosophical regress problems as follows:

Simply postulate a final term in the regress which is sufficiently similar to the previous term to satisfy, with respect to the penultimate term, the sort of need or impetus which originally generated the regress; but which is different enough from previous terms so as not itself to require satisfaction by a further term. (Bonjour 1978, 118)

Bonjour does not reject this strategy out of hand, but he does think that "the nature and possibility of such a convenient regress-stopper needs at the very least to be clearly and convincingly established and explained before it can constitute a satisfactory solution to any regress problem" (Bonjour 1978, 118). In other words, we need some independent reason for positing the proto-items of the relevant kind, and some explanation of what they are. King goes some way toward doing this by pointing out that anyone who accepts the Fregean picture in its classical form, on which propositions have their truth conditions independently of our acts of interpretation, will have to appeal to proto-intentional states to explain how subjects originally made cognitive contact with propositions (King 2007, 67). On the Fregean picture you must entertain a proposition in order to judge or believe it, which necessitates an appeal to proto-intentional states or proto-intentional actions to explain how we first began to entertain propositions. This may be dialectically effective against a philosopher who accepts the classical version of the Fregean picture, but it has no force against a philosopher who rejects that picture and the notion of entertainment that goes along with it. Indeed, the fact that the Fregean picture, in its classical form and in the form defended by King, is forced to posit mysterious proto-intentional states is a reason to be skeptical about this whole approach.

3

Predication and Unity

In this chapter I will begin to build a positive case for my alternative to the Fregean picture of propositional content. The basic explanatory element in this alternative is the concept of predication, understood as a kind of action that speakers perform in making judgments and assertions. It is because we perform these acts of predication that our judgments and assertions have truth conditions. Propositions are types of these actions, and they inherit their truth conditions from them. The goal of this chapter is to spell this out in detail and respond to objections. Another aim is to extend the account of propositions sketched in chapter 1 to relational and quantified propositions. Compound propositions, such as negations, disjunctions, and conjunctions, will have to wait for chapter 4, where I introduce the concept of cancellation.

3.1 Acts of Predication

Acts of predication are acts of sorting things into groups. When you predicate a property of an object you sort that object with other objects in virtue of their similarity with respect to the property. To predicate the property of being green of something is to sort that thing with other green things. This act of sorting can be done behaviorally, for example by picking the object up and putting it with other green things, or it can be done in thought, by mentally grouping the object with other green things, or in speech, by saying that it is green.

In psychology the term for this is *categorization*. "To categorize is to render discriminably different things equivalent, to group the objects and events and people around us into classes, and to respond to them in terms of their class membership rather than their uniqueness" (Bruner, Goodnow, and Austin 1956, 1; see also Smith 1995). The ability to categorize is basic, innate, and ubiquitous. The developmental psychologist Susan Gelman notes that "all

organisms form categories: even mealworms have category-based prefer-
ences, and higher-order animals such as pigeons or octopi can display quite
sophisticated categorical judgments" (Gelman 2003, 11). There are, of course,
vast differences in the number, variety, and character of the categories used
by different animals. Still, the *ability* to categorize is a basic biological
function that human beings share with the rest of the animal kingdom.
Without it, we would not be able to think or speak. As Quine put it, "surely
there is nothing more basic to thought and language than our sense of
similarity; our sorting of things into kinds" (1969a, 116).

   In human beings, acts of sorting/categorizing/predicating come in at
least three varieties: behavioral, mental, and linguistic (spoken or written). If a child picks up a yellow ball and puts it in a pile with other yellow
objects then he performs a behavioral act of predication. Alternatively, he
could simply look at the ball and mentally group it with the other yellow
objects; in this case he performs a mental act of predication. Or, if he
speaks English, he could point to the ball and say 'That is yellow' or 'It is
yellow'. It is tempting to say that the mental act is somehow more
fundamental than the behavioral or linguistic act, but it is difficult to
clarify what this means. It cannot be that in performing the behavioral or
linguistic act the subject must also perform, or have performed, the
mental act. It is possible to lie in performing a behavioral or linguistic
act of predication. One might retreat to the idea that in any sincere act of
behavioral or linguistic predication one must also perform the mental
act. But this is tautologous and uninteresting. A sincere behavioral or
linguistic act of predication is defined as one that is accompanied by the
corresponding mental act. Perhaps the idea is that the capacity to
perform the mental act is necessary for the capacities to perform the
behavioral or linguistic acts, but not vice versa. This seems plausible for
the linguistic capacity, but it is less clear for behavioral acts of predication. The ability to categorize is universal among animals and insects. For
example, by emitting the odor of TNT in the presence of sugarwater
wasps can be trained to detect land mines (Wynne 2004, 58). For this to
succeed the wasps must be sorting things according to the odors they
give off. These acts of sorting are behavioral. The wasp predicates the
property of smelling like TNT by flying to those things that have it.[1] It is

---

[1] Does this imply that the wasp makes judgments and has beliefs? Only in very
attenuated senses of 'judgment' and 'belief'. *We* say that the wasp judges that the landmines

unlikely, however, that the wasp can perform the kinds of purely mental acts of predication that human beings are capable of.

When someone predicates a property of an object the property provides a rule that determines correctness conditions for the act. For example, an act of predicating greenness of something is correct just in case that thing is green. Correctness and incorrectness here are just truth and falsity (cf. Boghossian 2005, 207–8). This means that the act is *true* just in case that thing is green. An act of predicating a property of an object is true or false insofar as it can satisfy or fail to satisfy the correctness conditions determined by the property.[2] Acts of predication have truth conditions and truth-values. On my approach, they are the primary and metaphysically basic bearers of truth conditions.

Some philosophers think that it is a category mistake to hold that *acts* are true or false.[3] This is the first point that Strawson makes in his reply to Austin in their symposium on truth:

The words 'assertion' and 'statement' have a parallel and convenient duplicity of sense. 'My statement' may be either what I say or my saying it. My saying something is certainly an episode. What I say is not. It is the latter, not the former, we declare to be true. (Strawson 1950, 162)

My statement that *x* is green, considered as an episode, is my act of stating that *x* is green. Strawson thinks that it is a "simple and obvious fact" (1950, 164) that when we attribute truth or falsity to statements, assertions, and the like, we are attributing truth and falsity to *what* is

---

smell like TNT, but the wasp can't say that—or anything else about what it is thinking. What exactly, then, is the content of the wasp's judgment? Absent the ability to use language to characterize its mental act, there is an irresolvable indeterminacy in the content of the wasp's judgment. Nothing fixes *what* the wasp judges or believes. The very concept of *determinate* content is tied to a linguistic specification of that content, and the wasp is not capable of providing that specification. I'll return to this in the conclusion.

[2]   I should reiterate a caveat from chapter 1 about reading these claims Platonistically (see footnote 2). I do not want to commit myself to the view that we latch onto Platonistic properties that determine the correctness conditions for acts of predication via their primitive satisfaction conditions. My talk of expressing or identifying a property in an act of predication should be taken as shorthand for whatever it is that we do to determine the correctness conditions for these acts.

[3]   The rest of this section and section 3.2 are improvements on (Hanks 2013b). Thanks to an anonymous reader for pointing out a number of problems and unclarities in an earlier draft.

stated, asserted, etc. and not to the acts of stating, asserting, etc.[4] Bar-Hillel agrees:

Since I find little, if any, point in talking about the truth of speech acts such as statings, assertings, or utterings, and of mental acts (or states) such as believings, I take it as close to self-evident that when one talks of true statements, assertions, utterances, and beliefs, one has the products of these acts in mind. (Bar-Hillel 1973, 304)

Bar-Hillel goes on to explain that by "product" he means "what is expressed" by a sentence—in other words, an abstract, non-linguistic proposition. Strawson and Bar-Hillel join the tradition in holding that it is propositions, and not the acts of stating or asserting propositions, that are the bearers of truth and falsity.

More recently, philosophers have begun to offer arguments for this view. These arguments point to the awkwardness of sentences in which 'true' and 'false' are combined with noun-phrases that denote actions. According to MacFarlane:

We say 'His aim was true', but not 'His aim*ing* was true' or 'What he did in uttering that sentence was true.' This suggests that when we say 'His assertion was false' or 'That was a true utterance', we are using 'assertion' and 'utterance' to refer to what was asserted or uttered, not to the act of asserting or uttering. Characterizing relativism as a thesis about the truth of assertions or utterances in the 'act' sense looks like a category mistake. (MacFarlane 2005, 322)

King makes essentially the same point about event tokens instead of actions:

Suppose I ask Vicky to think of o as red. As she is doing so, if I say 'The event of Vicky thinking of o as red is true (false)' or 'The event Vicky is now bringing about is true (false)' again this sounds like a category mistake. (King 2013, 90)

On the other hand, the sentence 'Vicky's assertion that *o* is red is true (false)' is "immaculate", as King puts it, but this is because the noun phrase 'Vicky's assertion that *o* is red' denotes the proposition she asserted, not her act of asserting it.

But these examples from MacFarlane and King really tell us very little. The question is whether it makes sense to attribute the properties of truth

---

[4] Echoing Strawson, Searle remarks that "the view that it is the act of stating which is true or false is one of the most serious weaknesses of Austin's theory of truth" (Searle 1968, 423). See also (Neale 2004, 100, fn. 45).

and falsity to acts of stating and asserting. Taken as a question about language, the question is: are there any sentences in which truth and falsity are felicitously applied to actions? MacFarlane and King provide a handful of bad sentences that fail in this regard. Clearly, though, we cannot conclude that there is *no* way to attribute truth and falsity to actions. You can't conclude that an existential claim is false from a few negative examples. If there is at least one construction that succeeds in attributing truth or falsity to an action, then the answer to our question is 'yes'.

Here is one such construction, (2a–b). It involves adverbial modification, as in (1a–b):

1a. Obama quickly stated that Clinton is eloquent.
 b. Obama loudly asserted that Putin is honest.
2a. Obama truly stated that Clinton is eloquent.
 b. Obama falsely asserted that Putin is honest.

Like 'quickly' and 'loudly', 'truly' and 'falsely' are verb modifiers that express properties of actions.[5] The mere fact that we have the adverbs 'truly' and 'falsely' in our language shows that we recognize properties of truth and falsity that apply to actions. In fact, we have a number such adverbs:

3a. Obama   rightly/correctly/accurately   stated   that   Clinton   is   eloquent.
 b. Obama   wrongly/incorrectly/inaccurately   asserted   that   Putin   is   honest.

The adverbs 'rightly', 'correctly', and 'accurately' in (3a) all have alethic senses. They can all be used to express the property of truth. Of course, they can also be used to express different sorts of normative properties. 'Rightly' and 'wrongly' have obvious moral meanings. My point is that there are also representational senses of these adverbs. Just as an action can be morally right or wrong, it can be representationally right or wrong—and being representationally right or wrong is just being true or false.

---

[5] See (Parsons 1990, ch.4). 'Truly' the verb modifier should not be confused with 'truly' the sentence modifier, as in "Truly thou art damned, like an ill-roasted egg, all on one side" (Shakespeare, *As You Like It*).

Perhaps the simplest sort of case in which truth or falsity is applied to an action occurs in (4a–b):

4a. Obama's statement was true.

  b. Obama's assertion was false.

I realize that these examples won't convince the philosophers I quoted earlier.[6] All of these philosophers recognize an act/object or act/content distinction in noun phrases like 'Obama's statement'. In the act sense these noun phrases denote acts of stating or asserting; in the object/content sense they denote the propositions stated or asserted. There is nothing wrong with this distinction (although, as I will argue in a moment, it is really just an instance of the token/type distinction). The problem occurs when these philosophers claim that examples like (4a–b) only make sense when the noun phrases are given their object/content readings. The act readings are allegedly unavailable because attributing truth and falsity to actions is supposed to be a category mistake. But as (2a–b) and (3a–b) show, there is no such category mistake. Why not, then, give the noun phrases in (4a–b) their act readings? I can see no compelling reason not to.

There may be lingering doubts due to the kinds of examples used by MacFarlane and King. If actions can be true or false, why can't we explicitly attribute truth and falsity to them with sentences such as the following?

5a. *What he did in uttering that sentence was true.

  b. *The act Obama is now performing is true.

  c. *The act of Obama asserting that Clinton is eloquent was true.

---

[6] Here are some examples I used in an earlier draft that did not convince some readers:

  4'a. Obama's statement lasted one minute and was true.

    b. Biden heard Obama's statement and thought it was true.

    c. Obama's true statement took place at precisely 9:37 am.

    d. Obama's statement, which was false, made him exhausted.

Prima facie, in these examples truth and falsity are predicated of noun phrases for statements, assertions, and judgments in their act senses. However, as an anonymous referee and Bjørn Jespersen pointed out, these look like cases of co-predication. Co-predication occurs when different predicates in a sentence apply to distinct meanings of a polysemous noun phrase, e.g. 'Lunch lasted two hours and was delicious'. 'Lunch' can mean the event or the food, and the predicates 'lasted two hours' and 'delicious' pick up these different meanings. To avoid the possibility of co-predication, I need examples in which only a single meaning is in play, such as 'Obama's statement was true'.

It is not difficult to see why these examples sound bad. Obama's assertion, considered as an action, is subject to both practical and theoretical norms. His assertion could be brilliant in a practical or pragmatic sense but false and theoretically unjustified. Conversely, it could be a tactical blunder but true and warranted. Some ways of talking about his action focus on its practical side, while others bring out its representational and theoretical sides. When we describe Obama's action as something he *did* or as an *act* we highlight its practical aspects. When we describe it as something he *asserted* or as an *assertion* we highlight its representational and theoretical aspects. Note the shift in the meaning of 'justified' between these two examples:

6a. What he did in uttering that sentence was justified.
  b. What he asserted in uttering that sentence was justified.

The justification in (6a) is practical justification; Obama had good reasons (or there are good reasons) for doing what he did. The justification in (6b) is theoretical justification; Obama had reasons (or there are reasons) that support the truth of his assertion. Substituting the verb 'asserted' for 'did' forces this switch in the interpretation of 'justified'. Note that the problems for (5a–c) disappear if we substitute predicates of practical rationality for 'true':

7a. What he did in uttering that sentence was irrational.
  b. The act Obama is now performing is reasonable.
  c. The act of Obama asserting that Clinton is eloquent was clever.

Similarly, the problems disappear if we substitute 'asserted' for 'did' in (5a), and 'assertion' for 'act' in (5b):[7]

8a. What he asserted in uttering that sentence was true.
  b. The assertion Obama is now performing is true.

Considered as something he *did*, as an *act*, Obama's assertion is subject to practical norms; considered as something he *asserted*, as an *assertion*,

---

[7] This doesn't work for (5c). *"The assertion of Obama asserting that Clinton is eloquent is true' is terrible. This must have something to do with the gerundive nominal 'Obama asserting that Clinton is eloquent'. 'The act of him moving attracted attention' is okay, but *"The movement of him moving attracted attention' is bad.

it is subject to theoretical norms. My suggestion, then, is that the reason (5a–c) sound bad is that they foreground the practical aspects of Obama's action, thereby making attributions of truth sound inappropriate.[8] This poses no threat to the claim that, when considered as an assertion, Obama's action is true or false and has truth conditions.

Bar-Hillel uses the terms 'act' and 'product' for what earlier I called the act/object or act/content distinction (henceforth just the act/content distinction). This is confusing terminology, since the terms 'act' and 'product' are best reserved for a different distinction. In the product sense the noun phrase 'Obama's statement' denotes the concrete sentence token he produced in making his statement. This is clearest in the case of written language. Suppose Obama writes 'Clinton is eloquent' on a chalkboard. Then 'Obama's statement' in the product sense denotes the chalk marks on the chalkboard. Statements, assertions, and judgments considered as products become more fleeting, and more metaphysically suspect, the farther away we get from this paradigm. If Clinton's assertion is spoken, then 'Clinton's assertion' in the product sense denotes the sounds she produced. 'Clinton's judgment', in the product sense, denotes, I suppose, the brain events that constituted her judgment— although saying this requires a hair-splitting distinction between these brain events and her act of judgment. In any case, there is no denying that noun phrases like 'Obama's statement', at least in some cases, exhibit the same kind of act/product ambiguity that we find in noun phrases like 'Obama's building' or 'Obama's writing'.

The act/product distinction for 'Obama's statement' is genuine, but it provides no help for the philosopher who wants to deny that acts of stating or asserting are true or false. Even if the noun phrases in (4a–b) can be read in the product senses, they do not have to be, and the act reading will be strongly preferred whenever the product reading is elusive or metaphysically questionable.

---

[8] Thanks to Michelle Mason for insightful comments that led to this idea. Note that (5a–c) are supposed to be about *token* acts of assertion. The suggestion is that these examples sound bad because they foreground the practical aspects of these token actions. Nothing I have said implies that propositions, considered as types of acts of assertion, are subject to practical norms.

The act/product distinction is, of course, also subject to the token/type distinction. There are tokens and types of actions, and tokens and types of products. 'Obama's statement' is thus four-ways ambiguous:

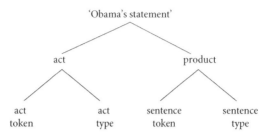

Adding the act/content distinction threatens to complicate the picture even further, but thankfully there's no need for that. The act/content distinction is already captured in our diagram in the form of the token/type distinction for the act reading of 'Obama's statement'. Obama's statement, in the content sense, is *what* Obama stated, and 'what Obama stated' typically (although not always) denotes the *type* of statement he made. We often use phrases of the form 'what S *v*'ed' to talk about types. For example, 'what Obama ate' can be used to denote a type of food he ate; 'what Obama wore' can be used to denote a type of clothing he wore, e.g. a blue suit. Now, compare these examples:

9a. Clinton did what Obama did.
 b. Clinton and Obama did the same thing.
 c. There's something Clinton and Obama both did.

10a. Clinton stated what Obama stated.
 b. Clinton and Obama stated the same thing.
 c. There's something Clinton and Obama both stated.

(9a–c), on their most natural readings, mean that Clinton and Obama performed the same type of action. 'What Obama did' in (9a), and 'the same thing' in (9b), denote this type of action. Similarly, 'what Obama stated' in (10a), and 'the same thing' in (10b), are naturally read as denoting a type, either the type of statement (action) that Obama performed, or perhaps the sentence type he produced. Given that propositions are not sentence types, if we use 'what Obama stated' to denote a proposition, then we should identify this proposition with the type of statement he produced—a type of action. Propositions are types of statements, assertions, judgments, and beliefs.

3.2 Tokens, Types, and Truth Conditions

I have just been arguing that token acts of predication, which can be token acts of judging, stating, or asserting, are true or false and have truth conditions. Someone might accept this and still deny that types of these actions have truth conditions. In this section I want to consider a more theoretical, less example-driven argument against the claim that types of acts of predication have truth conditions. Examining this argument will help clarify what it means for a type of action to inherit truth conditions from its tokens, and hence will clarify my explanation of how propositions have truth conditions.

The argument arises out of the metaphysical differences between tokens and types. Suppose we accept that token acts of predication are true or false. Any such token is true or false because it consists in a subject predicating a property of an object. When Obama asserts that Clinton is eloquent he predicates the property of being eloquent of Clinton. In doing so he sorts Clinton into the group of people who are eloquent. The truth conditions for his act of predication are determined by a rule given by the property of eloquence: his assertion is true iff Clinton is eloquent.

This explanation for the truth conditions of Obama's assertion depends on the fact that Obama performed an act of predication. He predicated eloquence of Clinton, and therefore his assertion is true iff Clinton is eloquent. But, of course, the *type* of action he performed doesn't predicate eloquence of Clinton. The type does not consist in a subject predicating a property of an object. If it did then it would be a token act of predication. Therefore, even if token acts of predication have truth conditions, it doesn't make sense to say that types of these actions do as well.

To see what is wrong with this argument it helps to consider the following parallel argument. Types of material objects are not themselves material objects. Therefore, types of material objects do not have material properties:

Argument 1

P_1. Only token material objects have material properties.

P_2. Types of material objects are not token material objects.

∴ Types of material objects do not have material properties.

This argument is unsound; premise 1 is false. Consider the Union Jack, the flag of the United Kingdom. Tokens of the Union Jack have material properties, but so does the type. The Union Jack, the type, is partly red, partly blue, and partly white. It is striped. It is rectangular. It is attached to flagpoles all over the United Kingdom. Works of art provide another rich source of examples. As Richard Wollheim observes:

> For though they may not be objects but types, this does not prevent them from having physical properties. There is nothing that prevents us from saying that Donne's *Satires* are harsh on the ear, or that Dürer's engraving of St. Anthony has a differentiated texture, or that the conclusion of "Celeste Aida" is pianissimo. (Wollheim 1980, 82).

In each of these examples a material property is attributed to a work of art considered as a type.

Let's stay with this analogy for a moment before returning to tokens and types of acts of predication. How could an abstract type of material object have material properties? There is really no great mystery here. Types of material objects have material properties in a secondary or derivative sense. Token material objects are the primary bearers of material properties, and types of material objects have material properties because their tokens do. The sense of 'because' here is metaphysical or constitutive. The fact that the Union Jack, the type, is flying from flagpoles all over the UK is constituted by the fact that tokens of the Union Jack are flying from flagpoles all over the UK. Dürer's engraving of St. Anthony has a differentiated texture in virtue of the fact that tokens of this engraving have differentiated textures.

In addition, for many material properties, the possession of the material property by the type does not depend on the existence of tokens of that type.[9] Suppose all the tokens of Dürer's engraving of St. Anthony are destroyed. We would still say that the engraving, the type, has a differentiated texture. In this case the fact about the type is constituted counterfactually. Dürer's engraving of St. Anthony has a differentiated

---

[9] This is true for many material properties, but not all. If no tokens of the Union Jack exist then the Union Jack, the type, is not flying from any flagpoles.

texture in the sense that if there were tokens of this engraving then those tokens would have differentiated textures. We explain what it is for the type to have a material property by appealing to the possession of that property by its actual or possible tokens.

All of this is consistent with the fact that we can often explain why an object has some property by saying that it is a token of a certain type. Suppose someone wants to know why a particular engraving is worth, say, $400,000. We can explain this by saying that it is an instance of Dürer's engraving of St. Anthony, and this type of engraving is worth $400,000. Here we explain why the token has a certain property by locating it under a type. This doesn't threaten the constitutive dependence of facts about the type on facts about its tokens since the nature of this explanation is not constitutive. The fact that the token engraving is worth $400,000 is not constituted by a fact about the type. It is constituted by some complicated fact about the art market. Saying that the engraving is a token of Dürer's engraving of St. Anthony explains why it is worth $400,000 by telling us what kind of engraving it is. The explanation is classificatory, not constitutive. Compare explaining why this apple is green by appealing to its surface reflectance properties versus saying that it is a Granny Smith.

All of these points carry over in a straightforward way to tokens and types of acts of predication. Types of acts of predication are not particular acts of predication, but this is no barrier to their sharing truth conditions with their tokens. Furthermore, the possession of truth conditions by a type is constituted by the possession of truth conditions by actual or possible tokens of that type. This is the sense in which a type of act of predication, a proposition, *inherits* truth conditions from its tokens.

Of course, the analogy between material objects and acts of predication is not exact. Acts of predication are not objects. What, then, is the analog of argument 1 for acts of predication? To answer this, we need an analog for material properties. In the case of acts of predication, that role can be played by the concept of an *evaluative* property. We evaluate token actions along rational, prudential, moral, and aesthetic dimensions, among many others. Actions are justified or unjustified, wise or foolish, morally right or wrong, beautiful or ugly. We apply these sorts of evaluative properties in the first instance to particular, token actions. In doing so, we evaluate what an agent did. This may lead one to think that, because types of actions are not constituted by agents performing actions, it is inappropriate to attribute evaluative properties to types of actions. Token actions may have evaluative properties, but types of actions do not. Here, then, is our analog for argument 1:

Argument 2
P_1. Only token actions have evaluative properties.
P_2. Types of actions are not token actions.
∴. Types of actions do not have evaluative properties.

As before, premise 1 is false. We regularly attribute evaluative properties to types of actions. Consider a skillfully executed, elegant pirouette. The token movement performed by the dancer is skillful and elegant, but so is that type of movement. It is easy to multiply examples. There are mechanically sound and unsound ways to swing a baseball bat, healthy and unhealthy ways to make an omelet, easy and hard ways to change a bicycle tire, effective and ineffective ways to deliver a lecture. In each case, evaluative properties are applied to *ways* of doing something—types of actions.

Truth and falsity are evaluative properties. To say that a judgment or assertion is true is to give it a positive evaluation. Whatever other features a token act of predication may have, being true is a positive feature and being false is a negative feature. As we have just seen, we regularly attribute evaluative properties not only to token actions but also to types under which these actions fall. The metaphysical differences between tokens and types therefore present no barrier to holding that types of acts of predication are true or false. And, of course, in order to be true or false a type of act of predication must have truth conditions.

Just as in the case of types of material objects and material properties, types of acts of predication inherit their truth conditions from their actual or possible tokens. A type of act of predication need not have any actual tokens in order for it to have truth conditions. Even if no one ever has or ever will predicate eloquence of Clinton, this type of act of predication is true iff Clinton is eloquent because if there were any tokens of this type, those tokens would be true iff Clinton is eloquent. The fact that types of acts of predication have truth conditions is constituted by the possession of those truth conditions by its actual or possible tokens.

The story is complicated by the fact that any token act of predication falls under an indefinitely large number of different types, only some of which inherit the truth conditions of the token. Consider a case of moral evaluation. Suppose Obama lies to Clinton during a Cabinet meeting on a Thursday. This token action is morally wrong, and it falls under a large range of types that are also morally wrong, e.g. lying to Clinton during a Cabinet meeting on a Thursday, lying to Clinton during a Cabinet meeting, lying to Clinton on a Thursday, lying to Clinton, lying, intentionally deceiving Clinton on a Thursday, intentionally deceiving Clinton, etc. But there are other types under which Obama's action falls that are morally neutral, e.g. saying something to Clinton during a Cabinet meeting on a Thursday, saying something to Clinton during a Cabinet meeting, saying something to Clinton, uttering a sentence of English, making noises with one's mouth, doing something on a Thursday, etc. This raises a question about why some types inherit a property from their tokens and some do not. I do not know how to answer this question for the moral case, although I have the beginning of an answer for the case of truth and falsity. But let's first get a better sense of the range of available types pertaining to acts of predication.

Using the notation I introduced in chapter 1, here is the proposition that Clinton is eloquent:

11. ⊢ <**Clinton**, ELOQUENT>

This is a type of action someone performs when she refers to Clinton, expresses the property of eloquence, and predicates this property of Clinton. '**Clinton**' stands for a type of reference act, 'ELOQUENT' stands for a type of expression act, and '⊢' stands for predication. Like its tokens, this type of action is true iff Clinton is eloquent.

This type, (11), sits roughly near the center of a range of types of varying degrees of fineness of grain. The reference type **Clinton** is an example of what I call a *semantic reference type*, which is more finely grained than the type that covers acts of reference to Clinton of any kind using any referential device whatsoever. Semantic reference types are defined in terms of the concept of semantic competence. Very roughly, two token acts of reference employing the names n_1 and n_2 fall under the same semantic reference type just in case anyone who is semantically competent with the names n_1 and n_2 will know, just in virtue of their competence, that these token acts of reference co-refer (I give a more precise definition in chapter 5). This entails that most acts of reference employing co-referential but distinct names, e.g. 'Mark Twain' and 'Sam Clemens', fall under different semantic reference types, since someone can be competent with both names and fail to realize that their uses co-refer. On the other hand, we can define a type of reference act solely in terms of the identity of the referent, in which case uses of 'Mark Twain' and 'Sam Clemens' would fall under the same reference type. Let's call this more coarsely grained type an *object dependent reference type*, since whether a token act of reference falls under it depends only on the identity of the object referred to. Uses of 'Mark Twain' and 'Sam Clemens' fall under different semantic reference types but the same object dependent reference type. Any token of a semantic reference type falls under the corresponding object dependent reference type, but not vice versa.

Let '$Clinton_{obj}$' stand for the object dependent reference type corresponding to the semantic reference type **Clinton**. Corresponding to (11), then, we have a more coarsely grained type:

12. ⊢ <$Clinton_{obj}$, ELOQUENT>

This is a super-type of (11): any token of (11) falls under (12), but not vice versa. In addition, there are indefinitely many sub-types of (11), each of which incorporates more details about how the reference act is performed. There is the type of act of referring to Clinton under the semantic reference type **Clinton** while thinking of her as a former senator from New York, or while thinking of her as the Secretary of State in President Obama's first term, or during a Cabinet meeting on a Thursday, etc. The more details we include, the more finely grained the resulting type will be. This generates sub-types of (11):

13a. ⊢ <$Clinton_{thought\text{-}of\text{-}as\text{-}a\text{-}former\text{-}senator\text{-}from\text{-}New\ York}$, ELOQUENT>
   b. ⊢ <$Clinton_{thought\text{-}of\text{-}as\text{-}the\text{-}Secretary\text{-}of\text{-}State\text{-}in\text{-}Obama's\text{-}1st\text{-}term}$, ELOQUENT>
   c. ⊢ <$Clinton_{during\text{-}a\text{-}Cabinet\text{-}meeting\text{-}on\text{-}a\text{-}Thursday}$, ELOQUENT>

Like (11), all of these types, (12) and (13a–c), are true or false depending on whether Clinton is eloquent. And there are many more that share these truth conditions. Intuitively, the idea is that a type like (11) is surrounded by an array of less or more finely grained types, all of which share the same truth conditions. I see no problem with calling all of the types in this array propositions.[10] Remember that propositions play a

---

[10] What about types that are impossible to perform, e.g. predicating eloquence of Clinton while drawing a round square? I am still inclined to say that this type is a

fundamentally classificatory role. In some contexts we want to classify a judgment or assertion quite broadly, in which case we will classify it under the type (12). In other contexts we want to classify a judgment or assertion more narrowly, in which case we could use the type (11), (13a–c), or any number of other more finely grained types. These acts of classification take the form of propositional attitude reports. When I say 'Obama asserted that Clinton is eloquent', the that-clause determines the type (11) and its surrounding array of less or more finely grained types. The truth of the attitude report in a context depends on whether Obama performed a token of one of the types in this array. So, in some contexts 'Obama asserted that Clinton is eloquent' is true iff Obama performed a token of (12), in others iff he performed a token of (11), or (13a–c), or some other more finely grained type. All of this allows us to capture the complicated and highly context sensitive facts about the truth conditions of propositional attitude reports. This is just a sketch of how to use this approach to propositions to give a semantic account of propositional attitude reports—I return to this topic in chapter 7. The point to emphasize is that all of the above types, and many more, are useful for classifying attitudes and speech acts in propositional attitude reports. This is why all of these types deserve to be called propositions.

The types (12) and (13a–c) all share the truth conditions of (11). By widening our scope we can arrive at super-types of (11) that do not share these truth conditions. Consider the type of act of referring to someone or other, expressing the property of eloquence, and predicating that property of the person referred to. This is also a super-type of (11), but it does not have a truth-value or truth conditions. This is because the reference type, the type of act of referring to someone or other, fails to determine a referent. There is also the type of act of referring to Clinton, expressing the property of eloquence, and combining that property with

proposition and that it is true iff Clinton is eloquent. The problem is that it has no actual or possible tokens, which blocks the inheritance account of how it has its truth conditions. But notice that this is a sub-type of the type of act of predicating eloquence of Clinton, and the inheritance account goes through for this more general type. In this case we can extend the truth conditions of the possible super-type to the impossible sub-type by courtesy. Are there impossible types that are not sub-types of possible ones? I am not sure. If there are, then I think we could safely not count them as propositions. Thanks to Jenn Asselin and other members of Ben Caplan's seminar at Ohio State for pressing these concerns.

Clinton in some way or other—not necessarily by predicating eloquence of Clinton, but perhaps by asking whether Clinton has this property, or ordering Clinton to have this property. This super-type of (11) also lacks a truth-value and truth conditions, because its tokens need not be cases of agents predicating eloquence of Clinton. There are many, many more such super-types. Why do some of these types have truth conditions and others do not? At a minimum, in order to be true iff Clinton is eloquent, a type has to determine Clinton, determine the property of eloquence, and determine that this property is predicated of Clinton. Super-types of (11) that fail to meet one of these conditions are not true or false and do not have truth conditions. More generally, in simple atomic cases, in order to inherit truth conditions from its tokens a type needs to be finely grained enough to determine a property or relation, the right number of objects, and predication.

3.3 Relational Propositions

To this point I have focused on very simple subject–predicate propositions in which a monadic property is predicated of an object. It is time to extend the view to more complicated propositions. In this section I will discuss relational propositions, e.g. the proposition that Obama admires Clinton, and in the next section quantified propositions.

As soon as we turn to relational propositions we immediately face a problem about non-symmetrical relations. The proposition that Obama admires Clinton is obviously different from the proposition that Clinton admires Obama. What is the difference between these propositions? In the present context this is a question about acts of predication. What is the difference between the acts one performs in judging that Obama admires Clinton versus judging that Clinton admires Obama?

It is very natural to say that the difference is a matter of the *order* in which admiration is predicated of these two individuals. To judge that Obama admires Clinton is to predicate admiration of Obama and Clinton in that order. To judge that Clinton admires Obama is to predicate admiration of Obama and Clinton in the opposite order. Alternatively, we might say that the difference between these judgments is a difference in the *direction* in which admiration is predicated of Obama and Clinton. In judging that Obama admires Clinton one predicates admiration *from* Obama *to* Clinton.

Russell uses both of these metaphors, order and direction, in an explanation of what it is to judge that Desdemona loves Cassio:

It will be observed that the relation of judging has what is called a 'sense' or 'direction'. We may say, metaphorically, that it puts its objects in a certain *order*, which we may indicate by means of the order of the words in the sentence. (In an inflected language, the same thing will be indicated by inflections, e.g. by the difference between nominative and accusative.) Othello's judgement that Cassio loves Desdemona differs from his judgement that Desdemona loves Cassio, in spite of the fact that it consists of the same constituents, because the relation of judging places the constituents in a different order in the two cases. Similarly, if Cassio judges that Desdemona loves Othello, the constituents of the judgement are still the same, but their order is different. This property of having a 'sense' or 'direction' is one which the relation of judging shares with all other relations. (Russell 1912, 126–7)

Russell is quite clear that these are metaphors, which come naturally to us because of the significance of word order in English. But what could it mean, literally, to predicate love of Cassio and Desdemona in a certain order? It cannot mean temporal order. In judging that Cassio loves Desdemona you do not have to mention Cassio *before* you mention Desdemona. The act of predication involved in judging that Cassio loves Desdemona is the same as that involved in judging that Desdemona is loved by Cassio. These judgments have the same content—they fall under the same type of predicative action—but the temporal order in which one refers to Cassio and Desdemona is switched in the two cases. The kind of order involved is logical or semantic, not temporal. Merely saying this, however, doesn't get us any closer to understanding what this sort of order amounts to.

Russell says that the relation of judging "puts its objects in a certain order". Perhaps his idea was something like the following. In Othello's judgment that Desdemona loves Cassio, the judgment relation is a four-place relation, which assigns different roles to its arguments. One argument role is for the subject (Othello), one for a subordinate relation (loving), and two for the relata of this relation (Desdemona, Cassio). This is still insufficient, since we do not have the resources for distinguishing the judgment that Desdemona loves Cassio from the judgment that Cassio loves Desdemona. To achieve this the judgment relation has to differentiate between the relata of its subordinate relation. It needs to have a first-relatum role and a second-relatum role. With loving as the subordinate relation, the first-relatum role is for the lover and the second for the one being loved. In Othello's judgment that Desdemona loves Cassio, the relation of judgment "puts its objects in a certain order" in the sense that it assigns its arguments to these various roles.

An obvious problem arises when we apply this account to judgments involving symmetrical relations. Suppose Othello judges that Desdemona is similar to Cassio. In this case, as before, Desdemona occupies the first-relatum role and Cassio the second-relatum role. This judgment is therefore distinct from Othello's judgment that Cassio is similar to Desdemona—but intuitively these are not distinct judgments, and Russell would not have regarded them as distinct. We could try to avoid this by distinguishing between judging relations, one for symmetrical subordinate relations and another for non-symmetrical ones. But even if that could be made to work, there is still something mysterious about this analysis. Russell's idea is that the relation of judgment assigns its arguments to various roles. Metaphorically speaking, the judgment relation takes its arguments and slots them into various roles. Surely, though, that is a job for the judging subject, not the relation of judgment.

The above passage comes from *The Problems of Philosophy*, published in 1912. One year later, in the unfinished manuscript *Theory of Knowledge*, Russell gave up the idea that the judgment relation "puts its objects in a certain order". He came to see that it is the subject who is responsible for this, not the relation of judgment. Speaking of understanding instead of judgment, where the former is an entertainment-like precursor to judgment, Russell implements this idea by including logical forms among the constituents of understanding:

What is the proof that we must understand the "form" before we can understand the proposition? I held formerly that the objects alone sufficed, and that the "sense" of the relation of understanding would put them in the right order; this, however, no longer seems to me to be the case. Suppose we wish to understand "*A* and *B* are similar". It is essential that our thought should, as is said, "unite" or "synthesize" the two terms and the relation; but we cannot *actually* "unite" them, since either *A* and *B* are similar, in which case they are already united, or they are dissimilar, in which case no amount of thinking can force them to be united. The process of "uniting" which we *can* effect in thought is the process of bringing them into relation with the general form of dual complexes. The form being "something and something have a certain relation", our understanding of the proposition might be expressed in the words "something, namely *A*, and something, namely *B*, have a certain relation, namely similarity". (Russell 1913, 116)

By "the general form of dual complexes" Russell means the logical form of facts involving two objects and a dyadic relation. Russell conceives of this logical form as a very general fact: the fact that something has some relation to something. He symbolizes this fact as '$R(x,y)$'. When a subject understands that A and B are similar she associates A with x, B with y, and similarity with R. This is what understanding that A and B are similar amounts to: associating these objects and relation with the positions in the logical form '$R(x, y)$'. On this version of Russell's multiple relation theory the relation of understanding is a five-place relation:

$U (S, A, B, \text{similarity}, R(x,y))$

The fifth argument place is reserved for the logical form '$R(x, y)$', which Russell regards as a simple object of acquaintance.

I do not want to get bogged down in the intricacies surrounding Russell's multiple relation theory of judgment in the *Theory of Knowledge* manuscript (see Hanks 2007; Pincock 2008). The key point for our purposes is Russell's idea that in making a judgment the subject associates objects with the argument places in a relation. Russell implements this idea by including logical forms as constituents of understanding and judgment complexes. I do not think we need to follow him in this. When predicating a relation of a pair of objects the subject assigns the objects to the argument places in the relation. There is no need to complicate the picture by including a Russellian logical form.

Acts of predication are directed. When Obama predicates the property of eloquence of Clinton, Clinton is the target of his act of predication. He applies the property of eloquence *to* Clinton. This is a necessary aspect of any act of predication. It makes no sense to perform an act of predication that is not targeted at anything. In performing an act of sorting or categorizing you must at least attempt to identify something to be sorted or categorized.

Now, consider an act of predication involving a symmetrical relation, e.g. the relation of being next-to. This relation calls for two arguments but does not distinguish between the roles played by these arguments. The argument places that are in the next-to relation are interchangeable. For this reason, an act of predication involving this relation can be indiscriminately targeted at two individuals. Suppose Biden judges that Obama is next to Clinton. Obama and Clinton both serve as targets for

Biden's act of predication, and they do so in exactly the same way. This is why Biden's judgment that Obama is next to Clinton and his judgment that Clinton is next to Obama both count as tokens of the same predicative type. This is the sense in which these judgments have the same propositional content.

Compare this with a case involving a non-symmetrical relation. Suppose Biden judges that Obama admires Clinton. The relation of admiration is a two-place relation; it calls for two arguments, and these arguments play different roles in the resulting state of affairs. One role is for the admirer and the other is for the person being admired. When you predicate the relation of admiration of two individuals, you have to target one of the individuals for the admirer role and the other for the admiree role. You cannot indifferently direct your act of predication at two individuals; one of them has to be selected as the admirer and the other as the admiree. This is why judging that Obama admires Clinton is different from judging that Clinton admires Obama. The two judgments differ in how the subject assigns Obama and Clinton to the argument roles in the admiration relation.[11]

There are a number of different ways of capturing these ideas with the notation I introduced in chapter 1. Here is one way to do so. We can represent the proposition that Obama is next to Clinton as follows:

14. ⊢ <(**Obama, Clinton**), NEXT-TO>

The parentheses, '(' and ')', indicate that this type does not differentiate between the ways in which Obama and Clinton serve as targets of the act of predication. These tokens include judgments that Obama is next to

---

[11] In a recent paper Gary Ostertag complains that "it is hard [for an act theorist like me or Soames] to give sense to the idea of assigning an entity to a 'position' in a relation," (Ostertag 2013, 528). Ostertag allows that if act theorists can make sense of relations with argument positions then we can make sense of assigning entities to these positions. The trouble is making sense of the relations. We cannot derive them from unified, Fregean propositions, since we reject the existence of such propositions. Nor can we derive them from types of acts of predication, since we presuppose these relations in making sense of these types. Ostertag concludes that relational propositions pose a decisive problem for the act theorist. But there is an option here that Ostertag overlooks. The act theorist can start with facts or states of affairs in which objects bear relations to one another, with the objects in those states of affairs playing different roles. We then derive relations by abstraction from these states of affairs. To assign entities to positions in a relation is, in effect, to sort a state of affairs containing those entities, playing their respective roles, alongside other similarly organized states of affairs.

Clinton and that Clinton is next to Obama. The propositions that Obama admires Clinton and that Clinton admires Obama can be represented, respectively, as follows:

15a. ⊢ < <**Obama, Clinton**>, ADMIRES>
  b. ⊢ < <**Clinton, Obama**>, ADMIRES>

The angle brackets around the reference types **Obama** and **Clinton** indicate that the acts of predication are targeted differently at Obama and Clinton. In (15a) Obama is targeted for the admirer role, Clinton for the admiree role, and vice versa for (15b).

Do not confuse (15a–b) with ordered pairs. I am using the angle brackets of ordered pairs to represent these propositions, but propositions like (15a–b) are not ordered pairs. There are other ways we might represent these types, but these different notational schemes do not correspond to different proposals about the natures of these propositions. This view does not face the Benacerraf problem.[12]

Think of the notation in (14) and (15a–b) as descriptions of different types of predicative actions. The notation in (14) tells us that this is a type of action in which a subject refers to Obama and Clinton, expresses the relation of being next-to, and predicates this relation of Obama and Clinton, where this act of predication is undifferentiated with respect to its targets. These last two features are represented by the single turnstile and the parentheses. The internal angle brackets in (15a–b) indicate that these acts of predication are not undifferentiated. The parentheses and angle brackets reflect differences in the acts of predication in tokens of these types. Tokens of (14) are different from tokens of (15a) not just in the fact that subjects express different relations, but also in the fact that subjects perform different kinds of acts of predication. We might call the predication in (14) *unsorted* predication and the predication in (15a–b) *sorted* predication. In an act of unsorted predication a subject targets various objects, but doesn't treat these objects any

---

[12] (Benacerraf 1965) argues against any reduction of numbers to sets based on the fact that there are many equally good ways of carrying out such a reduction, with no principled way to choose between schemes of reduction. Many proposals about the nature of propositions face a similar problem. See (Hanks 2009) for discussion. (Caplan and Tillman 2013) press the Benacerraf problem against King's theory of propositions.

differently as targets of predication. In an act of sorted predication the subject targets various objects and does treat them differently, by assigning them to different argument roles.

Before moving on to quantified propositions, let me say a bit about how these argument roles are related to the semantic concept of thematic roles. The kind of argument roles I am appealing to are specific to particular relations.[13] For example, the relation of admiration has a role for an admirer and a role for someone being admired. The relation of loving has a role for a lover and a role for someone loved. When a subject predicates one of these relations she assigns objects to these specific argument roles. Thematic roles, such as Agent, Patient, Experiencer, Theme, Source, and Goal, are generalized roles that are supposed to be shared across different verbs and relations. For example, the verb 'kick', in addition to assigning kicker and kickee roles, assigns the Agent role to the person who does the kicking and the Patient role to the thing that is kicked (or to the respective nouns). The verb 'give' assigns the Agent role to the giver, the Theme role to the object given, and the Goal role to the person to whom the object is given.[14] There is a great deal of disagreement among linguists about which thematic roles exist, how they should be characterized, how to justify assignments of nouns to the various roles associated with a verb, and even about whether thematic roles have any place in semantic theory. On the other hand, it is not controversial that particular verbs and relations assign particularized roles to their arguments. These more specific roles are the ones I am using in my account of relational propositions. It is questionable whether, in predicating admiration of Obama and Clinton, a subject targets Obama as the Experiencer and Clinton as the Patient or Theme. It should not be controversial that the subject targets Obama as the one doing the admiring and Clinton as the one being admired.

---

[13] See Dowty's concept of an "individual thematic role", in (Dowty 1989).

[14] There is also a closely related concept of thematic relations. Thematic *roles* are roles that verbs or relations assign to their arguments; thematic *relations* are relations that objects bear to the states of affairs in which they participate. Consider the state of affairs in which Caesar stabs Brutus with a knife. Caesar bears the Agent relation to this state of affairs, Brutus the Patient relation, and the knife the Instrument relation. See (Parsons 1990, 1995).

3.4 Quantified Propositions

Suppose Obama says that every politician is eloquent. How should we understand this act of predication? He did not refer to any particular object and so it can't be that he predicated the property of being eloquent of anything. He *expressed* the property of being eloquent, but he didn't predicate this property of anything. Remember that we have decoupled the act of expressing a property from the act of predication. This decoupling is necessary because there are different ways of combining a property with an object. You can predicate a property of an object, but you can also *ask* whether an object has a property, or *order* an object to have a property. In these different acts you express or single out a property for the purposes of combining it in some way with an object. The differences come in the different forms of combination. This is one reason why the act of expressing a property has to be kept distinct from the act of predication. Quantification provides another reason.

When Obama says that every politician is eloquent, he expresses the property of being eloquent, but *not* for the purpose of predicating that property of something. Rather, he expresses the property of being eloquent in order to provide a target for a second order act of predication. He predicates a second-order property, the property of being instantiated by every politician, of the property of being eloquent. This is just the familiar Fregean treatment of quantifiers as second-order concepts translated into act-theoretic terms. In a first-order act of predication, a first-level property is predicated of an object. In a second-order act of predication, a second-level property is predicated of a first-level property. When Obama says that every politician is eloquent he performs a second-order act of predication. This second-order act of predication is still predication. It is still sorting or categorizing. The first-order/second-order distinction is just a matter of whether you are sorting an object with other objects (first-order), or a property with other properties (second-order). This doesn't make for a fundamental difference in the act of sorting itself.

Given the detachment of property expression from predication, quantification does not present any special difficulties. In fact, it is easy to implement the familiar, standard approach to generalized quantification, as in, for example, (Keenan 1996), into act-theoretic terms. On this approach, quantificational determiners like 'every' and 'some' are assigned functions from first-level properties to second-level properties. In 'Every politician is eloquent', the function assigned to 'every' maps the property of being a politician to the second-level property of being a first-level property had by every politician. This sentence is true just in case the first-level property of being eloquent instantiates this second-level property.

As I said, it is not hard to implement this approach in the framework of act-types. Let EVERY be a type of action you perform when you express a function, call it $F_\forall$, from properties to second-level properties of properties. $F_\forall$ maps the property of being a politician to the second-level property of being a first-level property that holds of every politician. When Obama says that every politician is eloquent he expresses this function and applies it to the property of being a politician, thereby yielding this second-level property. He then predicates this second-level property of the property of being eloquent. This act of predication is true just in case every instance of the property of being a politician possesses the property of being eloquent, i.e. just in case every politician is eloquent.

We can represent this type of action, the proposition that every politician is eloquent, as follows:

16. $\vdash_2$ <<EVERY, POLITICIAN>, ELOQUENT>

I am representing EVERY with small caps, the notation for acts of expression. We are obviously not referring to anything with 'every', and so it wouldn't make sense to represent this as a type of reference act. There is a difference, however, between expressing a property and expressing a function like $F_\forall$. Acts of function expression are inherently applicative in a way that acts of property expression are not. In expressing the function $F_\forall$ you single out this function and apply it to a property to yield a second-level property. There is no corresponding act of application involved in expressing a property.

The notation for predication in (16), '$\vdash_2$' indicates that this is second-order predication. This tells us that the target for this act of predication is the property of being eloquent. Remember, though, that there is no difference in kind between first and second-order predication. First and second-order predication are sub-types of a more encompassing type of act, predication. The difference between these sub-types is just a difference in the ontological categories of their targets.[15]

This account extends in the obvious way to other quantificational determiners, such as 'some', 'no', 'few', 'many', and 'most', each of which is used to express a different function from first-level properties to second-level properties. For example, the proposition that few politicians are eloquent is a type of action in which someone expresses and applies the function F_{few} to the property of being a politician to yield the second-level property of being a property that holds of few politicians, and then predicates this second-level property of the property of being eloquent.

Let's finish with a quantified relational proposition. Suppose Obama asserts that every politician admires Clinton. We can represent this proposition as follows:

17. $\vdash_2$ <<EVERY, POLITICIAN>,<<∅, **Clinton**>, ADMIRES>>

In a token of (17) a subject targets Clinton for the admiree role in the admiration relation, leaving the admirer role open, as indicated by the empty set symbol. This yields the one-place property of admiring Clinton. The subject expresses and applies the function $F_\forall$ to the property of being a politician to yield the second-level property of being a property that applies to every politician, and then predicates this property of the property of admiring Clinton.

---

[15] This notation for second-order predication seems to demand that I add a subscript '1' to all cases of first-order predication, but I won't bother to do that. Read the un-subscripted '$\vdash$' as first-order predication.

4

Cancellation and the Content–Force Distinction

In this chapter I will extend my account of propositions to negated, conjunctive, and disjunctive propositions. To do this I have to introduce and explain the notion of cancelled predication. A cancelled act of predication is an act of predication that takes place in a context in which the usual requirements and commitments of predication have been overridden, and in which an act of predication does not have the status of a judgment or assertion. I call these 'cancellation contexts'. In a cancellation context a subject can predicate a property of an object without thereby judging or asserting that the object has that property. This happens, for example, when someone utters the disjuncts in a disjunction. Explaining and defending this notion of cancellation is the central element in my argument against the constitutive version of the distinction between content and force.

4.1 Cancellation Contexts

In chapter 1 I made a distinction between the taxonomic and constitutive versions of the content–force distinction. According to the taxonomic version, speech acts with different forces can have the same propositional content. To accept this version of the distinction is to hold that propositional contents are shared across speech acts with different kinds of satisfaction conditions, such as assertions, questions, and orders.

The main target of this chapter is the constitutive version of the content–force distinction. To accept this distinction is to hold that there is nothing judgmental or assertive about the propositional contents of judgments, assertions, and declarative sentences. We could put this by saying that there is no element of judgment or assertion in these propositional contents. Alternatively, we might say that in characterizing the natures of these propositional contents we do not need to use the concepts of judgment or assertion. On the Fregean picture, judgment and assertion are actions that subjects perform with propositions. These actions are not built into the nature of propositions themselves.

The view I am defending abandons this distinction. The contents of judgments and assertions have a distinctively assertoric element, in the form of predication (⊢). This is not to say that propositions literally perform acts of judgment or assertion. Propositions are assertive in the sense that they are types of actions whose tokens are judgmental or assertoric in character.

Adopting this position means that I have to confront Frege's arguments for the content–force distinction, the most powerful of which is based on the fact that one can sincerely and felicitously utter a conditional without judging or asserting its antecedent or consequent. Here is one of Frege's examples:

The thought contained in the sentence:
'If the accused was in Rome at the time of the deed, he did not commit the murder'
may be acknowledged to be true by someone who does not know if the accused was in Rome at the time of the deed nor if he committed the murder. Of the two component thoughts contained in the whole, neither the antecedent nor the consequent is being uttered assertively when the whole is presented as true. (Frege 1918b, 348)

Frege concluded that there is nothing assertive about the component propositions contained in the conditional. The argument is simple. A sentence does not change its propositional content when it is used as the antecedent or consequent of a conditional, but we do not assert this content when the sentence is so used. The propositional content must therefore be devoid of any assertive element. Otherwise, it would not be possible to use the sentence, without change in content, without asserting it.

The phenomenon is not limited to conditionals. The same sort of thing occurs when people utter negations or disjunctions, form hypotheses, act in plays, write poetry or fiction, make jokes, speak ironically, or read someone else's writing out loud. The general idea is that a proposition can be put forward assertorically or non-assertorically, with no difference in the nature of the proposition itself. Geach dubbed this the Frege point: "a thought may have just the same content whether you assent to its truth or not; a proposition may occur in discourse now asserted, now unasserted, and yet be recognizably the same proposition" (Geach 1965, 254). Geach followed Frege in concluding that assertion is not built into the nature of propositional content.

There is, however, another way to view all of this. We could take the fact that we do not assert the contents of sentences embedded inside conditionals and disjunctions etc. to show that there is something assertive about the propositional contents of these sentences, but this element of assertion is cancelled or overridden when the sentence is used in a conditional or disjunction etc. When you use a sentence inside a conditional, your use of 'if' cancels the assertive elements of the contents of the antecedent and consequent. Geach himself uses this language of cancellation in his discussion of conditionals:

> The conjunction "if", *which generally cancels all assertoric force in the "if" clause*, can grammatically be prefixed to any sentence of assertoric form without altering its grammatical structure or even the way it sounds; somebody who fails to hear the first word of my "if" clause may actually mistake what I say for an assertion, so that like Alice I have to explain 'I only said "if"'. (Geach 1965, 262, my emphasis)

Explaining conditionals as Geach does here actually requires us to give up the constitutive version of the content–force distinction. The idea that 'if' cancels assertoric force only makes sense if there is something there to be cancelled.

In thinking about cancellation I find it helpful to consider the case of the actor on stage. When the actor utters lines in a play he is not asserting those lines. Frege would say that the actor is merely expressing the propositions contained in the sentences he utters.

> When playing his part the actor is not asserting anything; nor is he lying, even if he says something of whose falsehood he is convinced. In poetry we have the case of thoughts being expressed without being actually put forward as true, in spite of the assertoric form of the sentence . . . . (Frege 1918a, 330)
> If I attach the word 'salt' to the word 'sea-water' as a predicate, I form a sentence that expresses a thought. To make it clearer that we have only the expression of a thought, but that nothing is meant to be asserted, I put the sentence in the dependent form 'that sea-water is salt'. Instead of doing this I could have it spoken by an actor on the stage as part of his role, for we know that in playing a part an actor only seems to speak with assertoric force. (Frege 1979, 251)

The actor's utterances fall short of assertion; they are missing something necessary for assertion. For Frege, the actor's utterances only seem to be assertions. They are like assertions but they lack a crucial assertive element that must be supplied by the actor.

As Dummett explains, Frege took these examples to demonstrate the necessity of his assertion sign.

In the course of a controversy between him and Peano about the respective merits of their logical notations, Peano dismissed the assertion sign as superfluous, since it preceded every theorem; Frege retorted that a correct logical analysis reveals the necessity for such a sign, and it is therefore a mistake to omit it even if no ambiguity results. Its necessity appeared to him to depend, not so much on there being, besides assertoric sentences, sentences of different forms which expressed the same thoughts but carried a distinct kind of force, but on the possibility of using assertoric sentences as complete sentences but stripped of their assertoric force. (Dummett 1981, 308).

For Frege, the actor's utterances provided examples of just this sort; the actor utters assertoric sentences but is not using them with assertoric force.

Dummett agrees, of course, that the actor's utterances are not assertions, "but not for a reason that justifies the use which Frege makes of it" (Dummett 1981, 310). It is not that the actor fails to do something required for the performance of an assertion. Rather, there is more going on than in a normal case of assertion:

The reason he is not making assertions is not that he is doing *less* than that— merely expressing thoughts, say—but that he is doing *more* than that—he is acting the making of assertions. What constitutes his doing this is his uttering the assertoric sentence—with the assertion sign if we have one—in a context which determines the significance of everything he does in that context—on the stage in a theatre at an announced time. (Dummett 1981, 311)

The additional factor in stage acting is that the actor is performing his utterances in a special sort of context created by theatrical conventions.

It is easy to see why Dummett must be right about this. Frege's view was that the actor's utterances are not assertions because they are performed without the necessary assertoric force. This implies that the actor's utterances would be assertions if the actor were to supply this missing element, for example, by using the assertion sign, or by intending to put thoughts forward as true. But there is *nothing* the actor can do to make his utterances count as genuine assertions. Even if he believes and endorses everything he says, takes himself to be manifesting his beliefs, intends to commit himself to the truth of his utterances, etc., he is still not performing genuine assertions—not even if he breaks the fourth wall and speaks directly to the audience. The actor can perform his own assertions only if he leaves the play behind and takes himself out of the theatrical context.

Stage acting is a good example of what I mean by a cancellation context. Suppose an actor says 'Clinton is eloquent' while acting in a play. In uttering these words the actor does exactly the same sort of thing that Obama does when he asserts that Clinton is eloquent. Both the actor and Obama predicate the property of being eloquent of Clinton. The difference is that when the actor performs this act of predication he is subject to conventions about stage acting that cancel the normal require-ments and consequences of acts of predication. The actor has not broken any rules if he does not know that Clinton is eloquent, or if he does not believe that Clinton is eloquent, or if Clinton is not eloquent. The actor does not undertake a commitment to providing reasons for thinking that Clinton is eloquent, and does not authorize others to assert that Clinton is eloquent on the basis of his authority. The actor's utterance is not subject to the usual requirements on acts of predication, and it does not have the usual consequences of predication. If the actor steps off stage and speaks for himself then all of these requirements and consequences are back in force. The actor moves out of the cancellation context and into one in which acts of predication once again count as assertions.

Cancellation contexts arise for all sorts of rule-governed activities, not just acts of predication. In Chapter 1 I discussed an example from chess in which one player makes a move with her knight in order to demon-strate how the knight moves. The player moved her knight in exactly the same way she would have done if she were making a real move, but because the move takes place in the context of a demonstration it does not have its usual status or consequences. Here is another example. In American football the referees will often allow play to continue even though a defensive player has committed a penalty that nullifies the results of the play.[1] Suppose this happens and the defense tackles the quarterback inside the offense's endzone. Normally this would count as a safety and the defense would get two points, but because of the penalty it does not count and the play is called back. The defense did exactly the same sorts of things they would have done if they had really scored a safety, but they did so in a context in which those actions do not have

---

[1] Thanks to Justin Kuster for help with this example.

their usual consequences. In this scenario the defensive team has clearly not done something *less* than score a safety. Rather, they did everything they needed to do in order to score a safety, but something else happened, the penalty, which serves to override the usual consequences of tackling an offensive player in the endzone. This is a cancellation context, in which a certain action does not have its usual status.

Just as the conventions about stage acting create a context in which acts of predication do not count as assertions, so does the use of 'if' in the utterance of a conditional. The use of 'if' creates a cancellation context. This is part of the meaning of 'if'. Anyone who understands the conditional use of 'if' knows that someone who prefaces a remark with 'if' is not asserting what follows. 'If' creates a linguistic setting in which acts of predication do not have their usual requirements and consequences.

What is the alternative to this way of understanding conditionals and stage utterances? Frege's view is that the actor is merely expressing propositions. Another option invokes Austin's distinction between locutionary and illocutionary acts (Austin 1975). Perhaps the actor performs a locutionary act but not an illocutionary act. Since locutionary acts are typically conceived of as components of illocutionary acts, this would be to side with Frege, and against Dummett and me, in maintaining that the actor does something less than a full-fledged assertion.

Austin's concept of a locutionary act is notoriously difficult to understand (Recanati 1987, 2013). It is usually introduced and explained as an act of *saying something* (Austin 1975, 94–5; Bach and Harnish 1979, 19; Cappelen 2011). Someone who utters 'I will be there' has *said* that she will be there (locutionary act), and in doing so has *promised* to be there (illocutionary act). But as Searle points out, the verb 'to say' is an illocutionary verb (Searle 1968, 411–2).[2] To say something is to perform a certain kind of assertion. The most natural way to interpret the report that Obama *said* that Clinton is eloquent is to take it to mean that Obama *asserted* that Clinton is eloquent. If this is not what 'saying something' means—if 'to say' has a technical meaning when used to explain locutionary acts—then until we hear more we are no closer to understanding locutionary acts.[3]

---

[2] Searle discards Austin's notion of a locutionary act and replaces it with what he calls the propositional act—an act of expressing a proposition (Searle 1968).

[3] To his credit, Recanati provides an interpretation of what it is to say something in the locutionary sense (Recanati 1987). For Recanati, to perform a locutionary act is to present

Even if we put this difficulty to one side, there is another problem with using Austin's concept of locutionary acts to explain what the actor is doing. Locutionary acts are not free standing actions that can be performed in isolation. They are abstractions from illocutionary acts. A locutionary act is an aspect or element of an illocutionary act, which we identify by intellectual abstraction from the total illocutionary act. Here's an analogy. Consider an act of hitting a tennis ball with a tennis racket. Within this act there is an act of moving one's arm, but the arm movement and the act of hitting the tennis ball are not discrete, independent actions. The arm movement is a component of the total intentional action that we arrive at by abstracting away from various other features, such as the subject's intentions, the movement of the tennis racket, the contact between the racket and the ball, etc. This is what locutionary acts are like. Bodily movements are to intentional actions as locutionary acts are to illocutionary acts. The analogy is not perfect, however, since there can be mere bodily movements that are not components of intentional actions, whereas that is not possible with locutionary and illocutionary acts.

yourself as performing a certain illocutionary act, and you can do that without performing the illocutionary act. He puts this in a number of different ways. To perform a locutionary act is to "indicate", "stage", or "act the making of" an illocutionary act:

> If the locutionary/illocutionary distinction is relevant, as I have tried to show, then a true assertion is really a kind of stage assertion with an additional element. The speaker who performs a locutionary act is acting the making of an assertion; the locutionary act becomes an illocutionary act in Austin's sense if the speaker genuinely subscribes to what he says and identifies with the theatrical part . . . he is playing. To say something, in the locutionary sense, is to act the performing of an illocutionary act; but if one seeks an understanding of the real pragmatic activity of the actors, as opposed to the characters they play on stage, one had better look behind the scenes. (Recanati 1987, 266)

This account of assertion is like Frege's in positing a neutral, non-commital core inside every assertion. Recanati calls the neutral core a locutionary act; for Frege it is an act of expressing a proposition. The neutral core amounts to a full-fledged assertion when it is accompanied by an extra, non-neutral act that boosts the total act to the making of an assertion. I have already mentioned the problem for this account of the actor: there is nothing the actor can do to make his lines in the play count as full-fledged assertions. No act of subscription or identification or endorsement can convert his stage utterances into real assertions. The only way for his utterances to count as genuine assertions is for the theatrical conventions to be lifted and the play to end. This drives home the fact that these conventions create a context that overrides the assertive character of the actor's utterances. No intentional actions on the part of the actor can restore that assertive character, at least not until the actor leaves the theatrical context.

It might be replied that the example of the actor provides exactly the sort of case in which it is possible to merely perform a locutionary act. The idea is that the theatrical context in which the actor performs his utterance filters out the illocutionary aspects of that utterance, leaving only the locutionary act. Suppose an actor shakes hands with another actor during the course of a play. The actor performs the various bodily movements involved in shaking hands, but the actor has not *greeted* the other actor (Dummett 1981, 311). The theatrical context filters out the aspects involved in an act of greeting, leaving just the bodily movement. Similarly, by uttering a declarative sentence onstage, the theatrical context cancels the assertoric features of the speech act, leaving just the locutionary act.

There are two things to say in response. The first is that it is not clear that this succeeds in isolating the locutionary act. The actor is *pretending* to make assertions, and his locutionary acts are elements or aspects inside these larger acts of pretended assertion. But secondly, and more importantly, this way of explaining what the actor is doing is just another way of stating my account of cancelled predication in Austinian terms. The thought is that the actor performs an action in which the usual illocutionary aspects are overridden or cancelled, leaving just a locutionary act. Substitute 'assertoric' for 'illocutionary' and 'act of cancelled predication' for 'locutionary act' and you have my account of the actor.

It is worth reiterating that my account of cancelled predication does not face the problem I raised in chapter 1 for Soames's concept of neutral predication. The problem for Soames is that his concept of predication incoherently combines the truth-evaluability of judgment with the neutrality of entertainment. Insofar as an act of predication is truth-evaluable it is capable of being correct or incorrect, which means that it is possible to make a mistake in performing that act of predication, and if it is possible to make a mistake in performing an act of predication then that act cannot be neutral. Someone might be tempted to think that my notion of cancelled predication faces a similar incoherence. It does not. The crucial point is that the concept of a mistake only applies to acts of predication that take place outside of cancellation contexts. Cancellation contexts make the concept of a mistake inapplicable. We do not charge the actor with a mistake if one of his lines is false. We do not accuse someone of being wrong if she utters a false disjunct as part of the assertion of a (true) disjunction. Cancellation contexts allow you to make false predications without thereby being wrong about anything. For that reason, there is no conflict in holding that acts of cancelled predication are truth-evaluable and yet neutral, in the sense that they do not commit the subject to the truth of her act of predication.

If this account of cancelled predication makes sense then Frege's arguments for the constitutive version of the content–force distinction are invalid. It does not follow from the fact that the actor is not performing assertions, or from the fact that we do not assert the antecedents of conditionals, that propositions are devoid of any assertive element. We can explain what is going on in stage acting and conditionals by invoking the concepts of cancellation contexts and cancelled acts of predication. This removes a residual concern left over after the arguments in chapter 2. There I argued that the Fregean picture fails in its task of explaining how our judgments and assertions have truth conditions. On the Fregean picture there is no good way to explain how propositions themselves have truth conditions, and hence the picture makes it mysterious how we represent the world in thought and speech. The residual concern is that we are still forced into the Fregean conception of propositional content by the arguments for the content–force distinction. The point of cancellation is to show that this is not so.

4.2 Truth, Negation, Target-shifting, and Anti-predication

Let's use the tilde, '~', to symbolize cancellation. Prefixing the tilde to the single turnstile indicates that tokens of the resulting type take place in a cancellation context. Here is the notation for the type of action the actor performs when he says on stage that Clinton is eloquent:

   1.   ~$\vdash$ <**Clinton**, ELOQUENT>

This is the type of action someone performs when she predicates eloquence of Clinton in a cancellation context. Note that the tilde does not stand for a type of action. There is no *act* of cancelling an act of predication. A cancellation context may be the *effect* of something that the subject does, e.g. use of the word 'if', but the act should be kept distinct from the context it generates. It is also incorrect to read '~$\vdash$' as the absence of predication. In a token of (1) a subject performs an act of predication, albeit one that takes place in a cancellation context.[4] This act of predication is no different than the kind of predication that takes place outside of cancellation contexts. Furthermore, cancelled predication is not predication minus commitment. There is no such thing as partial, non-committal predication. Cancelled predication is more than predication, not less.[5]

Suppose instead of saying that Clinton is eloquent, Obama asserts 'It is true that Clinton is eloquent'. In doing so he predicates the property of being true of the proposition that Clinton is eloquent. But, of course, he also asserts that Clinton is eloquent. The sentence modifier, 'it is true that' does *not* create a cancellation context. We can represent the proposition he asserts as follows:

2. $\vdash < \vdash$ <**Clinton**, ELOQUENT>, TRUE>

There is no tilde on the internal turnstile. This means that in a spoken instance of (2) a subject performs two acts of predication, both of which count as assertions. The inner turnstile represents the first act of predication, and the outer turnstile represents the second.

When Obama says 'It is true that Clinton is eloquent' he predicates the property of being true of the proposition that Clinton is eloquent. The target of this act of predication is the type $\vdash$ <**Clinton**, ELOQUENT>. In order to predicate truth of this type he has to somehow single it out, but he doesn't do that by referring to it. Rather, he singles it out by tokening it. He performs a token of $\vdash$ <**Clinton**, ELOQUENT> and thereby makes this type available as a target for predication.

I call this *target-shifting*. A target-shifted act of predication is one that is targeted, not at something the subject refers to, but at a type of action the subject performs. Let's represent it with the following notational modification to (2):

2′. $\vdash_\uparrow < \vdash$ <**Clinton**, ELOQUENT>, TRUE>

---

[4] I was confused about this when I wrote (Hanks 2011), and I said things that I now regret. For example, I wrote that in an assertion that George is clever or Karla is foolish, "a speaker neither predicates cleverness of George nor foolishness of Karla" (Hanks 2011, 21). This was a mistake.

[5] (Reiland 2013) and (Hom and Schwartz 2013) both rightly argue that cancellation cannot be understood as the absence of predication or predication minus commitment. They are wrong, however, in arguing that these exhaust the options for understanding cancelled predication.

Like second-order predication, target-shifted predication, represented by '$\vdash_\uparrow$', is no different in kind from normal predication. These are all sub-types of predication. The difference between normal first-order predication and target-shifted predication is whether the act of predication is targeted at an object the subject refers to or at a type of action the subject performs. In a token of (2), the subject does not refer to the proposition that Clinton is eloquent. She tokens it, and then predicates truth of the type of action she performs. As we will see, target-shifting occurs whenever one sentence is embedded inside another.

We are now ready to handle negation. Suppose Obama asserts, 'It is not the case that Clinton is eloquent'. Here is the proposition he asserts:

3. $\vdash_\uparrow<\sim\vdash$ <**Clinton**, ELOQUENT>, NOT-TRUE>

Note the tilde on the internal turnstile. Negation creates a cancellation context. Obama is obviously not asserting that Clinton is eloquent when he says that it is not the case that Clinton is eloquent. The expression type NOT-TRUE is the type of act of expressing the property of not being true. In a token of (3), a subject predicates this property of the proposition that Clinton is eloquent. This act of predication is target-shifted. When Obama says 'It is not the case that Clinton is eloquent', he performs a token of the proposition that Clinton is eloquent, albeit one that takes place in a cancellation context. This makes the type of action he performs, $\vdash$ <**Clinton**, ELOQUENT>, available as a target for predication.

The sentence modifier 'it is not the case that' is awkward, but unlike some other forms of natural language negation, it iterates. Suppose Obama says 'It is not the case that it is not the case that Clinton is eloquent'. This is a token of the following type:

4. $\vdash_\uparrow<\sim\vdash_\uparrow<\sim\vdash$ <**Clinton**, ELOQUENT>, NOT-TRUE>, NOT-TRUE>

This is truth-conditionally equivalent to the proposition that Clinton is eloquent—but still a different proposition. Even if their assertions have the same truth conditions, speakers perform different types of predicative actions in saying 'Clinton is eloquent' and 'It is not the case that it is not the case that Clinton is eloquent'. In performing a token of (4) a subject predicates the property of not being true of (3). That is the only uncancelled act of predication involved in a token of (4). Cancellation is not like double negation; iterated cancellation operators do not cancel each other out. When one tilde occurs in the scope of another, as in (4), we have a situation in which one cancellation context is embedded inside another. That does not add up to no cancellation context.

It is, of course, much more likely that Obama will say 'Clinton isn't eloquent' or 'Clinton is not eloquent' instead of using 'it is not the case that'. Let's start with 'Clinton is not eloquent'. Here 'not' functions as a predicate modifier that expresses a function from properties to properties. Applied to the property of being eloquent, the function yields the property of being non-eloquent. In an utterance of 'Clinton is not eloquent' a speaker applies this function to the property of being eloquent to yield the property of being non-eloquent, and then predicates this property of Clinton. Let's use 'NOT' to represent the type of act of expressing this property negation function. Like acts of quantifier expression, e.g. EVERY, NOT is an act of expressing a function, and is therefore inherently applicative. To perform a token of NOT is to identify a certain function and apply it to a property to yield another property. Here, then, is the proposition that Clinton is not eloquent:

5.   ⊢ <**Clinton**, <NOT, ELOQUENT>>

This commits me to the existence of negative properties, but this need not carry any heavy metaphysical implications. Think of the properties that we express in performing acts of predication as principles for sorting. Recall the analogy with sorting out the green marbles from a pile of marbles. One way to do this is to pick up the green marbles and put them in a separate pile. Another is to pick out the non-green ones and put those in a separate pile. In the first case you sort according to the property of being green, in the second according to the property of being non-green. Don't think of the negative property as a quality or universal shared by all the non-green marbles. Think of it as a rule that determines correctness conditions for your acts of sorting.

The difference between uttering 'Clinton is not eloquent' and 'Clinton isn't eloquent' is the difference between predicating a negative property of Clinton and *denying* that Clinton has a certain property (Horn 2012). The sorting analogy is again helpful in clarifying this distinction. To predicate being non-green of a marble is to sort it with the other non-green marbles. To *deny* that a marble is green is, among other things, to prevent, refuse, or undo an act of sorting the marble with the other green marbles. Suppose I pick up one of the marbles in the green pile and put it back in the unsorted pile. In doing so I undo an act of predicating greenness of the marble. Or suppose someone else picks up the marble and asks me whether it should go in the green pile. I say 'no', thereby denying that the marble is green.

Let's call these acts of denial *anti-predication*, which we can symbolize with the reverse single turnstile, '⊣'. Here is the proposition Obama asserts when he says that Clinton isn't eloquent:

6. ⊣ <**Clinton**, ELOQUENT>

A token of (6) is true iff Clinton is not eloquent, and so (6) has the same truth conditions as (3) and (5). Even so, these are different types of actions and hence different propositions.

Anti-predication is meant to capture the intuitive concept of denial. On reflection, however, it is clear that denial covers a wide range of cases. Utterances of any of the following could be reported by saying that the speaker denied that Clinton is eloquent:

7a. It is not the case that Clinton is eloquent.
 b. Clinton is not eloquent.
 c. Clinton isn't eloquent.
 d.—Is Clinton eloquent?—No.
 e. No politician is eloquent.

(The last example, (7e), depends on common knowledge among conversational participants that Clinton is a politician. If the parties to the conversation know this and someone asserts (7e) then that utterance could be reported as a denial that Clinton is eloquent.) The fact that utterances of (7a–e) can all be reported as denials that Clinton is eloquent shows that all of these utterances fall under the type (6). This means that (6) resides at a fairly high level of generality. (6) is a super-type of (3) and (5); all tokens of the latter are tokens of (6), but not vice versa. Anti-predication is therefore a more coarsely grained type of action than predication. There are more ways to anti-predicate eloquence of Clinton, e.g. utterances of (7a–e), than there are ways to predicate eloquence of Clinton.

Propositions are types we use to classify and individuate our thoughts and utterances. Given this conception of content, it should be unsurprising that there will be multiple ways of classifying any given utterance. An utterance of 'Clinton is not eloquent' can be classified as a token of (5) or as a token of (6). Both of these types provide ways of characterizing what the speaker did in making this utterance—and there is no reason why we have to choose between them. I have been talking about "the proposition" a speaker asserts in making a given utterance, but this way of speaking is misleading. Any given utterance will fall under a range of types, many of which count as propositions. How we choose to classify a given utterance in a given context will depend on all sorts of different factors. Suppose Obama says 'It is not the case that Clinton is eloquent' and Biden says 'Clinton is not eloquent'. In such a context it would be quite natural to say that Obama and Biden said the same thing—they both denied that Clinton is eloquent. In this instance we are classifying these utterances together under the type (6). On the other hand, if our interests are more logically or semantically oriented, we could insist that Obama and Biden said different things—after all, Obama used sentence negation whereas Biden used predicate negation. In this case we classify Obama's and Biden's utterances under different types, (3) and (5), respectively. It is pointless to say that one of these ways of classifying their utterances is correct and the other incorrect. Both are correct, and both can be perfectly appropriate relative to our interests and purposes in reporting these utterances.

Before moving on it is worth seeing how negation interacts with quantification. Suppose Obama asserts that some politician is not eloquent, with negation taking narrow scope. In this case we have to read the use of 'not' as an expression of property negation. Here is the proposition Obama asserted:

8. $\vdash_2$ <<SOME, POLITICIAN>, <NOT, ELOQUENT>>

This is the type of action in which a subject predicates the second-level property of being a first-level property that holds of at least one politician of the first-level negative property of being non-eloquent.

4.3 Conjunction and Disjunction

One of the interesting things about conjunction is that in the assertion of a conjunction a speaker *does* assert each conjunct. Conjunction is unlike disjunction in this respect. An obvious way to explain this difference is to say that 'or' cancels assertion and 'and' does not. Uses of 'or' create cancellation contexts; uses of 'and' do not. This would explain why we do not assert disjuncts but we do assert conjuncts.

You cannot say this if you accept the constitutive version of the content–force distinction. The notion of cancellation only makes sense under the assumption that there is an assertive element in propositional content that is there to be cancelled. The theorist who accepts this distinction cannot say that 'or' cancels assertion and 'and' does not. How, then, does the proponent of the content–force distinction explain this difference between 'and' and 'or'?

She might try to appeal to the logical difference between conjunction and disjunction. The reason an assertion that p and q is an assertion that p and an assertion that q is that p and q each follow obviously and trivially from 'p and q', which of course is not the case for disjunction. This explanation relies on the following general principle: if β follows obviously and trivially from α, then an assertion that α is also an assertion that β. This principle is false. For any q, 'p or q' follows obviously and trivially from p, but we do not assert that p or q in an assertion that p. The difference between 'or' and 'and' is not a matter of the logical differences between disjunction and conjunction. It is a difference in speech act effects that are built into the semantics of these expressions.

But perhaps it is not that disjunction cancels assertion and conjunction doesn't. Maybe it's that conjunction *adds* assertion. Perhaps 'and', unlike 'or', is governed by the following semantic rule: if you assert 'p and q', you must also assert p and assert q. This is right as far as it goes, of course. 'And' is governed by this semantic rule and 'or' is not. This isn't so much an explanation of this difference between 'and' and 'or' as a statement of the difference. We wanted an explanation for the fact that, unlike disjunctions, assertions of conjunctions are assertions of their conjuncts. Positing a semantic rule to this effect for conjunction does little more than reiterate this difference. More significantly, however, to invoke this kind of semantic rule is to abandon the spirit of the constitutive version of the content–force distinction. The distinction is based on the thought that the contents of words and sentences can be characterized without using any concepts from the theory of speech acts. The semantic rule proposed for 'and' violates this restriction, insofar as it uses the concept of assertion to characterize the content of 'and'. Given this semantic rule, to explain the content of 'p and q' we have to mention that any assertion of this content is also an assertion that p and an assertion that q. This breaks the separation between propositional content and assertion demanded by the content–force distinction. Once that separation has been breached it is hard to see how the defender of the content–force distinction can make a principled objection to the use of the concept of cancellation to explain the difference between 'and' and 'or'.

Let CONJ be the act of expressing the conjunction relation, a relation that two propositions bear to one another if and only if both are true.[6] When Obama says 'Clinton is eloquent and Biden is persistent' he asserts the following proposition:

9. $\vdash_\uparrow$<($\vdash$<**Clinton**, ELOQUENT>, $\vdash$ <**Biden**, PERSISTENT>), CONJ>

This is a type of action in which a subject predicates the conjunction relation of the propositions that Clinton is eloquent and that Biden is persistent. This is a target-shifted act of predication; it is directed at the types of acts Obama performs when he utters the two conjuncts. In a token of (9) a speaker predicates the conjunction relation of the types of actions she performs in predicating eloquence of Clinton and persistence of Biden. Note that the turnstiles inside (9) are not cancelled. A token of (9), therefore, counts as an assertion that Clinton is eloquent and an assertion that Biden is persistent. Note also the parentheses around the arguments to the conjunction relation. The parentheses indicate that the outermost act of predication is unsorted. Tokens of (9) include assertions of 'Clinton is eloquent and Biden is persistent' as well as 'Biden is persistent and Clinton is eloquent'.

Let's see how conjunction interacts with negation. Suppose Obama says that it is not the case that Clinton is eloquent and Biden is persistent. This is a token of the type:

10. $\vdash_\uparrow$<~$\vdash_\uparrow$<($\vdash$ <**Clinton**, ELOQUENT>, $\vdash$ <**Biden**, PERSISTENT>), CONJ>, NOT-TRUE>

The tilde on the second turnstile covers all the turnstiles in its scope. This reflects the fact that all of these acts of predication take place within a cancellation context. An utterance of 'it is not the case that' creates a cancellation context for all the acts of predication that occur within its scope.

Let DISJ be the act of expressing the disjunction relation, a relation that two propositions bear to one another iff one or the other is true. An

---

[6] In (Hanks 2011) I used 'AND' instead of 'CONJ'. Here I will use 'AND' for something else.

assertion that Clinton is eloquent or Biden is persistent is a token of the following proposition:

11. $\vdash_\uparrow$<(~$\vdash$<**Clinton**, ELOQUENT>, ~$\vdash$ <**Biden**, PERSISTENT>), DISJ>

Tokens of (11) are neither assertions that Clinton is eloquent nor that Biden is persistent. This is the significance of the tildes attached to the internal turnstiles. Of course, it is not that in a token of (11) a speaker asserts nothing at all. The outermost, target-shifted predication operator is uncancelled. In a token of (11) a speaker performs an uncancelled act of predicating the disjunction relation of the types of actions she performs in uttering the disjuncts.

A negated disjunction will work the way one might expect. An assertion that it is not the case that Clinton is eloquent or Biden is persistent is a token of:

12. $\vdash_\uparrow$<~$\vdash_\uparrow$<(~$\vdash$<**Clinton**, ELOQUENT>, ~$\vdash$<**Biden**, PERSISTENT>), DISJ>, NOT-TRUE>

This has the same truth conditions as its DeMorgan equivalent, the proposition that Clinton is not eloquent and Biden is not persistent. The difference is a matter of what gets asserted in tokens of these propositions. In an assertion of 'Not (p or q)' a speaker does not assert that not p. In an assertion of '(not p and not q)' a speaker does assert that not p.

On this view, to assert a conjunction is to predicate the relation ___ *and* ___ *are both true* of two propositions, and to assert a disjunction is to predicate the relation *either* ___ *or* ___ *is true* of two propositions. Performing these acts of predication requires having the concept of truth. Small children who lack this concept therefore cannot judge or assert propositions like (9) or (11). But, as in the case of negation, there are other types of actions in the vicinity of (9) and (11) that do not require the concept of truth.

Let AND be a type of action a subject performs when she expresses a function, F_{and}, that maps n-tuples of properties to n-place relations. For example, F_{and} maps the pair of properties of being eloquent and being persistent to the two-place relation ___*is eloquent and* ___*is persistent*. An assertion that Clinton is eloquent and Biden is persistent can then be classified as an act of predicating this relation of Clinton and Biden, as in (13):

13. $\vdash$ <<**Clinton, Biden**>, <AND, <ELOQUENT, PERSISTENT>>>

Like (9), a token of (13) is true iff Clinton is eloquent and Biden is persistent. The difference is that performing a token of (9) requires having the concept of truth, whereas a token of (13) does not. This extends in the obvious way to disjunctions. An assertion that Clinton is eloquent or Biden is persistent can be classified under (14):

14. $\vdash$ <<**Clinton, Biden**> <OR, <ELOQUENT, PERSISTENT>>>

Here OR is the type of act of expressing a function, F_{or}, that maps n-tuples of properties to n-place relations, e.g. the relation ___*is eloquent or* ___ *is persistent*. Like (13), and unlike (11), performing a token of (14) does not require having the concept of truth.

We are also going to need degenerate cases of F_{and} and F_{or} in which n-tuples of properties are mapped to one-place properties. Call these functions F_{and-d} and F_{or-d}, and let AND-D and OR-D represent the corresponding types of expressive acts. The function F_{and-d} maps the pair of properties of being eloquent and being persistent to the one-place conjunctive property of being eloquent and persistent. An assertion that Clinton is eloquent and persistent can then be classified as a token of the type:

15. $\vdash$ <**Clinton**, <AND-D, <ELOQUENT, PERSISTENT>>

In a token of (15) a subject applies the function F_{and-d} to the properties of being eloquent and being persistent to yield the conjunctive property of being eloquent and persistent, and then predicates this property of Clinton. This works in the same way with OR-D and disjunctive properties. Like negative properties, think of disjunctive properties as rules for sorting that determine correctness conditions for acts of predication.

Cases in which quantification combines with conjunction and disjunction reinforce the need for conjunctive and disjunctive properties. Suppose Obama asserts that every politician is eloquent and persistent:

16. $\vdash_2$ <<EVERY, POLITICIAN>, <AND-D, <ELOQUENT, PERSISTENT>>>

In a token of (16) a speaker predicates the second-level property of being a first-level property that holds of every politician of the first-level conjunctive property of being eloquent and persistent. Tokens of this type are thus true iff every politician is both eloquent and persistent. Quantified disjunctions will work in the same way, with OR-D in place of AND-D.

Now, if I were more ambitious I would go on to extend this approach to indicative conditionals. I am not going to attempt to do that in this book. Indicative conditionals are too difficult and the debate about them is too complicated—treating these issues properly would take us too far from our main themes. The only claim I will make about 'if' is that, at least on some of its uses, it creates a cancellation context for the utterances of sentences embedded inside it.

4.4 Supposition and Hypothesis

In addition to conditionals and stage-acting, Frege often mentions cases of supposition and hypothesis formation when motivating the constitutive version of the content–force distinction:

The separation of the act from the subject matter of judgement seems to be indispensable; for otherwise we could not express a mere supposition—the putting of a case without a simultaneous judgement as to its arising or not. (Frege 1891, 142)

A judgment is often preceded by questions. A mathematician will formulate a theorem to himself before he can prove it. A physicist will accept a law as an hypothesis in order to test it by experience. We grasp the content of a truth before we recognize it as true, but we grasp not only this; we grasp the opposite as well. (Frege 1979, 7)

In an assertoric sentence two different kinds of thing are usually intimately bound up with one another: the thought expressed and the assertion of its truth. And this is why these are not often clearly distinguished. However, one can express a thought without at the same time putting it forward as true. A scientist who makes a scientific discovery usually begins by grasping just a thought, and then he asks himself whether it is to be recognized as true; it is not until his investigation has turned out in favour of the hypothesis, that he ventures to put it forward as true. (Frege 1979, 138)

These are really just more instances of the Frege point. They are cases in which a propositional content occurs in thought or discourse without being judged or asserted. Frege took the fact that we can suppose or hypothesize that p, without judging or asserting p, and without any change to p, to show that judgment and assertion must be kept out of p. For Frege, to suppose or hypothesize that p is to merely entertain the proposition that p. This is pure entertainment—entertainment that occurs in the absence of judgment and assertion.

There are a number of different things we do that can be characterized as the making of suppositions or the formation of hypotheses. Here I will consider three such things, with the aim of showing that none of them requires the notion of Fregean entertainment or the content–force distinction. They are (i) wondering or asking whether p, (ii) merely thinking through p, without judging it, and (iii) supposing that p for *reductio ad absurdum*, or, more generally, for the purpose of inference or further inquiry.

Following some of Frege's remarks, one way to form a hypothesis is to ask a question. A scientist who asks 'Is oxygen condensable?' can be described as having formulated the hypothesis that oxygen is condensable. This is easily accommodated on my approach. The scientist's action is a token of the following interrogative type:

17.   ? <**Oxygen**, CONDENSABLE>

In tokens of (17) a subject combines the property of being condensable with oxygen by asking whether oxygen bears this property. After investigation, this interrogative act can be followed up with any of the following actions:

18.   ⊢ <**Oxygen**, CONDENSABLE>
19a.   ⊢ <~⊢ <**Oxygen**, CONDENSABLE>, NOT-TRUE>
  b.   ⊢ <**Oxygen**, <NOT, CONDENSABLE>>
  c.   ⊣ <**Oxygen**, CONDENSABLE>

(19a–c) are all ways of denying that oxygen is condensable. (Note that (19c) is a super-type of (19a–b). Tokens of the latter count as tokens of (19c), but there are tokens of (19c) that are not tokens of (19a–b), e.g. someone who responds to the question 'Is oxygen condensable?' by saying 'No'.) Along with (18), these are ways of answering the question posed by (17). Nothing here requires the idea that the subject enters into bare cognitive contact with a force-less, truth-conditional representation.

In Frege's discussions the interrogative act usually comes on the heels of an act of entertaining a thought. First the scientist grasps a proposition, then she asks whether it is true. It is the prior act, one might think, that is properly construed as an act of hypothesis formation. Forming a hypothesis is supposed to be something like thinking through a propositional content in a neutral state of mind. This is our second form of supposition.

Here's something someone might do prior to judging or asking whether *a* is F: contemplate the act of predicating being F of *a*. It is clearly possible to think about a certain type of action without performing a token of that type. I can think about getting up from my desk and going for a walk without actually doing it. A scientist can think about the act of predicating being condensable of oxygen without judging that oxygen is condensable. Sometimes our judgments, assertions, and questions are preceded by reflection on the act one would perform in making that judgment, assertion, or question. We do this for any number of reasons, e.g. to gauge the effects of an action, to survey our options, to prepare for the performance of the act, and so on. This kind of neutral contemplation of a type of action is an analog, in my theory, of the Fregean notion of pure entertainment. The crucial difference has to do with whether this sort of act is *required* in order to make a judgment or ask a question. You do not have to contemplate the act of predicating being F of *a* before judging or asserting or wondering or asking whether *a* is F. In fact, this probably happens quite rarely. In most cases you simply judge that *a* is F, or assert that *a* is F, or ask whether *a* is F, with no prior, reflective engagement with the act you are about to perform.

Asking or wondering whether something is the case, and contemplation of a certain predicative action are two forms that supposition can take in my framework. An example of the third occurs in proof by *reductio ad absurdum*. A math teacher says to her students 'Suppose that 2 has a rational square root'. What is the math teacher asking her students to do?

There are two ways I could go here. On the first, supposition is treated as a kind of assertion. To suppose that *a* is F is to perform an attenuated or provisional act of predicating F of *a*. Such an act of predication would generate a provisional commitment to *a*'s being F, which is removed when the supposition is discharged. When you suppose that *p* for the sake of *reductio*, you temporarily commit yourself to *p* for the purposes of drawing inferences from *p*. There is a promissory element to this. As Dummett observes, "supposition is different from other linguistic acts in that it is possible only as a preparation for further acts of the same speaker" (Dummett 1981, 312–3). In supposing that *p* for *reductio*, you provisionally commit yourself to *p*, and you undertake a commitment to drawing inferences from p and eventually discharging your commitment to p. This is to view the act of supposition as a special variety of assertion, which carries a different sort of commitment than ordinary assertion and has a commissive aspect built into it.

However, I prefer a different way of understanding supposition.[7] Instead of viewing supposition as a species of assertion, we can take it to generate a certain sort of cancellation context. When the math teacher says 'Suppose that 2 has a rational square root', she creates a cancellation context for her subsequent acts of predication. Once that context is in place, she and her students can predicate the property of having a rational square root of the number 2, and they can draw inferences from this predication, without being held accountable for these acts of predication. If you suppose that a is F for the sake of an inference or argument you do not break any rules if a is not F, or if you do not believe or know or have reasons for a's being F. You do not license others to assert that a is F on the basis of your authority, and you haven't made a mistake if a is not F. Making a supposition creates a context in which acts of predication are not subject to the usual rules and do not have their usual consequences. The contexts generated by acts of supposition have all the marks of cancellation contexts. One way in which these contexts are special is that, as we noted above, they require the subject to draw inferences or conduct further investigation on the basis of her act of predication. If I suppose that a is F for *reductio ad absurdum* then I am committed to drawing inferences from my act of predication until I reach a contradiction, at which point the supposition context is lifted and I assert that a is not F.

Suppositions often occur by way of utterances of the form 'Suppose that p' or 'Let's suppose that p'. What type of action does someone perform by making these utterances? To say 'Suppose that a is F' is, in part, to request an audience to perform an act of predication inside a cancellation context. But it is also to perform such an act of predication for yourself. Let '**You**' stand for the type of reference act you perform when you address an audience using an imperative. An utterance of 'Suppose that a is F' is a token of the following type:

---

[7] I am indebted here to David Taylor.

20.   ! <<**You**, ~⊢ <**a**, F>>, SUPPOSE>

In a token of (20) a speaker requests an audience to perform a token of ⊢ <**a**, F> inside the cancellation context she has just created. Note that the internal turnstile is cancelled. This reflects the fact that the speaker's use of 'suppose' creates a cancellation context for her own act of predicating F of *a*. In a token of (20), therefore, the speaker also performs a cancelled token of ⊢ <**a**, F>.

We have now seen that all three forms of supposition—asking whether *p*, thinking through *p*, and supposing that *p* for *reductio ad absurdum*— are easy to accommodate in my framework. There are probably other actions that can be reasonably characterized as the making of suppositions or hypotheses, but I won't try to explore any other examples. My aim has been to show that that we can use the resources of my framework to account for what is going on in the kinds of examples that Frege uses to motivate the content–force distinction.

5

Proper Names and Types of Reference Acts

The purpose of this chapter[1] is to introduce the concept of a semantic reference type and use it to give an account of the semantic contents of proper names. The resulting theory is neither Millian nor Fregean, although it is closer in spirit to the Fregean view. The contents of names, on my approach, are neither referents nor Fregean descriptive modes of presentation. They are types of reference acts. By carefully individuating these types it will be possible to explain the difference in content between distinct co-referential names without attributing any descriptive content to names. Typical cases of distinct co-referential names have different contents, not because they are associated with different descriptive conditions, but because they are used to perform different types of reference acts. This provides a new solution to Frege's puzzle about identity sentences, and it does so without threatening the thesis that names are rigid designators. This last point is independent of the details about semantic reference types and so provides a good place to begin.

5.1 Rigidity

The conception of content that I am defending in this book is that contents are types we use to classify and individuate our spoken and mental actions. Applied to linguistic expressions, this yields the view that the content of an expression is a certain type of action that speakers perform by using that expression. In the case of proper names, these

---

[1] Portions of this chapter are taken from (Hanks 2011).

types are types of reference acts. For example, the semantic content of the name 'Aristotle' is a certain type of action a subject performs when she refers to Aristotle. Obviously enough, this type of action is distinct from Aristotle himself, the referent of 'Aristotle'. This approach therefore shares with Fregean approaches the view that the semantic contents of names are distinct from the referents of names. Further, on my account, as on Fregean theories, the semantic content of a name determines the referent of that name. Just as a Fregean sense determines a referent but is not identical to that referent, types of acts of referring to Aristotle determine Aristotle as referent but are, of course, distinct from the man himself. On the other hand, unlike descriptive Fregean senses, the way in which a type of reference act determines a referent is not by way of satisfaction of properties or concepts. The reason for this will become clearer in a moment. The relevant point is that, on my view, the semantic contents of names determine referents but are not identical with referents. It is precisely because of this feature that the issue of rigidity is pressing. If the semantic content of a name were identical to its referent, as on Millian theories, then there would be no gap between semantic content and referent and consequently no way for the referent of a name to vary from world to world. Alternatively, if the semantic content of a name is not its referent then there is a chance that the semantic content will determine different referents with respect to different worlds, in which case the name would not designate rigidly.

Our question, then, is whether a type of reference act can determine different referents with respect to different worlds. The answer is 'no', it cannot. To see why, we need to distinguish between *referring* to an object and *denoting* that object. This is a distinction between two kinds of actions—two ways in which a speaker can designate an object in an utterance. Denotation is typically performed with definite descriptions. In an utterance of 'The inventor of bifocals was a statesman', the speaker denotes Benjamin Franklin. Uses of proper names are typically acts of reference. When a speaker says 'Benjamin Franklin was a statesman', the speaker refers to Benjamin Franklin. How should we distinguish between these two kinds of actions?

I don't pretend to have anything like necessary and sufficient conditions for either the act of referring or the act of denoting. Still, it is possible to go some way toward explaining reference by drawing out some differences between referring and denoting. In an act of denotation a speaker must have certain properties or conditions in mind that uniquely identify an object, and then the speaker designates whichever object satisfies those properties or conditions. A consequence of this is that acts of denotation are typically non-rigid, since the properties or conditions the speaker has in mind usually identify different individuals in different possible worlds. None of this is true for acts of reference. A speaker can refer to an object without knowing any properties or conditions that would uniquely identify that object.[2] In addition, even if a speaker does have uniquely identifying conditions in mind, she may not designate the bearer of those conditions.[3] Acts of reference determine objects in some way other than by satisfaction of associated properties or conditions. Perhaps they determine their referents by way of causal or historical chains (Kripke 1980), or perhaps by way of what Evans calls the "dominant source" of associated information (Evans 1973), or perhaps in some other way. The crucial point for our purposes is that, however an act of reference determines its designation, it does so in a way that does not allow the referent to vary across possible worlds. For any possible world w, a token act of reference refers to the same thing in w as it does in the actual world.[4] Token acts of reference rigidly designate their referents.

The argument for this is essentially the same one that Kripke used to argue that names are rigid designators (Kripke 1980, 6–7). The argument is based on the counterfactual truth conditions for sentences and assertions containing names. The sentence 'Aristotle was fond of dogs' correctly describes a counterfactual possible world if and only if a certain man, the same one in every case, is fond of dogs in that world. Assuming that truth conditions are determined compositionally, it

---

[2] This is the point of Kripke's Feynman example (Kripke 1980, 81–2).

[3] This is the point of Kripke's Gödel example (Kripke 1980, 83–92).

[4] As in the case of proper names, a token act of reference need not exist in a world in order for it to refer to something with respect to that world. To evaluate a token act of reference with respect to non-actual worlds we hold fixed the relevant semantic facts about the token in the actual world and then consider what those facts determine with respect to non-actual worlds. It is irrelevant to this determination whether the token act of reference exists in those other worlds. It is also irrelevant whether the referent exists in counterfactual worlds. A token act of reference still refers to its actual referent even with respect to worlds in which that referent does not exist. In Nathan Salmon's terminology (Salmon 1981, 32–41), token acts of reference are "obstinately rigid".

follows that the name 'Aristotle' refers to the same man with respect to every possible world. All of this holds *mutatis mutandis* for an assertion that Aristotle was fond of dogs. A token assertion that Aristotle was fond of dogs is true with respect to a counterfactual possible world if and only if a certain fixed individual, Aristotle, was fond of dogs in that world. Given the compositionality of truth conditions for assertions, it follows that the token act of reference performed in the course of making the assertion determines that same individual with respect to every world.

Types of reference acts determine their referents by way of their tokens. The referent of a type of reference act is determined to be that object that is the referent of its tokens. To find out what a type of reference act designates with respect to a possible world we simply ask what its tokens designate with respect to that world. Since its tokens will determine the same object with respect to every possible world, the type does as well. This is an instance of the more general fact that types inherit properties from their tokens. Just as the type $\vdash$ <**Aristotle**, FOND-OF-DOGS> inherits its truth conditions from its tokens, the type of reference act **Aristotle** inherits its referent from its tokens.

Therefore, types of reference acts rigidly designate their referents. If the semantic content of the name 'Aristotle' is a type of act of referring to Aristotle, then the referent of 'Aristotle' is the same individual, Aristotle, with respect to every possible world. The type of reference act always identifies Aristotle as the referent of 'Aristotle', regardless of what happens to be true of Aristotle in different possible worlds. Identifying the semantic contents of names with types of reference acts correctly implies that names are rigid designators.

5.2 Semantic Reference Types

When a speaker uses a name to refer to an object her act falls under an enormous range of reference types. The problem we now face is that of identifying one of the types in this range to serve as the semantic content of the name. At one end of the range we have what I call an *object dependent type*. Object dependent reference types are individuated by the objects that are their referents. Any act of referring to Clinton, using any kind of referential device, falls under the object dependent reference type determined by Clinton. Farther down in the range of types we have what

I call an *object-and-name dependent reference type*.[5] This type of reference act is individuated by an object and a name. All and only those acts
of reference to Clinton that employ the name 'Clinton' fall under the
name-and-object dependent reference type corresponding to the name
'Clinton'.

Neither of these types is well-suited to serve as the semantic content of
the name 'Clinton'. There is nothing distinctively semantic about either
one. Object dependent reference types are defined in terms of objects.[6]
Object-and-name dependent reference types are defined in terms of
objects and names. For a type of reference act to merit the label 'semantic' it should be defined in recognizably semantic terms, and neither of
these types meets this condition. Semantic reference types are types that
are identified using semantic concepts. Since we deploy no semantic
concepts when we individuate a reference type in terms of Clinton, or
in terms of Clinton and the name 'Clinton', the types we thus identify are
not properly thought of as semantic reference types—and that makes
them poor candidates to be the semantic content of the name 'Clinton'.

If we characterize semantic reference types simply as those that are
defined using semantic concepts then there is no guarantee that a
particular act of reference will fall under a unique semantic reference
type. Consider the fact that for any semantic reference type T there are
indefinitely many sub-types of T that are definable by adding conditions
to the definition of T, e.g. the type whose tokens are instances of
T performed using a certain name, or in a certain location, etc. Given
our general criterion for being a semantic reference type, all of these sub-
types count as semantic reference types. Any token act of reference
therefore falls under many semantic reference types. Our task, then, is
to identify, among all the semantic reference types, one to serve as the
semantic content of a name. Ideally, this semantic reference type will be
minimal, in the sense that it is not a sub-type of any other semantic
reference type. More importantly, the type should account for our

---

[5] In previous work, (Hanks 2011, 2013a), I called these 'name dependent reference
types', but as an anonymous reader pointed out, 'object-and-name dependent reference
type' is more appropriate, since the type is individuated both in terms of an object and a
name.

[6] The view that the semantic contents of names are object dependent reference types
would be the analog, in my framework, of the Millian view of names.

semantic intuitions about sentences containing names, i.e. our intuitions about truth conditions, validity, substitution phenomena, and so on.

The strategy I am going to follow takes its cue from Frege's criterion of difference for senses. Frege held that if it is possible for a speaker to take different attitudes towards two sentences S_1 and S_2, both of which she understands, then S_1 and S_2 must have different senses (Frege 1892a, 156). This uses the concept of understanding, or semantic competence, to give a criterion of difference for senses. This is the concept I will use to define semantic reference types. Suppose there are two co-referential names, n and m, such that any speaker who is semantically competent with both names is capable of realizing, solely by virtue of her competence, that acts of reference using these names have the same referent. If so, then token acts of reference using n and m fall under a certain type of reference act: the type of reference act such that all tokens of this type can be known by competent speakers to have the same referent.

We can approach this a bit more formally. Let's define a relation on token acts of reference using the concept of semantic competence, and then use this relation to individuate a type of reference act. Initially, let's restrict our attention to token acts of reference performed using non-empty names. I will extend the account to empty names, indexicals, and demonstratives in later chapters. Let x and y be two such token acts of reference, and let n_x and n_y be the names used in these acts, respectively. Define a relation, R, as follows:

xRy iff$_{def}$ anyone who is semantically competent with n_x and n_y will realize, under relevantly ideal conditions, that x and y have the same referent.

Given any token act of reference x and the relation R, there is a type of reference act of being an act of reference that bears R to x. Call this the *R-semantic reference type* of x. Tokens of this type include any token act of reference that bears R to x. R is an equivalence relation on the set of token acts of reference with names. (For now, at least. In section 5.6 I will refine the definition of R in such a way that R becomes intransitive.) For any token act of reference x, R determines an equivalence class of such tokens. All the tokens in this equivalence class fall under the same R-semantic reference type. For any name n, then, we can identify the semantic content of n with the R-semantic reference type of any token act of reference using n. In what follows I will drop the 'R' and simply call this the semantic reference type of n, but it should be kept in mind that there are many other semantic reference types, possibly minimal, under which uses of *n* fall.

I need to say something about the "relevantly ideal conditions" in the definition of R, but before doing so it will help to look at an example. Consider the spy novelist John Le Carré, who is better known to his friends and family as David John Moore Cornwell. Cornwell gave himself the pen name 'John Le Carré' to protect his identity as a secret agent for the British secret service agency MI6. As it turned out, Cornwell's cover was blown by the Soviet mole Kim Philby, who also worked for MI6.[7]

Suppose Philby was a fan of Le Carré's early novels, *Call for the Dead* and *The Spy Who Came in from the Cold*. Suppose he read these novels, read their reviews, talked about Le Carré with his friends, and read interviews with Le Carré in the newspaper (*sans* photographs, of course). All of this should lead us to say that Philby was semantically competent with the name 'John Le Carré'. This is despite the fact that, like virtually everyone else, Philby did not realize that Le Carré and Cornwell, his colleague at MI6, were the same person. Philby was competent with the names 'Le Carré' and 'Cornwell' but he did not realize that token acts of reference using these names have the same referent, and would not have realized this even under the ideal conditions relevant for R. Given the above definitions, it follows that token acts of reference using the names 'Le Carré' and 'Cornwell' fall under distinct semantic reference types, **Le Carré** and **Cornwell**, respectively. These semantic reference types, I submit, are the semantic contents of the names 'Le Carré' and 'Cornwell'.

This is an example of two co-referential names whose uses fall under different semantic reference types. Of course, uses of 'Le Carré' and 'Cornwell' fall under the same object dependent reference type. The semantic reference types **Le Carré** and **Cornwell** are both sub-types of the object dependent reference type: all tokens of the former fall under the latter, but not vice versa. It's also important to see that **Le Carré** and **Cornwell** are not object-and-name dependent reference types. The object-and-name dependent reference type corresponding to uses of 'Le Carré' is the type of reference act of referring to Le Carré/Cornwell

---

[7] My source here is the Wikipedia entry for John Le Carré, so these claims should be taken with a grain of salt (http://en.wikipedia.org/wiki/John_le_Carré).

using the name 'Le Carré'. This object-and-name dependent type is defined in a different way than the semantic reference type, and the two types correspond to different properties of their tokens. Even if co-extensive, these are different types of reference acts.

Are there examples of distinct co-referential names whose uses fall under the same semantic reference type? Maybe. We would need to find an example in which semantic competence with two names guaranteed knowledge of co-reference. That would rule out situations like Philby's, and one might think that such situations are always possible for any syntactically distinct co-referential names. Despite this, I do think there are examples of this kind. One variety of examples involves names in different languages, e.g. 'London' and 'Londres'. Another involves empty names, e.g. 'Zeus' and 'Jupiter'. I will return to the cross-linguistic case at the end of this chapter. Empty names have to wait until chapter 6.

5.3 Paderewski and Ideal Conditions

Kripke's Paderewski example presents a problem for this approach to names (Kripke 1979). Recall Kripke's Peter, who fails to realize that Paderewski the statesman is the same person as Paderewski the pianist. Because of this, Peter fails to realize that two token acts of reference using 'Paderewski', one to the statesman and the other to the pianist, refer to the same individual. Assuming Peter is competent with the name 'Paderewski', something I do not wish to deny, it would seem to follow that these token acts of reference do not bear R to one another, and hence that uses of the name 'Paderewski' fall under at least two different semantic reference types.[8] This is a problem. Paderewski was also a composer. Suppose Peter fails to realize that the statesman, pianist, and composer are all the same person. Then uses of 'Paderewski' would fall under three semantic reference types. Take any other property, F, had by Paderewski. Peter might fail to realize that Paderewski the statesman/ pianist/composer is Paderewski the F. Since there are indefinitely many such F's, there are, apparently, indefinitely many semantic reference

---

[8] Why not deny that Peter is competent with 'Padereswski'? Because semantic competence with the name would then require knowing that a certain statesman and a certain pianist are the same person. By varying the example we could show that competence with 'Paderewski' requires knowing everything there is to know about Paderewski.

types corresponding to uses of the name 'Paderewski'. Unless we are willing to say that the name has indefinitely many semantic contents, this renders semantic reference types useless for giving an account of the contents of names.

The ideal conditions in the definition of R are meant, in part, to avoid this sort of problem. Under the ideal conditions for R, speakers will know which names were used in the two token acts of reference under consideration. In particular, they will know whether the acts of reference employed tokens of the same or different name types. This sort of idealization is required for any non-trivial application of Frege's criterion of difference for senses. Peter takes different attitudes toward tokens of the sentence 'Paderewski had musical talent'. Assuming he is competent, it follows by Frege's criterion, without the use of ideal conditions, that this sentence has multiple senses. Using parallel arguments we could show, absurdly, that any sentence has multiple senses. To avoid this we are going to have to build an idealization into Frege's criterion that grants competent speakers knowledge of whether two sentences are tokens of the same type. We need the same sort of idealization for my definition of the relation R, in this case for names rather than sentences.

This means that we need a criterion of individuation of names. For the purposes of R, then, let name-types n_1 and n_2 be distinct if and only if n_1 and n_2 are syntactically different, have different referents, or have different origins. This implies that 'Le Carré' and 'Cornwell' are distinct names, since they are syntactically distinct. It implies that there are two names, 'Aristotle', one of which refers to the philosopher and the other to the shipping magnate. And it implies that there is only one name, 'Paderewski', in Kripke's example. Therefore, under the ideal conditions for R, Peter would know that the two token acts of reference using 'Paderewski' contain instances of a single name in the sense relevant for R, and would therefore realize that these acts of reference co-refer. This avoids the proliferation of semantic reference types.

I include origins in the individuation conditions for names in order to handle cases in which an object is dubbed with syntactically identical names on two separate occasions.[9] Suppose two separate groups of explorers approach a mountain from different sides and both give it

---

[9]   Thanks here to Michael Murez and Daniel Brigham.

the name 'Nadelhorn'. According to our criterion of individuation, we have two names, 'Nadelhorn', even though they are syntactically alike and have the same referent. Under the ideal conditions for R, speakers will know that these are two distinct names. Furthermore, competence with these names does not guarantee knowledge of co-reference. Someone might learn about both groups of explorers and fail to realize that it was the same mountain. Uses of the two names therefore fall under different semantic reference types and have different semantic contents.

This appeal to ideal conditions in order to avoid problems generated by Paderewski-style examples may appear ad hoc. It is not. Remember what we are doing. We are trying to define a type of reference act that is suitable to serve as the semantic content of a name. The suitability of the type will be determined by its ability to capture our intuitions about the semantic features of sentences containing names. In defining this type we can make use of whatever concepts and conditions we like (aside from the concept of semantic content, which would render the account circular). My definition uses the concept of semantic competence and a criterion of individuation for names that invokes the syntax, reference, and origin of a name. The definition is consciously designed to deliver the result that the various uses of 'Paderewski' fall under the same semantic reference type and, more generally, that names, as presently individuated, have unique semantic contents. This is exactly what an account of semantic content in terms of semantic reference types should do. There are, of course, many other types that we could define, some of which would classify different uses of 'Paderewski' under different types. For example, there is the type of act of referring to Paderewski while thinking of him as a statesman, and the type of act of referring to Paderewski while thinking of him as a pianist. These are perfectly legitimate types, which may be interesting or useful for various purposes. In fact, I will use them in my account of propositional attitude reports. But, assuming we want names to have unique semantic contents, these types are not viable candidates to be the semantic contents of names.

5.4 Semantic Competence with Names

The concept of semantic competence obviously plays a central role in this theory. I am defining the semantic contents of names in terms of semantic competence with names, but I am not going to attempt to give a theory or definition of semantic competence. Semantic competence plays the role of an unexplained explainer in my theory.

That said, I intend the conditions on semantic competence with a name to be fairly minimal. You do not have to possess uniquely identifying information about an individual in order to be competent with a name for that individual, nor must you be "acquainted" with the individual in any interesting sense (cf. Hawthorne and Manley 2012). It's possible to be competent with names for individuals with whom you have very tenuous causal connections and about whom you know, or believe, very little.

Semantic competence also tolerates many false beliefs about the referent of a name—witness Kripke's Peter. But there are limits. Someone who thinks that Paderewski is a city in Poland is not competent with the name 'Paderewski'. Competence with a name requires some number of true sortal beliefs about the referent of the name. This is an instance of a more general condition on semantic competence with any term (Davidson 1982). In order to be competent with the word 'tree', for example, you must have some minimum number of true general beliefs about trees, e.g. that trees are plants, that trees are alive, that trees grow and reproduce, and so on. Someone who lacks these beliefs, and who thinks, for example, that trees are rock formations formed by erosion, does not have the concept of a tree and does not understand the word 'tree'. But this is a vague and open-ended matter. There is no fixed list of beliefs you must have in order to be competent with the word 'tree', and no one belief is necessary for competence. The same goes for names. To be competent with the name 'Paderewski' you must have a certain number of true general beliefs about Paderewski, for example that Paderewski is a human being, but there is no single, unchanging set of such beliefs necessary for competence. Another way to put this is that you cannot be competent with a name if you are massively confused about its referent—but there is no single way *not* to be massively confused.

This should dispel the worry that this reliance on the concept of semantic competence entails a distinction between semantic and non-semantic knowledge or between analytic and synthetic truths. Among all the beliefs someone has about Paderewski, it is impossible to single out those that ground their semantic competence and those that do not. We cannot single out justified true beliefs that one acquires simply by acquiring competence with a name, nor can we identify sentences that owe their truth to the meaning of a name.

The kind of semantic competence I use in the definition of semantic reference types is semantic competence with name *types*, i.e. names considered as repeatable expressions in public languages, which are individuated in terms of syntax, reference, and origin. An alternative would be to use the concept of understanding as applied to name tokens, i.e. uses of names by speakers in particular contexts.[10] This would connect my definition of semantic reference types with the phenomenon of *de jure* co-reference (Fine 2007; Pinillos 2011; Recanati 2012). Two singular term tokens are *de jure* co-referential just in case anyone who fully understands the discourse containing those tokens knows that they co-refer if they refer at all. Examples of *de jure* co-reference often involve anaphoric pronouns, e.g. an utterance of 'The Prime Minister personally invited Smith, but he didn't show up' (Pinillos 2011, 303). Arguably, any competent speaker who fully understands this utterance knows that the occurrences of 'Smith' and 'he' co-refer.

It would be straightforward to define semantic reference types using this concept of *de jure* co-reference in place of semantic competence with name types. First, define a relation, call it R_{dj}, on token acts of reference: two token acts of reference bear R_{dj} just in case the name tokens used in their performance are *de jure* co-referential. That is, two token acts of reference bear R_{dj} just in case understanding the name tokens used in their performance guarantees knowledge of co-reference. Then we can define semantic reference types as before in terms of this relation. The semantic reference type of a token act of reference x is the type of act of being an act of reference that bears R_{dj} to x. The semantic content of a name *token* is then the semantic reference type of the token act of reference performed with that token. This opens the way to individuating name types purely syntactically. Only name tokens used in particular contexts would have semantic contents; name types would not. In addition, this alternative may allow us to dispense with the reliance on ideal conditions. Arguably, Kripke's Peter fails to fully understand the two utterances containing distinct tokens of 'Paderewski', e.g. two utterances of 'Paderewski had musical talent'. Although he is competent with

---

[10]   I am indebted here to François Recanati.

the name, he fails to fully understand the two utterances since he fails to realize that the two uses of 'Paderewski' co-refer. If that's right then there is no need to use ideal conditions in the definition of semantic reference types in order to avoid the sort of problems raised by Kripke's Paderewski example.

I am open to this alternative definition of semantic reference types. Our current aim is to find reference types that can serve as the semantic contents of names. Given the abundance of types, it should come as no surprise that there are different ways of defining types, all of which can serve equally well. The choice between these alternatives comes down to a choice between using the concept of *semantic competence with expression types* versus the concept of *understanding expression tokens in contexts* as the basic theoretical notion in the definition of semantic content. This makes contact with questions about whether the proper bearers of semantic content are public language expression types (perhaps relative to contexts) or uses of expressions in particular contexts by speakers with communicative intentions. That is to say, this choice makes contact with the debate about contextualism in philosophy of language (see, for example, Recanati 2004 and Stanley 2005). My definition of semantic reference types aligns with the non-contextualist view that the bearers of content are expression types (perhaps relative to contexts); the alternative I have just been sketching aligns with the contextualist view that only uses of expressions by speakers have content. This debate goes beyond the scope of this book. I will stick with my non-contextualist definition of semantic reference types, keeping in mind that there is an easily available contextualist alternative. The larger aim of this book is to get a type-theoretic framework for understanding content off the ground. It is an asset of this framework that it is flexible enough to accommodate either side of the debate about contextualism.

5.5 Frege's Puzzle About Identity

The identification of the semantic contents of names with semantic reference types provides a straightforward solution to Frege's puzzle about identity sentences. The puzzle is familiar. How can two identity sentences that are alike except for the substitution of distinct co-referential names differ in cognitive significance? For example, (1) is trivial and uninformative, whereas (2) is not:

1. Le Carré is Le Carré.
2. Le Carré is Cornwell.

The solution is that these sentences express different propositions:

1a. ⊢ <(**Le Carré**, **Le Carré**), IDENTITY>
2a. ⊢ <(**Le Carré**, **Cornwell**), IDENTITY>[11]

Although these types have the same truth conditions, they are distinct. This is because the semantic reference types **Le Carré** and **Cornwell** are distinct. In a token of (1a) a speaker refers to Le Carré twice, with each act of reference falling under the same semantic reference type. Because of this, any competent speaker under ideal conditions will know that these acts of reference have the same referent. This captures the relevant sense in which (1) is trivial and uninformative. Note that (1) could be informative to someone, like Kripke's Peter, who thinks that there are two authors named 'Le Carré'. Such a speaker might be competent with the name 'Le Carré' and yet learn something from an utterance of (1). For such a speaker an utterance of (1) is neither trivial nor uninformative. This draws out the fact that posing Frege's puzzle requires the same sort of idealization I used in the definition of semantic reference types. It is only under ideal conditions, in which speakers know whether two name-tokens are instances of the same or different name-types, that uses of (1) are trivial and uses of (2) are not. The puzzle is to explain how, even under these ideal conditions, (1) and (2) differ in cognitive significance.

In a token of (2a), on the other hand, a speaker refers to Le Carré/Cornwell twice, but under two distinct semantic reference types. Since it is possible for a competent speaker to fail to realize that tokens of these types co-refer, even under ideal conditions, tokens of (2a) can be quite informative.

As Nathan Salmon has pointed out, it's a bit of a misnomer to call this Frege's puzzle about *identity*, since it doesn't depend in any essential way on the identity relation (Salmon 1986, 12). The same puzzle arises for examples that do not contain an identity predicate, such as:

---

[11] The parentheses, as opposed to angle brackets, represent the fact that these are unsorted acts of predication, with the consequence that (2a) is also the content of 'Cornwell is Le Carré'. See section 3.3.

3. Le Carré is an author if Le Carré is.
4. Cornwell is an author if Le Carré is.

The pair (3) and (4) exhibit the same contrast in cognitive significance as (1) and (2). Once again, this contrast depends on an idealization, since it is possible for someone who thinks there are two people named 'Le Carré' to learn something from an utterance of (3). The puzzle is to explain how, under ideal conditions in which a competent speaker knows the identities of the names involved, (3) is trivial and (4) is not. My solution, as before, is to distinguish the propositions expressed by these sentences:

5. $\vdash_\uparrow$< <~ $\vdash$ <**Le Carré**, AUTHOR>, ~ $\vdash$ <**Le Carré**, AUTHOR>>, COND>
6. $\vdash_\uparrow$< <~ $\vdash$ <**Le Carré**, AUTHOR>, ~ $\vdash$ <**Cornwell**, AUTHOR>>, COND>

(To avoid distracting issues about conditionals, let's stipulate that 'if' in (3) and (4) expresses the material conditional. Then COND is the type of act of expressing the material conditional relation that holds between two propositions, p and q, iff either p is false or q is true.) Tokens of (5) are uninformative for any competent speaker under ideal conditions, whereas tokens of (6) are not.

One of the attractive features of this approach to the semantic contents of names is that an explanation for the difference in cognitive significance in pairs like (1–2) and (3–4) falls directly out of this conception of semantic content. It is easy enough to find different semantic values for distinct co-referential names. For example, we could associate distinct causal or historical chains with the names 'Le Carré' and 'Cornwell' (Devitt 1974, 1981, 1989, 1996), or we could treat semantic contents as primitive and assign different contents to these names (Ackerman 1979, 1989). These views are similar to mine, insofar as they associate non-descriptive senses with names. The problem is that it is not clear how these other theories can account for the differences in cognitive significance that senses are meant to capture. The names 'Le Carré' and 'Cornwell' have different origins and different historical trajectories. How does that difference explain the difference in cognitive significance in sentences containing these names? The answer is obscure, and even more so for views on which the non-descriptive senses of names are primitive. To capture these differences an account of the senses of names needs to be based on, or at least entail, Frege's criterion of difference for sense. My account of semantic reference types is consciously designed to meet this condition.

5.6 Names and Translation

Cases in which a name in one language is translated by a syntactically different name in another language, e.g. 'London' and 'Londres', present another problem. Someone can be competent with both names and fail to realize that they co-refer. Given our current definitions, uses of these names would fall under different semantic reference types and the propositions in which these types occur would be distinct. This is a result I would like to avoid. It would be preferable to individuate semantic reference types in such a way that pairs like 'London' and 'Londres' are assigned the same semantic reference type as content. As things presently stand, my definition of semantic reference types does not deliver this result.

In previous work, (Hanks 2011), I used John Burgess's concept of *bilingual competence* to solve this problem (Burgess 2005). Bilingual competence with two languages L_1 and L_2 is competence with each language individually along with knowledge of the translation conventions between the two languages. Someone who is merely competent with both English and French might fail to know that 'London' and 'Londres' are names for the same city. By contrast, someone who is bilingually competent with English and French will know that 'Londres' is the French translation of 'London', and will therefore know that uses of the two names refer to the same city. Using the concept of bilingual competence, we can rewrite the definition of the relation R in such a way that token acts of reference using 'London' and 'Londres' bear R to one another, and so fall under the same semantic reference type. The idea is that two token acts of reference x and y with names n_x and n_y bear R iff anyone who is competent with n_x and n_y, or bilingually competent with these names if they belong to different languages, will realize, under ideal conditions, that x and y co-refer.

This solution works because it restricts our attention to bilingually competent speakers who know that 'London' and 'Londres' are translations of one another. A more direct route to the same result is to build this knowledge into the ideal conditions for R. This is the strategy I will take here. Let's add to the ideal conditions for R the stipulation that, when the names used in two token acts of reference belong to different languages, a competent speaker knows whether these names are translations of one another. Under these ideal conditions, competent speakers will know that 'Londres' translates 'London' and will therefore know that token uses of these names co-refer. This implies that uses of 'London' and 'Londres' fall under the same semantic reference type, and therefore that these names have the same semantic content.

It is worth reiterating that there is nothing circular, ad hoc, or otherwise illegitimate about this use of ideal conditions. When speakers use the names 'London' and 'Londres' their acts of reference fall under countlessly many different types of reference acts. Our present aim is to single out types to serve as the semantic contents of these names. In doing so we want pairs of names that are translations of one another to have the same semantic content. I have rigged the definition of semantic reference types to get this result. There is nothing inappropriate about this. The project is to define a reference type that reflects our judgments about the semantic contents of names, one of which is that translating a name from one language to another preserves semantic content.

This judgment is a reflection of the decision, made by translators and bilinguals, to classify together utterances containing a name and its translation. To say that one sentence is a *translation* of another is to make such a classification. As Burgess points out (Burgess 2005, 201), the English translation of the Greek name '$E\lambda\lambda\alpha\delta\alpha$' is 'Greece', not the etymologically and phonetically more appropriate 'Hellas'. 'Greece is pretty' is a translation of the corresponding Greek sentence; 'Hellas is pretty' is not. To say this is to classify utterances of 'Greece is pretty' together with the corresponding Greek utterances, and to classify utterances of 'Hellas is pretty' separately. This classification deserves the label 'semantic' because it is backed by a convention among translators and bilinguals. Contents are types we use for classifying and individuating our mental states and speech acts. Semantic contents are types we use when we classify linguistic utterances according to their conventional meanings. The reason a name and its translation should have the same semantic content is that we classify uses of that name and its translation together when our purposes for such classification are meant to reflect conventional, semantic facts about those names.

This adjustment to the ideal conditions for R has the interesting consequence that R is no longer transitive and hence no longer an equivalence relation. Consider a case in which a name in one language is conventionally translated by two different names in another language. At one time the English translation for the Chinese name of the capital of China was 'Peking'. Now it is 'Beijing'. Let's imagine that the earlier translation convention is still in effect, so that we could now correctly translate the Chinese name either as 'Peking' or 'Beijing'. Let C be the Chinese name for the capital of China. According to our amended definition of R, uses of C and 'Peking' bear R, as do uses of C and 'Beijing'. However, uses of 'Peking' and 'Beijing' do not bear R. It is possible for a monolingual English speaker who is competent with both names to fail to realize that uses of these names refer to the same city, even under ideal conditions. This means that R is not transitive.

Consider the semantic reference type of the name C, i.e. the type of reference act of being an act of reference that bears R to token acts of reference using C. This type has among its tokens uses of 'Peking' and uses of 'Beijing', but these tokens do not bear R to one another. The semantic reference type for C is a super-type of the semantic reference types for 'Peking' and 'Beijing'. Any use of 'Peking' is a token of the semantic reference type of C, but there are tokens of the semantic reference type of C, namely, uses of 'Beijing', that are not tokens of the semantic reference type of 'Peking'. We might say that the semantic contents of 'Peking' and 'Beijing' are *nested* inside the semantic content of C—but this should not be understood in a set-theoretical or mereological sense. The semantic content of 'Peking' is nested in the semantic content of C in the sense that the latter is a super-type of the former. However, this situation is somewhat unusual, insofar as it involves a scenario in which a name in one language is conventionally translated by distinct, non-synonymous names in another language. If we restrict our attention to a single language then we won't find cases in which the semantic content of one name is nested inside another. That is to say, if we restrict ourselves to a single language, the relation R is transitive, and it divides the space of token acts of reference into equivalence classes.

6

Empty Names

In chapter 5 I defined semantic reference types and used them to give an account of the semantic contents of proper names. The account was restricted to non-empty names. In this chapter I extend the view to empty names. The basic idea, as before, is that the semantic content of an empty name is a certain type of reference act. Even if they lack referents, empty names are still used to perform acts of reference. These acts of reference fall under types, one of which is the semantic content of the empty name. This avoids the familiar problem of empty names for the Millian theory of names. The contents of names are not referents, and so there is no problem about empty names having contents. In addition, by combining this approach with the concept of target-shifting (section 4.2), I will be able to give a new solution to the problem of true negative existentials.

6.1 Empty Names and Semantic Reference Types

One of the questions that came up in chapter 5 was whether there are examples of syntactically distinct names whose uses fall under the same semantic reference type. Here I want to suggest that "co-referential" empty names provide a source of such examples. "Co-referential" empty names are pairs of empty names that purport to refer to the same thing. 'Zeus' and 'Jupiter' are two names for the same Greco-Roman god.[1] Of course, there is no such god. Plausibly, however, anyone

---

[1] In earlier work (Hanks 2011) I used 'Bigfoot' and 'Sasquatch' as examples. The problem is these aren't proper names at all, but rather something like natural kind terms for a legendary species of ape-like creatures reputed to inhabit the forests of the Pacific Northwest.

who is semantically competent with both names knows that these names purport to refer to the same thing. Someone who thinks there are two gods, one named 'Zeus' and the other 'Jupiter', does not fully understand these names. There is no referent for the subject to be confused about; there are only the two names and their uses. Telling someone that Zeus and Jupiter "are the same god" can't provide new information about the world, since there is no god that is Zeus/Jupiter. The information must be about how these names are used—it must be about their meanings. Telling someone that Zeus and Jupiter are the same god serves to clear up this semantic confusion.

Legends, myths, fairy tales, and fiction offer many similar examples. Consider someone in the real world, not in the fictional world of the comic books, who thinks that 'Superman' and 'Clark Kent' are names for different comic book characters. Someone inside the fiction, like Lois Lane, can be competent with both names and fail to realize that they co-refer. But outside the fiction, understanding the names 'Superman' and 'Clark Kent' requires knowing that their uses purport to refer to the same character. If this is right then the pairs of names in these examples, 'Zeus' and 'Jupiter', and 'Superman' and 'Clark Kent', should be assigned the same semantic contents.

An advantage of assigning semantic contents in this way is that it can explain certain facts about empty names that have been emphasized by Anthony Everett (2000). Even though none of the names in (1a–b) and (2a–b) refer to anything, there is a strong intuition that the sentences in (1a–b) are "about" the same thing, and likewise for (2a–b), but these pairs are "about" different things:

1a. Zeus is fond of dogs.
 b. Jupiter is fond of dogs.

2a. Superman is fond of dogs.
 b. Clark Kent is fond of dogs.

Similarly, there is a strong intuition that someone who utters (1a–b) has said something different from someone who utters (2a–b). It is easy to explain these intuitions if we assign the pairs of names in these examples the same semantic contents, that is, if we classify their uses under the same semantic reference types. Utterances of (1a–b) are "about" the same thing in the sense that people who utter these sentences have performed tokens of the same semantic reference type. We classify utterances of (1a–b) together and (2a–b) together, but we classify utterances taken from different pairs apart. These classifications cannot reflect judgments about co-reference, since none of the names in these examples refers to anything.[2] Rather, these classifications must reflect judgments about how they are conventionally used. The classifications are semantic in nature, which should be reflected by assignments of the same semantic contents to the names in each pair.

To achieve this I need to make an adjustment to the definition of semantic reference types. In chapter 5 I defined semantic reference types in terms of a relation R on token acts of reference using names. I'll repeat that definition here for convenience. Let x and y be token acts of reference performed using the non-empty names n_x and n_y respectively:

$x R y$ iff$_{def}$ anyone who is semantically competent with n_x and n_y will realize, under relevantly ideal conditions, that x and y have the same referent.

The semantic reference type of a token act of reference x is the type of reference act of being an act of reference that bears R to x. The semantic content of a name n is the semantic reference type of token acts of reference using n.

The task now is to extend the definition of R to cover token acts of reference using empty names. Let's allow, then, that n_x and n_y can be empty. Define a relation R′ as follows:

$x R' y$ iff$_{def}$ anyone who is semantically competent with n_x and n_y will realize, under relevantly ideal conditions, that x and y have the same referent, or, in case x or y lacks a referent, that if x and y had referents then they would have had the same referent.

Anyone competent with names 'Zeus' and 'Jupiter' should realize, under ideal conditions, that uses of these names would refer to the same individual if they referred at all. Consequently, uses of 'Zeus' and 'Jupiter'

---

[2] Philosophers who believe in the existence of mythical and fictional entities might try to explain the intuitions emphasized by Everett by pointing to the fact that 'Zeus' and 'Jupiter' refer to the same mythical entity, which is different from the fictional entity referred to by 'Superman' and 'Clark Kent'. But this seems to get the order of priority wrong. The judgment that there is a single mythical entity, Zeus/Jupiter, is based in part on the intuition that uses of 'Zeus' and 'Jupiter' are "about" the same thing. The way we individuate mythical and fictional entities is driven by the way we classify and individuate the uses of mythical and fictional names, not the other way around.

fall under the same semantic reference type, and these names have the same semantic content. On the other hand, anyone competent with 'Zeus' and 'Superman' will realize, under ideal conditions, that if uses of these names had referents then these referents would have been different. It follows that uses of 'Zeus' and 'Superman' fall under different semantic reference types and hence these names have different semantic contents.

This commits me to the claim that competent users of 'Zeus' and 'Jupiter' will realize, under ideal conditions, that if uses of these names had referents then they would have had the same referent. This is supposed to capture the intuitive idea that competent users of these names know that they purport to refer to the same thing, or that sentences containing these names are "about" the same thing. Like R, the ideal conditions for R′ endow competent speakers with knowledge of the identities of the names under consideration. Also like R, for the purposes of R′ I am individuating names in terms of syntax, reference, and origin. Reference drops out for empty names, and so names like 'Zeus' and 'Jupiter' are individuated solely in terms of syntax and origin. This is how these names should be individuated when considering the counterfactual in the definition of R′. Applied to 'Zeus' and 'Jupiter', the counterfactual says: if token acts of reference using 'Zeus' and 'Jupiter' had referred at all, then they would have referred to the same thing.[3] In terms of possible worlds, this means that in the closest worlds in which these names, with the same origins as in the actual world, have referents, they have the same referent. Consider a world in which the names 'Zeus' and 'Jupiter' have the same origins but in which there are two gods, one named 'Zeus' and the other 'Jupiter'. Intuitively, this world is further away from actuality than a world in which there is one god referred to by

---

[3] What about names for impossible characters, e.g. a god who exists in and out of time, or a superhero who can make a round square? Given the standard Lewisian analysis, the relevant counterfactuals containing such names all come out vacuously true since they contain impossible antecedents (see Lewis 1973, 24–6). This isn't a problem. Let 'G' be the name for the impossible god, and 'S' the name for the impossible superhero. The key issue is whether competent speakers under ideal conditions would *realize* that if uses of 'G' and 'S' had referred at all, then they would have referred to the same thing. Some competent speakers, unaware of the Lewisian analysis, won't judge this to be the case and hence won't realize that this counterfactual is (vacuously) true (assuming it is). That is enough for uses of 'G' and 'S' to fall under different semantic reference types. Thanks to an anonymous reader for raising this concern.

both names. This is what competent speakers will judge under ideal conditions. Of course, they do not need to put their judgment in terms of possible worlds. It is enough for them to judge that if uses of 'Zeus' and 'Jupiter' had referents at all then they would have had the same referent. Even a competent speaker who believes that Zeus/Jupiter exists will accept this counterfactual.[4]

Following our notational convention, let's use '**Zeus**' for the semantic reference type of token acts of reference using the name 'Zeus'. If what I've just been arguing is correct, this is also the semantic reference type of token acts of reference using the name 'Jupiter'. So we could also call this type '**Jupiter**'. This type, **Zeus/Jupiter**, is the semantic content of the names 'Zeus' and 'Jupiter'. This bypasses the problems about empty names that plague the Millian theory of names. The name 'Zeus' has a content, and sentences in which this name occur express propositions. The only remaining issues concern the truth-values of these propositions.

6.2 Existence and Target-shifting

Acts of predication are acts of sorting or categorizing. To predicate the property of being green of something is to sort that thing with other green things. This act is correct, or true, just in case the object is green. These truth conditions for the act of predication depend on the fact that an object and property have been identified, and the property is predicated of the object. If one of these conditions is not met then no truth conditions are determined. This is often what happens with uses of empty names. Someone who says that Zeus is mighty hasn't referred to anything and so hasn't successfully identified an object for sorting. Consequently, the act of predication lacks truth conditions and is neither true nor false.[5]

---

[4] It is, of course, possible to be competent with the names 'Zeus' and 'Jupiter' while believing that Zeus/Jupiter exists. I am claiming that it is not possible to be competent with these names while thinking that they refer, or purport to refer, to different gods.

[5] Another option would be to treat this act of predication as false. Advocates of Negative Free Logic adopt this policy (Burge 1974; Sainsbury 2005). In Negative Free Logic, all simple, atomic sentences containing empty names are treated as false. Negative Free Logic is often contrasted with Fregean Free Logic, which holds that any sentence containing a term that lacks a referent is neither true nor false. The view I am advocating does not fit into either of these categories, although it is closer to Fregean Free Logic. On my view, some simple, atomic sentences containing empty names are neither true nor false, e.g. 'Zeus is mighty', but, as we will see, others are false, e.g. 'Zeus exists'.

This does not entail that the speaker hasn't asserted a proposition. An assertion that Zeus is mighty falls under the following type:

3. ⊢ <**Zeus**, MIGHTY>

Since **Zeus** and **Jupiter** are the same semantic reference type, (3) and (4) are identical:

4. ⊢ <**Jupiter**, MIGHTY>

This type, (3)/(4), is the proposition that Zeus is mighty. This type lacks truth conditions, but on the present approach that is no reason to deny that it is a proposition. The type (3)/(4) can serve its classificatory role just as well as any other proposition containing a non-empty reference type.

This leads immediately to questions about how it is possible to say something true or false using an empty name. The clearest examples of this are existential claims. 'Zeus exists' is false; 'Zeus does not exist' is true. A speaker who asserts these sentences does not refer to anything using the name 'Zeus'. How is it possible for these assertions to have these truth-values?

In chapter 4 I introduced the concept of target-shifting. In cases of target-shifting the target of an act of predication shifts away from what the subject refers to and is redirected at a type of action the subject performs. When Obama asserts that it is true that Clinton is eloquent he predicates the property of being true of the proposition that Clinton is eloquent. This proposition is the type of action he performs when he predicates eloquence of Clinton in the course of saying that it is true that Clinton is eloquent. Here is the proposition someone asserts by saying that it is true that Clinton is eloquent:

5. ⊢$_\uparrow$ <⊢ <**Clinton**, ELOQUENT>, TRUE>

The subscript on the outermost turnstile indicates that this is a target-shifted act of predication. The target of this act of predication is the type ⊢ <**Clinton**, ELOQUENT>. In a token of (5) a subject predicates truth of this type. Target-shifting also occurs in assertions of conjunctions:

6. ⊢$_\uparrow$ <(⊢ <**Clinton**, ELOQUENT>, ⊢ <**Biden**, PERSISTENT>), CONJ>

Again, the outermost turnstile represents a target-shifted act of predica-tion. In this case, the targets for this act of predication are the two types

⊢ <**Clinton**, ELOQUENT> and ⊢ <**Biden**, PERSISTENT>. In a token of (6) a subject predicates the conjunction relation of these two propositions.

All the examples of target-shifting we have seen so far involve compound sentences, i.e. cases in which one sentence is embedded inside another. In these cases the target of an act of predication shifts to the type of action a subject performs by using the embedded sentence. But there is no reason in principle why target-shifting should only occur with sentence embedding. Perhaps there are cases of target-shifting for non-compound sentences. This is what I want to suggest about existence claims. If target-shifting occurs in existence claims then we have the resources to solve the problem of true negative existentials.

Consider the false positive existential 'Zeus exists'. In asserting that Zeus exists the subject does not refer to anything, yet she still performs a type of reference act, the type **Zeus**. If the predicate 'exists' creates a target-shifted environment, then the target of her act of predicating the property of existence is the type **Zeus**. We can represent this type of act of predication as follows:

7. $\vdash_\uparrow$ <**Zeus**, EXIST>

In a token of (7) a subject performs a token of the reference type **Zeus**. The target for her act of predicating the property of existence is this type. Since the type **Zeus** exists, (7) is capable of having a truth-value. The subscript up-arrow on the single turnstile in (7) represents the fact that this act of predication is target-shifted. Its target is the type **Zeus**, not anything the subject attempts to refer to in performing this type of reference act.

The same goes for existence claims using non-empty names. Here is the proposition someone asserts by saying that Clinton exists:

8. $\vdash_\uparrow$ <**Clinton**, EXIST>

Like (7), in tokens of (8) the target of the act of predication is a type of reference act, in this case the type **Clinton**. The predicate 'exists' triggers target-shifting, not the names 'Zeus' or 'Clinton'. Uses of 'exists' create a target-shifted environment.

Although there are similarities between this concept of target-shifting and Frege's concept of an indirect context, the two concepts must be kept distinct. Frege thought that certain words, e.g. 'believes', created indirect contexts in which names do not have their customary referents (Frege

1892a). In Fregean indirect contexts the targets of acts of *reference* shift. This violates Davidson's principle of semantic innocence (Davidson 1968). Translated into the present framework, the principle of semantic innocence says that the type of action a speaker performs by the use of a word does not change from one linguistic setting to another. Using a name inside a that-clause in a belief sentence, for example, does not change the nature of the act of reference one performs by using that name. Frege's doctrine of indirect contexts violates this principle, since it implies that we use names inside that-clauses to perform different types of reference acts than the types we perform with other uses of names. By contrast, my concept of target-shifting poses no threat to semantic innocence. In what I am calling target-shifted environments, the targets of acts of *predication* shift. When someone utters 'Clinton exists' she uses the name 'Clinton' to perform the same type of reference act that she performs with any other use of this name. The difference is that in the existence claim her act of predication is directed at the type of reference act she performs. Her use of the predicate 'exists' is responsible for this difference. As we will see in chapter 7, something similar happens in propositional attitude reports.

We're now ready to see how this account handles true negative existentials. Suppose someone says that Zeus does not exist. Here is the type of action she performs:

9. $\vdash_\uparrow$ <**Zeus**, <NOT, EXIST>>

Recall from chapter 4 that NOT is a type of act of expressing a function from properties to negative properties. In this case, the function maps the property of existence to the negative property of non-existence. In a token of (9), a subject predicates non-existence of the type **Zeus**. This is a target-shifted act of predication.

Alternatively, someone might say that it is not the case that Zeus exists. This assertion is a token of the following type:

10. $\vdash_\uparrow$ <~$\vdash_\uparrow$ <**Zeus**, EXIST>, NOT-TRUE>

In a token of (10) a subject predicates the property of not being true of the proposition that Zeus exists. This target-shifted act of predication, represented by the outermost turnstile, is directed at the type $\vdash_\uparrow$<**Zeus**, EXIST>. Uses of the operator 'it is not the case that' create a cancellation context, and so the subject's token of $\vdash_\uparrow$<**Zeus**, EXIST> is cancelled.

Saying all of this commits me to the view that existence is not a property of individual objects. Existence is a property of types of reference acts (among other things).[6] This is not as strange as it may sound. When you say that Zeus does not exist it cannot be that you refer to something and predicate a property of it, since there is nothing there to refer to. Instead, your remark is a comment about a certain referential practice, the practice people engage in when they make claims using the names 'Zeus' or 'Jupiter'. To deny Zeus's existence is to say that this referential practice is empty; token instances of the practice fail to designate anything in reality. The type **Zeus** is this referential practice. This type lacks the property of existence in the sense that it fails to refer to anything in reality.[7] As usual, the type inherits this property from its tokens. The fact that the type **Zeus** fails to refer to anything in reality is constituted by the fact that tokens of this type fail to refer to anything in reality. Roughly speaking, to say that Zeus does not exist is ultimately a way of saying that people who talk about Zeus fail to refer to anything in the real world.

The view that existence is not a property of individuals is not new. It was held, in a different form, by Frege and Russell. For Frege, "existence is a property of concepts" (Frege 1884, 103). For Russell, "existence is essentially a property of a propositional function" (Russell 1918, 98). Fregean concepts are not the same things as Russellian propositional functions, but we can gloss over these differences by saying that, for Frege and Russell, existence is the second-level property of *being instantiated*. To say that unicorns exist is to say that the property/concept/

---

[6] By "among other things" I have in mind the types of actions we perform using general terms like 'unicorn' or 'politician'. When you assert 'Unicorns exist' you predicate the property of existence of a type of action you perform using the word 'unicorn'. This is not a type of reference act, in the strict sense of 'reference' that pertains to proper names. Perhaps it is a type of act of reference to a kind. Or it may be a type of expression act—a type of act of expressing the property of being a unicorn. If so, then on the present view, existence is both a property of types of reference acts and types of expression acts.

[7] Earlier I remarked that the type **Zeus** exists and can serve as a target for predications of existence. Here I say that **Zeus** lacks the property of existence. Isn't that a contradiction? There's a ladder here that can be kicked away, namely the claim that **Zeus** lacks the property of existence. The point of this claim is to clarify my account of existence. Strictly speaking, however, **Zeus** exists. Note that this claim itself needs to be analyzed along the lines of this approach to existence. In saying that **Zeus** exists, I predicate a property of a second-order reference type that refers to the type **Zeus**. Thanks to an anonymous reader for raising these issues.

propositional function *unicorn* is instantiated. In other words, *unicorn* has at least one instance. This is not the view of existence I am proposing here, which is that existence is a property of types of reference acts. One of the disadvantages of the Frege/Russell view of existence is that it only helps solve problems about existence claims if we adopt a descriptivist theory of names (Nelson 2012). If existence were the property of being instantiated, then to make sense of 'Clinton exists' we would have to find properties or concepts or propositional functions in the content of 'Clinton' to serve as the bearers of instantiation. Treating existence as a property of types of reference acts does not have this problem.

Another advantage of the present approach is that we avoid the threat of Meinongianism. We can view 'Zeus' as a device of reference without having to posit a non-existent entity to serve as its referent. 'Zeus' is a device of reference in the sense that it is used to perform a type of reference act, albeit one that fails to designate anything in reality. 'Zeus does not exist' is true precisely because of this failure.

There is a fairly straightforward argument for the claim that existence is not a property of individuals. The argument is based on the fact that it is pointless to predicate a property that is known to hold of everything in the domain of objects one is talking about. Suppose I am sorting a pile of marbles, and I know that everything in the pile is a marble. It would be trivial, uninteresting, and pointless to sort the marbles with respect to the property of being a marble. Or suppose we're watching a professional baseball game, and it is mutually known among everyone involved that everyone on the field is a Major League baseball player. It would be utterly pointless to point to someone on the field and say that he is a baseball player.

Now, suppose existence were a property of individuals. If it were, then, barring Meinongianism, it would have to be a universal property that everything has and nothing lacks. Furthermore, anyone who under-stands the word 'exists' would know that it expresses this universal property. But then it would be pointless to predicate the property of existence. Everyone who understands the predicate 'exists' would know ahead of time that everything has this property. But it is *not* pointless to predicate the property of existence. Learning that something exists, e.g. Neptune, or the Higgs boson, can be a momentous scientific discovery.

Here is a somewhat different argument for the same conclusion. Suppose that existence were a universal property of individuals. Then every atomic predication of existence, i.e. every simple, non-modal, positive act of predicating the property of existence of something one attempts to refer to, would either be true or neither true nor false because of reference failure. In other words, atomic acts of predicating the property of existence could not be false.[8] But they can be false. An assertion that Zeus exists is false. So, existence is not a universal property of individuals.

Russell used this argument in his lectures on logical atomism. He put it by saying that if existence were a property of individuals then it would be "absolutely impossible for it not to apply":

There is no sort of point in a predicate which could not conceivably be false. I mean, it is perfectly clear that, if there were such a thing as this existence of individuals that we talk of, it would be absolutely impossible for it not to apply, and that is the characteristic of a mistake. (Russell 1918, 108)

Kripke criticizes Russell's argument in the following passage:

The premise Russell is using here can be construed to be correct. It *is* necessary that everything exists, or that for every x there is a y, such that y is x. It by no means follows that existence is a trivial property, in the sense that everything has necessary existence. Symbolically, the difference is between $\Box(x)Ex$ (the fact that Russell invokes) and $(x)\Box Ex$, which does not follow. Only if the second formula were true would the predicate attributing existence to individuals be trivial. (Kripke 1973, 55)

Kripke is obviously right that, from the fact that necessarily everything exists, it does not follow that existence is "trivial", in the sense that everything necessarily exists. But Russell is not guilty of this mistake. His argument is not that if existence were a property of individuals then everything would necessarily exist. His argument is that if existence were a property of individuals, then *predications* of existence could not possibly be false. (Let x range exclusively over atomic acts of predication

---

[8] Advocates of Negative Free Logic, who hold that all simple atomic sentences containing non-referring terms are false and their negations true, will reject this claim. Negative Free Logic has intuitive advantages and disadvantages. An advantage is that it captures the falsity of 'Zeus exists' and truth of 'Zeus does not exist'. A disadvantage is that 'Zeus is not identical to Zeus' comes out true, but 'Zeus is distinct from Zeus' comes out false (see Sainsbury 2005, 69). In the end, the decision to adopt Negative Free Logic is driven by considerations of theoretical fruitfulness, often in the context of constructing a truth-theoretical semantic theory. Evaluating the merits of this decision would take us very far afield, something I have no intention of doing. So, the argument in this paragraph should be taken as conditional on the rejection of Negative Free Logic.

of the property of existence, and let 'F*x*' symbolize '*x* is false'. The claim is that $(x)\Box\sim Fx$.) For any simple, atomic act of predicating existence, you either refer to something and say something true, or you fail to refer to anything and say something that is neither true nor false. This is what Russell means when he says that 'exists' would be a predicate that "could not conceivably be false". His argument is straightforward:

P₁. If existence were a universal property of individuals, then atomic predications of existence could not be false.
P₂. Atomic predications of existence can be false.
∴. Existence is not a property of individuals.

It is useful to compare existence with a genuine universal property, such as the property of being self-identical. Atomic predications of self-identity cannot be false. For any name or referential device *t*, if you say that *t* is self-identical then you've either said something true or you failed to refer to anything and your assertion lacks truth conditions. Note also the pointlessness of the predicate 'is self-identical'. Anyone who understands this predicate knows ahead of time that everything is self-identical. Only a philosopher would say that something is self-identical.

Existence, then, is not a universal property of individuals. Frege and Russell held that it was the second-level property of being instantiated, but we don't have to follow them in this. By holding that existence is a property of types of reference acts, and that predications of existence involve target-shifting, we can make good sense of how it is possible for existence claims with empty names to be true or false.

6.3 Problems and Objections

One of the advantages of this approach to empty names is that it explains the sense in which, as Mark Crimmins put it, uses of empty names "*feel just like ordinary uses of names*" (Crimmins 1998, 33). It feels like we are referring to something when we use empty names. On my account this is captured by the fact that when you use an empty name you perform an act of reference, the same sort of action you perform when you use a non-empty name. Non-empty and empty names alike are used to perform acts of reference. This is true for any use of an empty name, including existential claims. A speaker who says that Zeus does not exist performs a token act of reference using the name 'Zeus'. This is the same kind of action a speaker performs when she uses a non-empty name like 'Clinton' or 'Obama'.

This account of negative existentials also satisfies a constraint proposed by Fred Kroon. The constraint is that "the terms in negative existentials are used rather than mentioned, exactly as grammar tells us, and furthermore are used as devices of reference, purporting to identify a referent rather than serving as shorthand for quantificational constructions that say what there is not" (Kroon 2000, 98). One of Kroon's targets is the Russellian account of existence claims, which analyzes 'Zeus does not exist' as a quantified claim meaning something like 'There is no unique god who throws lightning bolts and rules Mt. Olympus'. Another target is the meta-linguistic view that 'Zeus does not exist' means ''Zeus' does not refer'. My view is not a meta-linguistic view of this kind. I am not saying that 'Zeus does not exist' is about the name 'Zeus', nor that in an utterance of this sentence a speaker mentions rather than uses the name 'Zeus'.

Nevertheless, there is a still a concern that my account is vulnerable to the same kinds of problems that arise for the meta-linguistic account. One problem I do not face involves translation. Nathan Salmon (Salmon 1998) has argued that the meta-linguistic theory of negative existentials is refuted by an analog of the translation argument that Church (Church 1950) used to refute Carnap's analysis of belief reports. According to the meta-linguistic theory of negative existentials, (11a–b) express the same proposition:

11a. London does not exist.
  b. 'London' does not refer.

The problem is that when we translate these sentences into another language, e.g. French, the resulting sentences clearly do not express the same proposition:

12a. Londres n'existe pas.
  b. 'London' ne réfère pas.[9]

---

[9] As Salmon (2001) explains, it is irrelevant to the argument whether actual translators would translate (11b) as (12b). All the argument needs is that (11b) and (12b) express the same proposition. (11a) and (12a) express the same proposition, and so do (11b) and (12b). Since (12a–b) don't express the same proposition, neither do (11a–b).

A competent, monolingual speaker of French could accept (12b) without accepting (12a), or vice versa.

David Braun makes a related point. He argues that on the meta-linguistic view, "negative existentials that use different names (for instance, 'London does not exist' and 'Londres n'existe pas') cannot express the same proposition" (Braun 1993, 455). On the meta-linguistic account, 'London does not exist' and 'Londres n'existe pas' are about different names, 'London' and 'Londres' respectively, and so the propositions these sentences express must be distinct.

It is easy for me to avoid Braun's objection. Recall from chapter 5 (section 5.6) that uses of the names 'London' and 'Londres' fall under the same semantic reference type. Call this type **London**. (We could also call it **Londres**.) It follows that utterances of 'London does not exist' and 'Londres n'existe pas' express the same proposition:

13. $\vdash_\uparrow$ <**London**, <NOT, EXIST>>

In a token of (13) a speaker predicates non-existence of the semantic reference type **London**. Since this is the semantic reference type a speaker performs with either a use of 'London' or a use of 'Londres', utterances of 'London does not exist' and 'Londres n'existe pas' are assertions of the same proposition.

The Church translation problem is also easily dealt with. Applied to my theory, the analog of Church's argument would be that (14a–b) express the same proposition, but their respective translations, (15a–b), do not:

14a. London does not exist.
  b. **London** does not refer.
15a. Londres n'existe pas.
  b. **London** ne réfère pas.

This argument cannot get started. (14a–b) do *not* express the same proposition on my theory. Utterances of (14a) and (14b) are very different types of actions. In a token of (14a) a speaker refers to London and performs a target-shifted act of predicating non-existence of this type of reference act. In a token of (14b) a speaker refers to **London**, the semantic reference type, and performs a *non*-target-shifted act of predicating non-reference of this type. Since these are very different types of actions, the propositions a speaker asserts with utterances of (14a–b) are not the same. The same goes for (15a–b).

The examples (14a–b) raise a different problem, however. (14a) is false but contingent; London might not have existed. On the other hand, (14b) is false but not contingent. There are no possible worlds relative to which **London** fails to refer. Types of reference acts, like their tokens, are *obstinately* rigid.[10] The reference type **London** still refers to London even with respect to worlds in which London does not exist. Suppose someone asserts that London was never founded. This assertion is true with respect to many possible worlds—call one of them *w*. For this assertion to be true with respect to *w* it has to be that the speaker's token act of reference refers to something, namely London, with respect to *w*. It follows that a token act of reference to London still refers to London with respect to worlds in which London does not exist. The type of reference act **London** inherits its reference from its tokens. Since these tokens are obstinately rigid, the type is as well.

It follows that (14a) is contingently false and (14b) is necessarily false. This is potentially a problem, even though, as we have just seen, (14a) and (14b) express different propositions. These sentences are used to perform different types of actions, but one might think that these types of actions have the same truth conditions and are necessarily equivalent. In an utterance of (14a) a speaker predicates the property of non-existence of the type **London**. In an utterance of (14b) a speaker predicates the property of not having a referent of this same type. If the property of non-existence is the property of not having a referent, then in both utterances a speaker predicates this property of the type **London**. If so then these types of acts of predication should be necessarily equivalent.

This shows that the property of existence cannot simply be identified with the property of having a referent. These properties have to be distinct. When I was introducing this approach to negative existentials I was careful to say that **Zeus** lacks the property of existence in the sense that it *fails to designate anything in reality*. I put it that way in the hope that it would avoid suggesting that the property of existence is the same as the property of having a referent. The distinction between

---

[10] The term "obstinately rigid" is due to (Salmon 1981). See (Kaplan 1989a, 1989b; Salmon 1981; and Branquinho 2003) for defenses of the view that proper names are obstinately rigid.

these properties reveals itself when we consider non-actual worlds. With respect to a world w in which London was never founded, the type **London** fails to designate anything in reality. The reality in question is the world w. There is nothing in w that **London** designates, and hence this type fails to designate anything in reality with respect to w. On the other hand, since **London** is obstinately rigid, **London** still refers to London with respect to w.

I can clarify this with what Soames calls the "actually*" operator (Soames 2002, 46–9). Unlike the standard indexical actuality operator, the actually* operator can be coindexed with another modal operator in the sentence in which it occurs. An utterance of 'Necessarily, the actual 42nd First Lady is a philosopher' is true iff in every world w, Hillary Clinton is a philosopher. An utterance of 'Necessarily$_i$, the actual*$_i$ 42nd First Lady is a philosopher' is true iff in every world w, the 42nd First Lady in w is a philosopher. Suppose Ross Perot won the 1992 presidential election in w_1. Then, 'In w_1, the actual*$_1$ 42nd First Lady is a philosopher' is true iff in w_1, Margot Birmingham, Ross Perot's wife, is a philosopher. To say that possibly, **London** fails to designate anything in reality is to say that there is a world w_i, such that **London** fails to designate anything actual*$_i$, i.e. **London** fails to designate anything in w_i. This can be true even though **London** still refers to London with respect to w_i. It follows that (16a) is true, while (16b) is false:

> 16a. Possibly, **London** fails to designate anything in reality.
> b. Possibly, **London** fails to refer.

This captures the modal difference between (14a) and (14b). (14a) is contingently false because (16a) is true. (14b) is necessarily false because (16b) is false. The property of designating something in reality is world relative in a way that the property of reference is not. The type **London** has the property of designating something in reality relative to some worlds but not others. That is why it is contingently true that London exists. But, since **London** is obstinately rigid, this type refers to something relative to every world. That is why it is necessarily true that **London** refers.

The claim, then, is that the property of existence is the property of designating something in reality. In saying this I am deliberately exploiting the variability in the meaning of 'reality', which parallels the variability in the meaning of 'exists'. 'Exists' is context-sensitive; its extension expands or contracts depending on the context of use. Sometimes we use the term 'exists' in a restricted way to talk solely about things in the concrete material universe. On other occasions we use 'exists' in a more expansive way to cover fictional, mythical, imaginary, and other varieties of non-concrete objects. A number of philosophers have argued, plausibly in my opinion, that when authors write fiction they create fictional characters.[11] These philosophers think that fictional characters like Hamlet and Sherlock Holmes exist, and were brought into existence by Shakespeare and Conan Doyle. At the same time, though, these philosophers have to acknowledge the strong inclination to say that Hamlet and Sherlock Holmes do *not* exist. Kripke captures the predicament nicely:

> What I have said above about fictional characters gives us some respite. A name of a fictional character has a referent. One might then suppose that the name definitely has a referent (the fictional character)....However, I find myself uneasy about invoking this as a complete solution. There is an inclination to say 'Sherlock Holmes never existed'. (Kripke 1973, 71)

Kripke wants to say, virtually in the same breath, that Sherlock Holmes exists and that Sherlock Holmes does not exist. This has to involve distinct senses of 'exist'. 'Sherlock Holmes exists' is true in the expansive sense of 'exists' that applies to concrete, material things, as well as fictional entities and other non-concrete things. 'Sherlock Holmes exists' is false in the restricted sense of 'exists' that applies only to concrete, material things.

The term 'reality' is context-sensitive in exactly the same way. Sometimes by 'reality' we just mean the concrete, physical universe. On other occasions we use the term 'reality' to cover a larger domain that includes fictional, mythical, imaginary, and other sorts of non-concrete things. When I say that existence is the property of designating something in reality, I don't intend my use of 'reality' to be pinned down to one or another of these senses. A philosopher might argue that Zeus exists as a mythical being, but that does not make her a true believer in Zeus. She holds that Zeus exists, but she will surely also deny that the ancient

---

[11] For example (Braun 2005; Kripke 1973; Salmon 1998; Searle 1979; Soames 2002; Thomasson 1999; van Inwagen 1977). See (Yagisawa 2001) for criticisms. Ben Caplan has argued (Caplan 2004) that the arguments for fictional entities extend to mythical and imaginary entities.

Greeks were right in their belief that Zeus exists. On my view, when this philosopher says that Zeus exists, she predicates the property of designating something in reality of the type **Zeus**, in the expansive sense of 'reality' that includes non-concrete things. When she asserts that Zeus doesn't exist, she predicates the property of failing to designate anything in reality of the type **Zeus**, in the narrow sense of 'reality' that only includes concrete, material things. There is no one property of existence, then. The extension of 'exists' expands or contracts depending on the context of use. In this respect 'exists' is like the predicates 'flat' or 'straight', whose extensions expand or contract depending on the standards for flatness or straightness. It is not hard to imagine situations in which Kripke's predicament would arise for these predicates. Suppose there are multiple standards of precision at work in a single conversation. In such as case, we might find ourselves inclined to say that something is flat and also not flat, or that it is straight but also not straight. Because of the varying standards of precision these claims are not contradictory. I am suggesting that something similar is going on with our inclination to say that Sherlock Holmes exists but also does not exist.

7

Propositional Attitude Reports

One of the advantages of the approach to propositional content that I am defending in this book is the enormous flexibility afforded by the identification of contents with types. Types are abundant. Any type is situated in a virtually limitless range of more or less finely grained types. In this chapter I exploit this flexibility to give an account of propositional attitude reports.[1] Roughly stated, the idea is that when a speaker utters a that-clause in a propositional attitude report she performs a token of a type, a proposition, which sits in the middle of a range of related types. The report is true in a context depending on whether the subject of the report bears the relevant attitude to one of the types in this range. This will allow us to capture, in a fairly simple and straightforward way, the complex and highly context-sensitive facts about the truth conditions of attitude reports.

7.1 That-clauses and Target-shifting

Let's start with a familiar and widely held relational analysis of attitude reports. Consider an attitude report of the form 'S v's that p'. The relational analysis makes the following three claims:

i. The attitude verb 'v' is used to express a binary relation between subjects and propositions.
ii. 'That p' is used to designate the proposition that p.
iii. 'S v's that p' is true iff S bears the v'ing relation to the proposition that p.

---

[1] Portions of this chapter are taken from (Hanks 2011).

In this section I will propose an alternative to (ii), and in the next section a modification to (iii).

The alternative to (ii) uses the concept of target-shifting:

ii*. 'That p' is used to perform a token of the type p. Along with the subject S, this type (or a suitably related type) is the target of the speaker's act of predicating the v'ing relation.

For the moment let's ignore the qualification about suitably related types—more on this in the next section. The point to focus on now is the idea that attitude reports involve target-shifting. Here is the proposition someone asserts when she says that Obama believes that Clinton is eloquent:

1. $\vdash_\uparrow$ < <**Obama**, ~$\vdash$ <**Clinton**, ELOQUENT>>, BELIEVE>

The outermost turnstile represents the speaker's act of predicating the belief relation. In this case, the speaker predicates the belief relation of Obama and the proposition that Clinton is eloquent, which is the type $\vdash$ <**Clinton**, ELOQUENT>. In a token of (1), a speaker performs a (cancelled) token of this proposition by uttering the sentence 'Clinton is eloquent'. By uttering the that-clause 'that Clinton is eloquent', the speaker uses the sentence 'Clinton is eloquent' to perform exactly the same type of action she would use this sentence to perform on any other occasion.

This is a mixed case of target-shifting. In a token of (1), the act of predicating the belief relation is target-shifted for the speaker's token of $\vdash$ <**Clinton**, ELOQUENT>, but not for the speaker's token of **Obama**. The speaker is not saying that the reference type **Obama** believes that Clinton is eloquent. Remember that target-shifting occurs whenever one sentence is embedded inside another. When that happens the target for predication shifts to the type of action the speaker performs by uttering the embedded sentence. In an utterance of 'Obama believes that Clinton is eloquent' the speaker uses the name 'Obama' to refer to Obama, and the sentence 'Clinton is eloquent' to perform a token of $\vdash$ <**Clinton**, ELOQUENT>. The speaker's use of the embedded sentence triggers target-shifting, but her use of the name 'Obama' does not. Note that there can be uses of attitude reports that do not involve target-shifting. Let's use 'Logicism' as a proper name for the proposition that mathematics is reducible to logic. Here is the proposition someone asserts by uttering 'Obama accepts Logicism':

2. $\vdash$ <<**Obama, Logicism**>, ACCEPT>

There is no subscript up-arrow on the outermost turnstile, which means that there is no target-shifting in this case. In a token of (2) a speaker refers to the proposition that mathematics reduces to logic and predicates the acceptance relation of Obama and this proposition. There is no target-shifting in this example because there is no sentence embedded inside 'Obama accepts Logicism'. Similar remarks apply to other examples in which attitude verbs take noun-phrase complements, such as 'Obama believes Clinton'.

This preserves semantic innocence, both for names and for sentences used inside that-clauses. In terms of my framework, Davidson's principle of semantic innocence is that the type of action we use an expression to perform does not change from one linguistic setting to another. This applies to sentences just as much as it does to names. Using a sentence inside a that-clause does not change the type of action someone performs by uttering this sentence. In an utterance of 'Obama believes that Clinton is eloquent' a speaker uses the embedded sentence to perform a token of the type $\vdash$ <**Clinton**, ELOQUENT>. She does not refer to or somehow designate this type using the that-clause. Rather, she performs a token of it, and her act of predicating the belief relation is targeted in part at this type. In this respect, attitude reports are like any other utterances in which a speaker uses a sentence inside another sentence.

So it is not the verb 'believes' that is responsible for target-shifting, but the fact that a speaker uses a sentence inside a larger sentence. On the other hand, the verb 'believes' is responsible for creating a cancellation context for the embedded act of predication. This is indicated by the tilde on the internal turnstile in (1). A speaker who says that Obama believes that Clinton is eloquent is not herself asserting that Clinton is eloquent. In the course of uttering this attitude report the speaker's act of predicating eloquence of Clinton takes place in a cancellation context. In this respect, 'believes' is like 'it is not the case that' and 'or'.

This raises a question about whether there are attitude verbs that do not generate cancellation contexts. The verb 'knows' seems like a good candidate. Perhaps 'knows' does not create a cancellation context. If not, then someone who asserts that Obama knows that Clinton is eloquent would also assert that Clinton is eloquent. If that were right, then an utterance of 'Obama knows that Clinton is eloquent' would be true only if Clinton is eloquent, which would account for the factivity of 'knows'. This is appealing, since it would allow us to view the non-factive/factive distinction as an instance of the more general distinction between sentence-embedding expressions that create cancellation contexts and those that do not.

Unfortunately this won't work. Like 'believes', uses of 'knows' must also create cancellation contexts. Consider an example in which 'knows' takes an interrogative complement:

3.   Obama knows whether Clinton is eloquent.

According to my theory, the content of the whether-clause is the interrogative proposition (4):

4.   ? <**Clinton**, ELOQUENT>

This is a type of action in which someone *asks* whether Clinton has the property of eloquence. The question mark '?' represents the type of act of combining an object and property in the interrogative mode, which can be done by asking or wondering whether Clinton is eloquent. Now, if 'knows' does not generate a cancellation context, then in an assertion of (3) a speaker would ask whether Clinton is eloquent, and it is clear that the speaker does no such thing. The proposition expressed by (3) has to be the following:

5. $\vdash_\uparrow$ <<**Obama**, ~? <**Clinton**, ELOQUENT>>, KNOW>

If the use of 'knows' cancels in this case, then uniformity demands that it cancels in all cases. There is more to be said about propositions like (5), but let's postpone that until we fill in the rest of this approach to attitude reports.

7.2 Standard and Super-standard Contexts

Let's now turn to clause (iii) in the relational analysis of attitude reports. According to this clause, an attitude report of the form 'S *v*'s that *p*' is true iff S bears the *v*'ing relation to the proposition that *p*. Here is my proposed modification:

iii*. 'S *v*'s that *p*' is true iff S bears the *v*'ing relation to a proposition suitably related to the proposition that *p*.

This is going to give us the flexibility we need to capture the context-sensitivity in the truth conditions of attitude reports. The propositions suitably related to p will vary with context. In some contexts, which I call *standard*, the only proposition suitably related to p is p itself. In a standard context, 'Obama believes that Clinton is eloquent' is true iff Obama bears the belief relation to the proposition $\vdash$ <**Clinton,** ELOQUENT>.

Standard contexts account for many examples of substitution failure in attitude reports. Let's use the Le Carré/Cornwell example from chapter 5. The Soviet double-agent Kim Philby was a colleague of Cornwell's in the British secret service in the 1950s and 60s. Let's imagine that Philby was a fan of Le Carré's early novels but, like most everyone else, did not know that his colleague Cornwell was Le Carré. Regarding the time before Philby learned that Cornwell was Le Carré, (6a) is true but (6b) is false:

6a. Philby believed that Le Carré was a novelist.
b. Philby believed that Cornwell was a novelist.

This is a familiar case of substitution failure in an attitude report. Now, the relevant context for (6a–b) is what I am calling a standard context. This means that, relative to the intended context, (6a) is true iff Philby bears the belief relation to $\vdash$ <**Le Carré,** NOVELIST>, whereas (6b) is true iff Philby bears the belief relation to $\vdash$ <**Cornwell,** NOVELIST>. The semantic reference types **Le Carré** and **Cornwell** are distinct, and hence these are different propositions. That explains how it is possible for (6a) to be true and (6b) false.

In other contexts, which I call *super-standard*, the propositions suitably related to p are more coarsely grained super-types of p. Recall that every semantic reference type determines a more coarsely grained object-dependent super type. **Le Carré** is a semantic reference type, which determines the object-dependent reference type $\text{LeCarré}_{\text{obj}}$. **Le Carré**$_{\text{obj}}$ is the type of reference act of referring to Le Carré/Cornwell in any way whatsoever, using any name or referential device. Every token of **Le Carré** is a token of **Le Carré**$_{\text{obj}}$ but not vice versa. That is why the object-dependent type is a super-type of the semantic reference type. Consequently, (7b) is a super-type of (7a):

7a. ⊢ <**Le Carré**, NOVELIST>
  b. ⊢ <**Le Carré**$_{obj}$, NOVELIST>

In a super-standard context, an utterance of 'Philby believes that Le Carré is a novelist' is true iff Philby bears the belief relation to the object-dependent super-type (7b).

Super-standard contexts account for cases of substitution *success* in attitude reports. Here is the example I used in (Hanks 2011). Suppose Philby sees a man running to catch a bus. The man happens to be Cornwell, although Philby does not recognize him. Commenting on what he sees, Philby says 'He's going to miss the bus'. Describing this scene later on, in a conversation in which everyone knows that Cornwell and Le Carré are the same person, someone can truly assert both (8a) and (8b):

8a. Philby said that Le Carré was going to miss the bus.
  b. Philby said that Cornwell was going to miss the bus.

In this case substitution of the names 'Le Carré' and 'Cornwell' doesn't seem to make any difference to the truth-value of the attitude report. This is a case of substitution success. Another sort of example would be one in which we are discussing the time *after* Philby learned that Cornwell was LeCarré. If everyone in the conversation knows that Cornwell is LeCarré, then it shouldn't make a difference which name we use when we are attributing beliefs and other attitudes to Philby.

The relevant contexts for cases of substitution success are super-standard contexts. Relative to a super-standard context, (8a) and (8b) are true iff Philby bears the belief relation to the object-dependent proposition (9):

9. ⊢ <**Le Carré**$_{obj}$, MISS-THE-BUS>[2]

Since **Le Carré**$_{obj}$ and **Cornwell**$_{obj}$ are the same object-dependent reference types, (9) is identical to (10):

10. ⊢ <**Cornwell**$_{obj}$, MISS-THE-BUS>

Tokens of (9)/(10) are cases in which someone refers to Le Carré/Cornwell, in any way whatsoever, and predicates the property of missing

---

[2] I am ignoring complications about tense and aspect. I am also pretending that the predicate 'was going to miss the bus' is used to express a simple monadic property. Nothing turns on these simplifications.

the bus of him. Philby's utterance of 'He is going to miss the bus' counts as a token of this type, and hence relative to a super-standard context (8a–b) are both true.

Returning to our modified clause (iii*), in super-standard contexts the propositions suitably related to p are object-dependent super-types of p. These object-dependent super-types are obtained by substituting corresponding object-dependent reference types for one or more of the semantic reference types in p. Note that if p contains more than one semantic reference type then p will have more than one corresponding object-dependent super-type, depending on how many of the semantic reference types in p are changed to object-dependent reference types.

7.3 Extra Super-standard Contexts and Designation Types

Suppose Philby says 'The author of *The Spy Who Came in from the Cold* is a spy'. Reporting this utterance later on in a conversation in which everyone knows that Cornwell is the author of *The Spy Who Came in from the Cold*, someone could truly assert (11):

11. Philby said that Cornwell is a spy.

Relative to this context (11) is true. Note, however, that Philby did not *refer* to Cornwell, and so didn't perform a token of any of the reference types **Le Carré**, **Cornwell**, or **Le Carré$_{obj}$**. Philby used the definite description 'the author of *The Spy Who Came in from the Cold*' to denote Cornwell, not to refer to him. How are we to account for the truth of (11)?

Let Le Carré be the type of act of *designating* Le Carré/Cornwell. (We could also use 'Cornwell' for this type.) This is an even more coarsely grained type than the object-dependent reference type **Le Carré$_{obj}$**. In fact, the designation type Le Carré is a super-type of both **Le Carré** and **Le Carré$_{obj}$**. Tokens of Le Carré can be acts of referring to Le Carré, but they can also be acts of denoting him using a definite description. When Philby uses the description 'the author of *The Spy Who Came in from the Cold*' he performs a token of Le Carré, but not a token of any reference type. Philby's utterance is therefore a token of (12):

12. $\vdash$ < Le Carré, SPY>

Relative to an *extra super-standard context*, an utterance of (11) is true iff Philby bears the saying relation to (12). In a token of (12) a speaker designates Le Carré, and predicates the property of being a spy of the person so designated. Since this is what Philby did in his utterance of 'The author of *The Spy Who Came in from the Cold* is a spy', we can truly report this utterance by uttering (11) in an extra super-standard context.

By expanding the concept of designation we can account for even more examples. Let's imagine that Cornwell worked on the third floor of the MI6 building. Suppose Philby says 'Everyone who works on the third floor is a spy'. Intuitively, since Cornwell works on the third floor, Philby said something about Cornwell. Let's extend the concept of designation to cover this kind of example. I won't try to make this perfectly precise, but the idea is that a speaker designates an object *a* whenever she says something that is intuitively about *a*. Since Cornwell works on the third floor, Philby said something that is intuitively about Cornwell when he said that everyone who works on the third floor is a spy, and so he designated Cornwell in our extended sense of 'designate'. It follows that Philby performed a token of (12) in his utterance of 'Everyone who works on the third floor is a spy', which means that we can truly report his utterance with (11) in an extra super-standard context. And that seems right. Consider a conversation in which everyone knows that Cornwell works on the third floor of the MI6 building. Relative to this context, we can give a partial report of Philby's claim that everyone who works on the third floor is a spy by saying that Philby said that Cornwell is a spy.

Relative to extra super-standard contexts, then, the propositions suitably related to *p* are obtained by substituting coarsely grained designation types for the corresponding semantic reference types in *p*. As before, if *p* contains more than one semantic reference type then there will be more than one corresponding designative super-type.

7.4 Sub-standard Contexts and the Paderewski Puzzle

In all the cases considered so far an attitude report of the form 'S *v*'s that *p*' is true iff S bears the *v*'ing relation to *p* or some *less* finely grained super-type of *p*. As one might expect, there are also cases in which 'S *v*'s that p' is true iff S bears the v'ing relation to a *more* finely grained sub-type of p. This happens in *sub-standard* contexts. In a sub-standard context, 'S v's that p' is true iff S bears the v'ing relation to a sub-type of p. These sorts of contexts explain how it is possible for an attitude report to change its truth-value *without* any substitutions in its that-clause. This is what happens in Kripke's Paderewski puzzle (Kripke 1979).

Peter, the subject in Kripke's Paderewski case, does not realize that Paderewski the pianist is the same person as Paderewski the Polish statesman. In a conversation about Paderewski the pianist, Peter assents to 'Paderewski had musical talent'. In a conversation about Paderewski the statesman, Peter does not assent to this sentence. Given the strong, biconditional form of Kripke's disquotation principle, it follows that (13) is true in the first conversation but false in the second:[3]

13.   Peter believes that Paderewski had musical talent.

These conversations take place in sub-standard contexts. The truth conditions for (13) relative to these contexts require Peter to bear the belief relation to different sub-types of the proposition that Paderewski had musical talent. What are these sub-types?

In the first conversation, Peter performs a token of **Paderewski** while thinking of Paderewski as a pianist. This act falls under a sub-type of **Paderewski**, the type of act of performing a token of **Paderewski** while thinking of Paderewski as a pianist. Let's represent this sub-type with '**Paderewski**$_{pianist}$'. In the second conversation, Peter performs a token of **Paderewski** while thinking of Paderewski as a statesman. This falls under a different sub-type of **Paderewski**—the type of act of performing a token of **Paderewski** while thinking of Paderewski as a statesman. Call this type '**Paderewski**$_{statesman}$'. Substituting these sub-types into the proposition that Paderewski had musical talent generates the following propositions:

---

[3] Kripke's strong, biconditional disquotation principle is that a normal English speaker who is not reticent will be disposed to sincere reflective assent to 'p' if and only if he believes that p (Kripke 1979, 113). I am only going to consider the version of Kripke's puzzle that employs this principle. The version of the puzzle that employs the weak disquotation principle raises issues about rationality and contradictory beliefs that I cannot adequately address here.

14a. ⊢ <Paderewski$_{pianist}$, MUSICALLY TALENTED>
   b. ⊢ <Paderewski$_{statesman}$, MUSICALLY TALENTED>

Relative to the first conversation, in which Peter is thinking of Paderewski as a pianist, (13) is true iff Peter bears the belief relation to (14a). Relative to the second conversation, in which Peter is thinking of Paderewski as a statesman, (13) is true iff Peter bears the belief relation to (14b). Since (14a) and (14b) are different types, it is possible for (13) to be true in the first conversation but false in the second.

Kripke sums up the London/Londres version of his puzzle by asking "Does Pierre, or does he not, believe that London is pretty?" (Kripke 1979, 124). We can ask the same thing about Peter. Does Peter, or does he not, believe that Paderewski had musical talent? This question is not as simple as it looks. There is no one belief that is the belief that Paderewski had musical talent. We individuate beliefs in terms of their propositional contents, and propositional contents come in varying degrees of fineness of grain. To answer the question about Peter, we need to know how the belief that Paderewski had musical talent is being individuated, i.e. what level of fineness of grain is intended. Relative to extra super, super, and standard contexts, the answer is 'yes'. These contexts require Peter to bear the belief relation to the following types, respectively:

15a. ⊢ <$\overline{\text{Paderewski}}$, MUSICALLY TALENTED>
   b. ⊢ <Paderewski$_{obj}$, MUSICALLY TALENTED>
   c. ⊢ <Paderewski, MUSICALLY TALENTED>

Peter believes each of these propositions in the sense that he has performed acts of judgment that fall under these types, or he would readily perform these judgments if queried, or at least he behaves as though he has performed judgments of these types. (This employs an account of attitude relations that I will develop in the next section.) Relative to sub-standard contexts, the answer can be 'yes' or 'no', depending on which sub-type of ⊢ <Paderewski, MUSICALLY TALENTED> is relevant. If the salient sub-type is (14a) the answer is 'yes'. If it is (14b) the answer is 'no'. But there is no context in which the answer to Kripke's question is both 'yes' and 'no'.[4]

---

[4] One consequence of this approach is that Kripke's strong disquotation principle has to be relativized to contexts, and once we do that it comes out false relative some kinds of

Let me try to sum up where we are at this point. The modified clauses (ii*) and (iii*), along with the distinction between extra super, super, standard, and sub-standard contexts, present the following picture. When someone utters an attitude report of the form 'S v's that p' she uses 'that p' to perform a token of the type p. This type sits near the center of a large range of less or more finely grained types. Depending on the context, the truth of the attitude report depends on whether S bears the v'ing relation to one of the types in this range. In extra super-standard contexts, 'S v's that p' is true iff S bears the v'ing relation to a designative super-type of p. In a super-standard context, 'S v's that p' is true iff S bears the v'ing relation to an object-dependent super-type of p. In a standard context, 'S v's that p' is true iff S bears the v'ing relation to the type p. In a sub-standard context, 'S v's that p' is true iff S bears the v'ing relation to some sub-type of p, where the particular sub-type is determined in context.

Extra super-standard $\vdash$ <Clinton, ELOQUENT>
Super-standard $\vdash$ <Clinton$_{obj}$, ELOQUENT>
Standard $\vdash$ <Clinton, ELOQUENT>
Sub-standard $\vdash$ <Clinton$_{\ldots}$, ELOQUENT>

contexts and true relative to others. As originally formulated, the principle says that a normal English speaker who is not reticent will be disposed to sincere reflective assent to 'p' if and only if he believes that p (Kripke 1979, 113). The right hand side of the biconditional is an attitude report, which has to be evaluated relative to a context. This generates different versions of Kripke's principle, depending on how we fill in the following blank:

Relative to any _____ context, a normal English speaker who is not reticent will be disposed to sincere reflective assent to 'p' if and only if he believes p.

If we fill in the blank with 'extra super-standard', 'super-standard', or 'standard' then the principle is false. Let 'p' be 'Cornwell is a novelist', and let Philby be our normal English speaker. Before he learned that Cornwell is LeCarré, Philby would not have assented to 'Cornwell is a novelist', even though at that time he bore the belief relation to designative and object-dependent super-types of $\vdash$ <Cornwell, NOVELIST>. Relative to extra super- and super-standard contexts, therefore, the principle is false. Kripke's Peter illustrates why the principle comes out false for standard contexts. There are standard contexts in which Peter does not assent to 'Paderewski had musical talent', even though he bears the belief relation to $\vdash$ <Paderewski, MUSICALLY TALENTED>. On the other hand, the principle is true if we fill in the blank with 'sub-standard'. Peter won't assent to 'Paderewski had musical talent' when he is thinking about Paderewski as a statesman, and he does not bear the belief relation to $\vdash$<Paderewski$_{statesman}$, MUSICALLY TALENTED>. The sub-standard version of the principle is the one we need in order to generate Kripke's Paderewski puzzle, and so it can still serve that purpose.

It is *not* part of this view that that-clauses are ambiguous. I am not claiming that the that-clause in 'Obama believes that Clinton is eloquent' changes its content from one context to another. In any utterance of 'Obama believes that Clinton is eloquent' the speaker uses the embedded sentence to perform a token of ⊢ <**Clinton**, ELOQUENT>. In context, the speaker's act of predicating the belief relation is targeted at this proposition or at one of the propositions in the surrounding range.

Speakers' intentions determine whether the context is standard, super-standard, etc., and hence which proposition figures in the truth conditions of the report. In sub-standard contexts, the speaker intends to make a finely grained, detailed claim about the type of attitude possessed by the target subject. Suppose I hear Peter say 'Paderewski had musical talent', and I happen to know that when he said this he was thinking about Paderewski as a pianist. When I report his assertion I intend the truth of my report to depend on whether Peter performed a token of a finely grained type of reference act that involves thinking of Paderewski as a pianist. This intention is responsible for the fact that the context for my report is sub-standard. On the other hand, in many cases I lack detailed information about how the target subject thought about or referred to the relevant objects, and even if I have such information I may not intend to tie the truth of my attitude report to the subject's having performed a token of a type that incorporates this information. In such cases the context for my report can be standard, super-standard, or extra super-standard. The context will be standard if I intend to make a report that is not sensitive to the details about how the subject was thinking about the relevant objects, but still won't tolerate substitutions of co-referential names. I don't really know anything about how Philby thought about his colleague Cornwell prior to learning that Cornwell was Le Carré. Nevertheless, when I say 'Philby believed that Cornwell worked for MI6', I intend the truth conditions for my report to be such that substituting 'Le Carré' for 'Cornwell' would change its truth-value. This intention entails that the context for my report is standard. In other cases I intend the truth of my report to be indifferent to how Cornwell/Le Carré is referred to or designated, in which case the relevant contexts will be super-standard or extra super-standard. Often it will be possible to tell which sort of context is involved by querying the speaker about what sorts of substitutions she will tolerate in her that-clause.

7.5 Propositional Attitude Relations

In giving this account of attitude reports I have been implicitly relying on a certain conception of the nature of attitude relations. Roughly speaking, attitude relations are tokening relations. The judgment relation is a good example. Suppose someone asserts 'Obama judges that Clinton is eloquent' in a standard context. On my account, this is true iff Obama bears the judgment relation to the type ⊦ <**Clinton**, ELOQUENT>. What is it to bear the judgment relation to this type? The answer is obvious. Obama bears the judgment relation to ⊦ <**Clinton**, ELOQUENT> insofar as he has performed a judgment that is a token of this type. Assertion is similar. Relative to a standard context, 'Obama asserted that Clinton is eloquent' is true iff Obama performed an assertion that is a token of the type ⊦ <**Clinton**, ELOQUENT>.

This is *not* to view relations like judgment and assertion as multiple-relations in the manner of Russell's multiple relation theory of judgment. Attitude relations, on my theory, are binary relations to propositions. Judgment, for example, is a relation a subject bears to a type. To judge that Clinton is eloquent is to perform a token judgment of the type ⊦ <**Clinton**, ELOQUENT>. In order to perform a token of this type you have to predicate the property of eloquence of Clinton, and in performing that act of predication the subject is multiply related to Clinton and the property of eloquence. The relation of predication is a multiple relation, but the relation of judgment is not. A subject bears the judgment relation to a proposition in virtue of the fact that she has performed an act of predication. The act of predication grounds the judgment, but the predication relation is not identical to the judgment relation.

There is an important and historically significant reason why attitude relations have to be viewed this way, i.e. as binary relations to propositions and not as multiple relations to objects, properties, and relations. The reason goes to the heart of an objection that Wittgenstein used to refute Russell's multiple relation theory of judgment. Here is how Wittgenstein put his objection:

I can now express my objection to your theory of judgment exactly: I believe it is obvious that, from the proposition 'A judges that (say) a is in a relation R to b', if correctly analysed, the proposition 'aRb. ∨. ~aRb' must follow directly *without the use of any other premiss.* This condition is not fulfilled by your theory.

(Wittgenstein 1995, 29)

5.5422 The correct explanation of the form of the proposition, 'A makes the judgement p', must show that it is impossible for a judgement to be a piece of nonsense. (Russell's theory does not satisfy this requirement.) (Wittgenstein 1961a, 65)

These remarks have received a great deal of attention among historians of analytic philosophy. Predictably, there is no consensus about the nature of the problem that Wittgenstein was raising for Russell. I do not want to get involved in this controversy here. Instead, I will just say what I think Wittgenstein's point was. It is very simple. (In fact, it has to be simple, in order to account for the powerful effect Wittgenstein's objection had on Russell. A complicated or highly technical objection would not have had the power to move Russell in the way that Wittgenstein's objection did. See (Hanks 2007) for discussion.) Whenever you judge that p, your judgment can be characterized as a judgment that p is true. To judge that p is to judge that something is true. This something— that to which you bear the judgment relation—must therefore be capable of being true or false. Judgment is a relation to truth-bearers. When Wittgenstein says that "it is impossible for a judgement to be a piece of nonsense," he means that whatever we bear the judgment relation to must have a *sense*. It must be true or false. Treating judgment as a multiple relation violates this restriction, since it takes the relata of the judgment relation to be various, disconnected items.

In his early work "Notes on Logic" Wittgenstein made the following remark about judgment:

When we say that A judges that etc., then we have to mention a whole proposition which A judges. It will not do to mention only its constituents, or its constituents and form, but not in the proper order. This shows that a proposition itself must occur in the statement that it is judged; however, for instance, "not-p" may be explained, the question what is negated must have a meaning. (Wittgenstein 1913, 94)[5]

---

[5] Wittgenstein dictated "Notes on Logic" to Russell in Cambridge in September 1913. There are two different published versions of the notes, which appear in the first and second editions of *Notebooks 1914–1916* respectively (Wittgenstein 1961b, 1979). The first version was published in the *Journal of Philosophy* in 1957 by H. T. Costello, who got the notes from Russell during Russell's visit to Harvard. The second is a reorganization of the Costello version due to Brian McGuinness, aimed at bringing the order of the notes closer to the original. As McGuinness argues in (McGuinness 1972), the Costello version is Russell's reconstruction and organization of Wittgenstein's notes. Interestingly, Wittgenstein's remark about negation, "however, for instance, 'not-p' may be explained..." appears in

This analogy with negation is very helpful in understanding the point of Wittgenstein's objection to Russell's multiple relation theory. Suppose we try to give a multiple relation theory of 'not p'. To do so, we have to break up p into its constituents and treat negation as a multiple relation between these constituents. For example, 'It is not the case that a is F' would be analyzed as 'Not (a, F)'. The problem with this theory of negation is obvious. It does not make sense to negate an object and a property. Whatever negation applies to has to be true or false. Negation operates on unified, truth-bearing propositions, not the disconnected components of propositions. Wittgenstein's point is that judgment works the same way. It does not make sense to bear the judgment relation to an object and a property. Like negation, judgment can only apply to something with a truth-value.

This is the basic problem for Russell's multiple relation theory of judgment. According to Russell's theory, a subject bears the judgment relation to a disconnected collection of objects, properties, and relations, such as the collection of Clinton and the property of eloquence. This disconnected collection is not a bearer of truth and falsity. Clinton and the property of eloquence are not true or false—not even if we put them together into a set or ordered pair. This is why the judgment relation cannot be analyzed as a multiple relation. Judgment has to be a relation to a unified proposition that is capable of being true or false.

Predication, by contrast, can be viewed as a multiple relation. We can take predication to be a poly-adic relation that a subject bears to various, disconnected entities. Russell's mistake was to confuse the relation of judgment with the relation of predication. Facts about predication ground facts about judgment, but the two kinds of facts must be kept distinct from one another.

The view that attitude relations are tokening relations applies in the first instance to actions such as judgment and assertion. How does the view

different places in the two versions of the notes. In the Costello version it appears immediately before Wittgenstein's objection to Russell's multiple relation theory (Wittgenstein 1961b, 96). In the McGuinness version the two remarks are separated by more than a page (Wittgenstein 1979, 94–5). If McGuinness is right, this means that when Russell was organizing Wittgenstein's notes, he put the remark about negation immediately before the objection to the multiple relation theory of judgment. I take this to be a bit of evidence in favor of the reading of Wittgenstein's objection that I defend here and in (Hanks 2007). Russell understood Wittgenstein's remarks about negation to be making essentially the same point as his objection to the multiple relation theory of judgment.

apply to *states*, such as belief? The interesting question for our purposes is not about the nature of belief—for example, whether beliefs are dispositional or functional or representational. As I mentioned in the introduction, I doubt that we can learn much about the metaphysics of belief from the classificatory conception of content. Rather, the question we must face is about how we can use types of actions to characterize states of belief that are not themselves actions. How is it possible to characterize someone's belief state by relating him or her to a type of action?

The most straightforward cases of belief are ones in which (i) at some point in the past the subject explicitly judged that *p*, (ii) the subject remembers that *p*, and (iii) the subject behaves in ways that are consistent with *p*. In these cases a belief state originates in a judgment, and we characterize the resulting state in terms of the type of action the subject performed in making the judgment. This is still to view the belief relation as a kind of tokening relation. To believe that *p* is to have performed a token judgment that *p*, to be capable of remembering that *p*, and to behave in ways that are consistent with that judgment.

Not all beliefs are like this, however. Perhaps there are cases of tacit or implicit belief, in which the subject has never explicitly judged that *p*. Barack Obama has, I presume, never explicitly judged that there are no giraffes in orbit around Mars, but this is still something he believes. (If not then these cases do not pose a problem.) Of course, he would immediately judge this to be the case if he thought about it or if he were asked, and he wouldn't need to gather any new evidence or engage in any kind of investigation (cf. Gertler 2011). This suggests that there is a modal aspect to the way we characterize implicit beliefs. Implicit beliefs are characterized not by judgments that the subject *has* performed, but by ones they *would* perform. Someone implicitly believes that *p* just in case she would readily and unhesitatingly perform a token of the type *p* if queried, and would do so on the basis of her current evidence.

A more difficult kind of example that has received attention in recent philosophy of mind involves subjects who explicitly judge that *p* but behave in ways that are contrary to *p*.[6] Here is an example due to Eric Schwitzgebel. Juliet explicitly and consistently avows that all races are

---

[6] See, for example, (Gendler 2008), (Sommers 2009), (Schwitzgebel 2010), and (Gertler 2011).

intellectually equal and is prepared to argue the point vigorously. Yet she behaves and reacts in ways that are systematically racist.

When Juliet is on the hiring committee for a new office manager, it won't seem to her that the black applicants are the most intellectually capable, even if they are; or if she does become convinced of the intelligence of a black applicant, it will have taken more evidence than if the applicant had been white. When she converses with a custodian or cashier, she expects less wit if the person is black. And so on. (Schwitzgebel 2010, 532)

It is hard to know what to say about this example. Does Juliet believe that all races are intellectually equal? Schwitzgebel's answer is 'yes and no'. He thinks this is a case of in-between belief, somewhat like in-between baldness. Juliet falls into a vague, penumbral area between believing and not believing that all races are intellectually equal. He does allow, however, that in some contexts it will be correct to make one or the other attitude report. Suppose a black student is advising another black student about whether to take a course from Juliet. In that context, it would be fair for the black student to say that Juliet thinks that black people are not as smart as white people (Schwitzgebel 2010, 537). If this report is true in this context then we have a problem, since the proposition that black people are not as smart as white people is not something that Juliet has or would ever explicitly judge. Still, Juliet behaves and reacts *as though* she had made this judgment.[7] The point of the belief report is not to characterize a judgment that Juliet has or would make, but to character- ize a pattern in her behavior that is typical of people who have made that judgment. Juliet believes that p, not in the sense that she has or would ever perform a token judgment that p, but in the sense that she exhibits patterns of behavior that we would expect to find in people who have judged that p.

To summarize, there are three ways in which we use types of acts of predication to characterize states of belief. Roughly, S believes that p if (i) S *has* performed a token of p, or (ii) S *would* perform a token of p, or (iii) S behaves *as though* she has performed a token of p. The same holds for other kinds of mental states, such as states of wondering or states of desire. In these cases we use types of acts of asking (?) or ordering (!) to

---

[7] There may also be a normative dimension to the belief report: given her behavior, Juliet *ought* to admit that she thinks that black people are not as smart as white people.

characterize the relevant states. (Recall that as I am using the term 'ordering', the type of act of ordering resides at a level of generality high enough to cover not just orders and commands, but also desires and intentions and promises.) Again roughly, if someone wants *a* to be F then either she has performed a token of !<**a,** F>, or she would do so if queried, or she behaves as though she had performed a token of this type.

7.6 Denial

The attitude of denial presents a different kind of problem for this approach to attitude relations. Someone who denies that Clinton is eloquent has obviously not performed a token of ⊢ <**Clinton,** ELOQUENT>. Denial looks like a clear counterexample to my claim that attitude relations are tokening relations. In fact, though, denial can be smoothly integrated into this approach to the attitudes.

In chapter 4 I analyzed denial using the concept of anti-predication, represented by the reverse single turnstile '⊣'. Anti-predication is a type of action that occurs at a level of generality higher than that of predication. You can anti-predicate eloquence of Clinton by uttering any of the following:

16a. It is not the case that Clinton is eloquent.
  b. Clinton is not eloquent.
  c. Clinton isn't eloquent.
  d. No politician is eloquent.
  e. —Is Clinton eloquent?—No.

Utterances of each of these sentences fall under the following anti-predicative type:

17. ⊣ <**Clinton,** ELOQUENT>

This means that there can be token acts of anti-predication that are themselves acts of predication. Utterances of (16a–d) are examples. The utterance of 'No' in (16e), by contrast, is best taken as a pure case of anti-predication—an act of anti-predication that is not a token act of predication. In a pure case of anti-predication the speaker prevents, blocks, refuses, or undoes an act of sorting an object according to a property. If I pick up a marble from the pile of green marbles and put it back in the unsorted pile then I anti-predicate greenness of this marble. Similarly, if someone asks whether the marble should go in the green pile and I say 'no', then I have anti-predicated greenness of the marble. In this case, I prevented an act of predicating greenness of the marble. If someone is in the process of putting the marble in the green pile and I stop them from doing so, then I anti-predicate greenness of the marble. In this case I block an act of sorting the marble with the other green marbles.

The issue we now face is how to make sense of a report of a denial, e.g. 'Obama denied that Clinton is eloquent'. According to our modified clause (iii*), this report is true just in case Obama bears the denial relation to the proposition $\vdash$ <**Clinton**, ELOQUENT>, or some suitably related proposition. Corresponding to this predicative proposition we have the anti-predicative proposition $\dashv$ <**Clinton**, ELOQUENT>, obtained by substituting anti-predication for predication. It is this anti-predicative proposition, or one of the less or more finely grained anti-predicative propositions in the surrounding range, that figure in the truth conditions for 'Obama denied that Clinton is eloquent'. If the context is standard, then 'Obama denied that Clinton is eloquent' is true iff Obama performed a token act of denial of the type $\dashv$ <**Clinton**, ELOQUENT>. If the context is super-standard, 'Obama denied that Clinton is eloquent' is true iff Obama performed a token act of denial of the object-dependent type $\dashv$ <**Clinton**$_{obj}$, ELOQUENT>. If the context is extra super-standard, then 'Obama denied that Clinton is eloquent' is true iff Obama performed an act of denial of the type $\dashv$ <<u>Clinton</u>, ELOQUENT>. This can happen, for example, if Obama asserts (16d).

As in all other cases, when a speaker utters 'Obama denied that Clinton is eloquent', she uses the embedded sentence 'Clinton is eloquent' to perform a token of the type $\vdash$ <**Clinton**, ELOQUENT>. Her use of the verb 'deny' forces a shift over to the corresponding anti-predicative proposition, which determines a range of less or more finely grained propositions.[8] The attitude report is true in a context just in case the subject of the report, Obama, bears the relation of denial to one of the propositions in this range. The only difference between this case and the ones we've already examined is the shift from the predicative type to the anti-predicative one.

---

[8] This shift bears affinities to the broader semantic phenomenon of coercion. See (Pustejovsky 1995) and (Ginzburg and Sag 2000).

This sort of shift occurs with many other attitude reports. Recall example (3):

3.   Obama knows whether Clinton is eloquent.

In an utterance of (3) a speaker performs a token of (5):

5. $\vdash_\uparrow$ <<**Obama**, ~? <**Clinton**, ELOQUENT>>, KNOW>

In a token of (5) a speaker performs a cancelled token of the interrogative proposition ?<**Clinton**, ELOQUENT>. This interrogative proposition determines the corresponding predicative and anti-predicative propositions as its answers:

18a. $\vdash$ <**Clinton**, ELOQUENT>
  b. $\dashv$ <**Clinton**, ELOQUENT>

In a token of (5) the speaker's use of 'knows' forces a shift over to either (18a) or (18b), depending on which is true. This is similar to the way in which a use of 'deny' forces a shift to an anti-predicative type. In context, a token of (5) is true iff Obama bears the knowledge relation to one of the propositions in the ranges surrounding (18a) or (18b). Let's stipulate that Clinton is eloquent. If so, then relative to a standard context, an utterance of (3) is true iff Obama is in a knowledge state that is appropriately related to a token of (18a). In chapter 9 I extend this to cover cases of embedded wh-questions, e.g. 'Obama knows which politicians are eloquent'.

Another related example involves an embedded infinitive clause in a belief report, such as:

19.   Obama believes Clinton to be eloquent.

On my approach, speakers use embedded infinitive clauses to perform tokens of imperative propositions. In this case, the imperative proposition is (20):

20.   ! <**Clinton**, ELOQUENT>

In a speech act token of (20) a speaker orders, commands, or requests Clinton to be eloquent. Obviously, a speaker can assert (19) without doing any of these things. As always, 'believes' creates a cancellation context for the speaker's utterance of the embedded clause. In an utterance of (19), then, the speaker performs a token of the following proposition:

21.   ⊢ <<Obama, ~! <Clinton, ELOQUENT>>, BELIEVE>

In this case the speaker's use of 'believes' forces a shift to the predicative proposition determined by !<Clinton, ELOQUENT>, namely ⊢ <Clinton, ELOQUENT>, obtained by substituting predication, ⊢, for ordering, !. Depending on whether the context is standard, super-standard, etc., an utterance of (19) is true iff Obama believes one of the propositions in the range surrounding this predicative proposition. This is another instance of the more general phenomenon in which there is a mismatch between an attitude verb and the type expressed by its complement. In all of these cases, the attitude verb forces a shift over to the appropriate type of content, which is obtained by substituting one type of combinatorial act for another.

One interesting case of this kind occurs in belief reports with reflexive pronouns and infinitive clauses:

22.   Obama believes himself to be eloquent.

In all likelihood, an utterance of (22) is meant to attribute a *de se* belief to Obama. Compare (22) with (23):

23.   Obama believes that Obama is eloquent.

Suppose Obama is listening to a recording of one of his speeches but doesn't recognize his own voice. Commenting on the speech, Obama says that the speaker is eloquent. In this case we could report Obama's belief with (23) but not (22). Obama has the non-*de se* belief that Obama is eloquent but not the *de se* belief that he himself is eloquent. An utterance of (22) is used to attribute a *de se* belief, the kind of belief Obama expresses by saying 'I am eloquent'. Up to now we do not have the resources to handle this sort of belief report, but that is something I will remedy in the next chapter.

8

First-person Propositions

In chapter 5 I defended the view that the semantic contents of proper names are semantic reference types. In this chapter I extend the view to indexicals and demonstratives.[1] Once the necessary modifications are in place it will turn out that the propositional contents of judgments and assertions expressed with context-sensitive expressions are very finely grained—so finely grained that it won't be possible for there to be multiple tokens of these types. I call this *non-repeatability*. When someone asserts 'I am on fire' the propositional content of her utterance is a non-repeatable type. No one else can perform a token of this type, and not even the original speaker can perform another token of this type on a different occasion. This propositional content is a first-person proposition, a proposition that only a single subject can believe or assert. These first-person propositions solve the problem of *de se* belief—the problem of distinguishing between the contents expressed using the first-person pronoun versus those expressed using non-first-person designators. They also avoid the problems that beset the Fregean account of first-person thoughts, including the problem of incommunicability. Although first-person propositions can only be believed or asserted by a single subject, there is no reason a hearer cannot grasp one of these propositions when it is asserted by someone else. In this chapter I distinguish the concept of grasping, something hearers do when they are interpreting the utterances of others, from the traditional Fregean concept of entertainment. I also draw a contrast between the picture of communication on my approach and the one given to us by the Fregean picture of content.

---

[1] Portions of this chapter are drawn from (Hanks 2013a).

8.1 Context Sensitive Reference Acts

The first order of business is to extend the account of semantic reference types to indexicals and demonstratives. This requires a revision in the definition of the relation R, which I introduced in chapter 5 (section 5.2). As before, let x and y be token acts of reference, but this time ones that may employ context-sensitive terms. Let d_x and d_y be the possibly context-sensitive terms used in x and y respectively, and let c_x and c_y be the contexts of interpretation for x and y respectively. Following Kaplan (1989a, 1989b), we can model a context of interpretation as an n-tuple of an agent, time, location, and world, along with sequences of demonstrata for pure demonstratives, e.g. a sequence of addressees for occurrences of 'you'. Define a relation R^* as follows:

xR^*y iff$_{def}$ anyone who is semantically competent with d_x and d_y, and can identify the applicable parameters in c_x and c_y, will realize, under relevantly ideal conditions, that x and y co-refer.

The applicable parameters in c_x and c_y are those parameters that fix the referents of d_x and d_y relative to their respective contexts.[2] For example, if d_x is 'I' then the applicable parameter in c_x is the agent, if d_x is 'now' the applicable parameter in c_x is the time, and so on. If d_x is not context-sensitive, e.g. if it is a proper name, then there are no applicable parameters in c_x. The semantic reference type of a token act of reference x is the type of reference act of being an act of reference that bears R^* to x. If the term d_x used in x is context-sensitive then the semantic content of d_x relative to c_x is the semantic reference type of x.

Perry's *Enterprise* example is a good case to consider (Perry 1977, 12–3). Suppose Perry and a friend are in downtown Oakland looking at the harbor. The bow and stern of the aircraft carrier *Enterprise* are both clearly visible, but the middle of the ship is hidden behind a building. The name of the ship is clearly printed on the bow but not on the stern.

---

[2] The idea that the parameters in a context "fix" the referents of context-sensitive terms should not be taken literally. It is speakers' communicative intentions that do the fixing. The "applicable" parameters in a context are just the items determined by these communicative intentions. My use of Kaplanian n-tuples to model contexts should not be taken to suggest that these n-tuples play any genuine role on either the speaker's or hearer's side in communicative exchanges. For example, the idea that a hearer has to identify the applicable parameters in a context is just a roundabout way of saying that the hearer has to figure out what the speaker intended to refer to.

Pointing at the bow, Perry says 'This is the *Enterprise*' and his friend agrees. Pointing at the stern, Perry says 'That is the *Enterprise*', but his friend disagrees, thinking there are two ships instead of one. Perry's friend is competent with the words 'this' and 'that' and she can identify the objects Perry intended to demonstrate, e.g. by pointing. But Perry's friend does not realize that Perry's two token acts of reference refer to the same ship. Because of this, Perry's token acts of reference using 'this' and 'that' do not bear R* to one another and so these acts fall under different semantic reference types. It follows that Perry asserted different propositions in his two utterances.

The same thing can happen when only a single subject is involved. In Perry's messy shopper example (Perry 1979), Perry is walking around a supermarket spilling sugar from a torn sack. At first he does not realize that he is the shopper spilling the sugar, even after he sees himself in a mirror followed by a trail of sugar. While pointing at himself in the mirror Perry says 'He is making a mess' followed by 'I am not making a mess'. Perry is competent with the words 'he' and 'I' and can obviously identify the intended referent for his use of 'he' and the agent of the context for his use of 'I'. But Perry does not realize that his acts of reference using 'he' and 'I' refer to the same person and thus these terms have different semantic contents relative to their respective contexts.

Perry's examples illustrate a general fact about context-sensitive reference acts. Competence, and the ability to identify the applicable contextual parameters, are virtually never sufficient for knowing that two context-sensitive reference acts co-refer. It is always possible for a competent speaker to fail to realize that the applicable parameters are identical. The only exceptions occur when multiple instances of an indexical or demonstrative must be interpreted with respect to a single context of interpretation, e.g. multiple instances of 'now' in the premises and conclusion of an argument. If there is a single context of interpretation for multiple occurrences of an indexical, as there must be for the premises and conclusion of an argument, then competent speakers cannot fail to realize that these occurrences co-refer. A similar situation arises for multiple occurrences of the same indexical in a single utterance. Both uses of 'I' in an utterance of 'I think I am on fire' must be interpreted with respect to a single context, and hence competent speakers cannot fail to realize that they co-refer. The same goes when an argument or utterance contains multiple uses of a demonstrative that share the same directing intention, e.g. 'You$_i$ thought you$_i$ were on fire'. This obviously involves an idealization, since actual hearers might fail to realize that an utterance is part of an argument or that several uses of a demonstrative share a directing intention. To handle these sorts of cases I need to add to the ideal conditions for R* the fact that competent speakers know when the context of interpretation must be held fixed for distinct token acts of reference. In other words, under ideal conditions a competent speaker will know when distinct utterances take place in an argument or when multiple uses of an indexical or demonstrative belong to the same utterance.

The more common situation is one in which distinct token reference acts have distinct contexts of interpretation. Whenever that is the case it will be possible for a competent speaker to fail to realize that the applicable contextual parameters are identical, and hence fail to realize that token acts of reference co-refer.[3] It follows that the semantic reference types of context-sensitive reference acts are very finely grained. In general, each such type is *non-repeatable*, in the sense that it has, at most, a single token. The semantic reference type of Perry's use of 'this' in the *Enterprise* example has as its only token Perry's use of 'this' in that utterance. Perry's utterance is not part of an argument and there is no other reason for holding the context of interpretation fixed for other reference acts. A competent speaker can therefore fail to realize that any other token reference act co-refers (if it does) with Perry's use of 'this'. That is why the semantic reference type of Perry's use of 'this' is non-repeatable.

Suppose Perry comes to realize that he is the one spilling the sugar and says 'I am making a mess'. Call the context of interpretation for this utterance *a*. Here is the proposition that Perry asserted.

---

[3] This clarifies the distinctive challenge that context-sensitive expressions pose for broadly Fregean approaches to content, and thereby answers the recent charge by Cappelen and Dever that "no evidence has been provided that we need to be revisionary about content to accommodate indexicality" (Cappelen and Dever 2013, 59). Even when we impose the idealizations needed to handle Paderewski-style cases, it is still possible for a competent and informed speaker to fail to realize that distinct occurrences of an indexical or demonstrative co-refer. This is why these expressions have to have a special kind of content that is different from that for proper names.

1. $\vdash <\mathbf{I}^a, \text{MAKING-A-MESS}>$[4]

Since the semantic reference type $\mathbf{I}^a$ is non-repeatable, the entire type (1) is non-repeatable. Any other assertions that Perry might make, e.g. 'He is making a mess', 'Perry is making a mess', 'The man in the brown suit is making a mess', etc., will be assertions of different propositions. The content of Perry's assertion of 'I am making a mess' is therefore different from the content of any other utterance of the form 'a is making a mess', where 'a' is any other term designating Perry, including names, descriptions, and other indexicals and demonstratives. Even if Perry makes a second utterance of 'I am making a mess' in a later context he asserts a different proposition. A competent speaker could hear both utterances and fail to realize that the agents of these two contexts are identical, and hence fail to realize that Perry's uses of 'I' co-refer. Perry himself might fail to realize this (suppose he has a bout of amnesia between utterances and fails to recognize himself in a recording of his earlier utterance). Let b be the context for Perry's second assertion of 'I am making a mess'. Here is the proposition Perry asserted in this second utterance:

2. $\vdash <\mathbf{I}^b, \text{MAKING-A-MESS}>$

These propositions, (1) and (2), are first-person propositions. No one other than Perry can perform tokens of these types, and hence no one else can believe or assert these propositions. Not even Perry can perform additional tokens of them on later occasions. This is in contrast to the proposition Perry asserts by saying 'Perry is making a mess':

3. $\vdash <\mathbf{Perry}, \text{MAKING-A-MESS}>$

The semantic reference type in (3), **Perry**, is repeatable. Anyone can perform a token of this type and hence anyone can assert this proposition. This proposition, (3), is a third-person proposition—a proposition that is accessible to anyone, in the sense that it can be believed or asserted by anyone.

Let's reserve the term 'first-person proposition' for those non-repeatable propositions that speakers express using 'I' and other forms of the

---

[4] For the sake of clarity I am treating 'is making a mess' as an unstructured predicate that speakers use to express a monadic property. I will do the same for some other examples. Nothing turns on this.

first-person pronoun, e.g. 'me' and 'myself'. (This is not a definition of first-person propositions. I will give a definition in section 8.3.) It is worth noting that many other propositions are non-repeatable and are therefore also inaccessible to anyone other than the original speaker. Let c be the context of interpretation for Perry's utterance of 'This is the *Enterprise*'. Here is the proposition he asserts in this utterance:

4. $\vdash$ <**This**^{c}, IS-THE-ENTERPRISE>

The semantic reference type **This**^{c} is non-repeatable; no one else, including Perry, can perform another token of (4). On this account there is inaccessibility in all of the propositions expressed with indexicals and demonstratives.

This is as it should be. The problems posed by *de se* assertions and beliefs arise for any assertions and beliefs expressed with indexicals and demonstratives. The problem about *de se* belief is that it is possible for a perfectly competent and rational subject to a have a *de se* belief without having any of the corresponding non-*de se* beliefs (Perry 1979). If, because of dementia or amnesia, I do not realize that I am Peter Hanks then I might believe that I am on fire without believing that Peter Hanks is on fire, or vice versa. More generally, the *de se* belief that I am on fire cannot be identified with any belief of the form 'a is on fire', where 'a' is any singular term or definite description that designates me. Since beliefs are individuated in terms of their contents, the *de se* belief that I am on fire must have a different content than any belief of the form 'a is on fire'. Exactly the same situation arises for assertions and beliefs expressed using any other indexical or demonstrative. The belief Perry expresses with 'This is the *Enterprise*' cannot be the same as any belief expressed by 'ψ is the *Enterprise*', where 'ψ' is another term or description for the *Enterprise*. It is always possible for someone to fail to realize that ψ and the referent of Perry's use of 'this' are identical. The non-repeatability of context-sensitive semantic reference types captures the uniqueness of the contents of utterances containing indexicals and demonstratives.

8.2 *De Se* Reference

No two people ever believe the same non-repeatable proposition, and no one person ever believes the same non-repeatable proposition on more than one occasion. Despite this, there is no trouble accounting for the intuition that two people can make the 'same' *de se* assertion or have the 'same' *de se* belief (Lewis 1979, 142; Turner 2010). Suppose Heimson says 'I am David Hume', and Hume says 'I am David Hume'. In an intuitive sense, Heimson and Hume said the same thing, even though Heimson is wrong and Hume is right. On my account they asserted different propositions. So in what sense did they say the same thing? In the sense that Heimson and Hume each made a *de se* assertion about himself to the effect that he is Hume. Let **I** be the type of reference act in which someone makes *de se* reference to herself. (More on this type below.) Anytime someone refers to herself using 'I' her action falls under the type **I**. Heimson's and Hume's assertions are both tokens of the type:

5.   ⊢ <**I**, BEING-HUME>

This is a super-type of the propositions asserted by Heimson and Hume. Even though their assertions have different propositional contents, these contents are the same kind of proposition in the sense that each is a sub-type of (5) (cf. Markie 1988, 575–9). This is enough to capture the intuitive sense in which Heimson and Hume asserted the same thing.

Both Hume's and Heimson's acts of self-reference fall under the type **I**, the type of action in which someone makes *de se* reference to herself— but what type of reference act is that? How is making *de se* reference to yourself different from any other act of self-reference? One possible answer is that when you make *de se* reference to yourself you cannot fail to know that you are referring to yourself in that act of reference. Heimson may be confused about who he is, but he cannot fail to know that he is talking about himself when he says 'I am Hume'. Similarly, when Perry says 'I am making a mess' he must know that he is talking about himself. On the other hand, when Perry says anything of the form 'α is making a mess', where 'α' is some term or description for Perry other than 'I', it is possible for him to fail to realize that he is referring to himself. The messy-shopper example depends on this possibility. Perhaps, then, we should define the *de se* reference type **I** as the type of reference act in which a subject refers to herself without the possibility of failing to know that she refers to herself in that act of reference.

The problem, though, is that for any *de se* reference act, this requires the subject to have a higher order belief to the effect that she referred to herself in that act of reference. This rules out the possibility of unconscious acts of *de se* reference, and it leads to a worrisome regress, since forming the required higher order belief involves performing *de se* reference acts. A judgment of the form 'I referred to myself in that act of reference' involves two *de se* reference acts, one for 'I' and one for 'myself'. These *de se* reference acts will require their own higher order beliefs with further *de se* reference acts, which will require further higher order beliefs, and so on.

To avoid this, let's instead define I by saying that when you make *de se* reference to yourself, it is impossible to believe that you did not refer to yourself in that act of reference. This avoids the need for the subject to have the problematic higher order belief about her act of self-reference. Instead, what's required is that the subject *lacks*, and could not have, the belief that she did not refer to herself in her act of self-reference. When Perry says 'I am making a mess' he lacks this belief, and, assuming he is competent with 'I', he could not have this belief about his act of self-reference. On the other hand, for any utterance of the form 'α is making a mess', where 'α' is any term for Perry other than 'I', it is possible for Perry to believe that he is not referring to himself in his use of 'α'.

This allows me to give a definition of the *de se* reference type I: I is the type of reference act in which someone refers to herself without the possibility of believing that she did not refer to herself in that act of reference. The modal component in this definition is important. It is not enough for an act of self-reference to be *de se* that a subject in fact lacks the belief that she did not refer to herself. If Perry knows that he is Perry then he won't believe that he is not referring to himself when he says 'Perry is a philosopher', but this is still not a *de se* assertion. For an act of reference to be *de se*—for it to fall under I—it has to be *impossible* for the subject to believe that she did not refer to herself in that act of reference. In other words, for any token act of self-reference z, z is *de se* just in case there is no possible world in which the subject performs z and believes that she did not refer to herself in z. This requires conceiving of acts of self-reference in such a way that they can occur in different worlds with different features. For example, it requires thinking that there is a possible world in which Perry performs his utterance of 'Perry is a philosopher' but mistakenly thinks that he did not refer to himself. To avoid triviality, however, we will have to hold fixed certain facts about the act of self-reference, in particular the fact that the subject is competent with the term she uses in the act of self-reference. The existence of possible worlds in which Perry is not competent with 'I', e.g. worlds in which he thinks 'I' is a proper name for Barack Obama, should not imply that Perry's uses of 'I' are not *de se*. It is plausible to think that anyone who is semantically competent with 'I' will always lack the belief that she does not refer to herself on any occasion in which she uses 'I'.[5] If so, and if we hold fixed the fact that the subject is semantically competent with 'I', it follows that any act of reference a subject performs with 'I' is *de se*.

The *de se* reference type I is not a semantic reference type, but it can have semantic reference types as sub-types. The semantic reference types I^a and I^b are examples. These are the semantic reference types of the token acts of reference that Perry performs when he makes distinct utterances of 'I am making a mess' in the contexts a and b. In each such token, Perry refers to himself in such a way that he cannot believe that he referred to someone else in that token (even though he might falsely believe that the two tokens do not co-refer.) Both tokens therefore fall under the type I, and of course each falls under its respective semantic reference type, I^a or I^b. The semantic reference types I^a and I^b are both sub-types of I. This fact about I^a and I^b is not built into the definitions of these semantic reference types, but it is something we can observe about them after defining them using the relation R*. Compare these types with the type of reference act Perry performs when he points at himself in a mirror and says 'He is making a mess', without realizing that he is the one in the mirror. Call the context for this utterance d. In this case Perry's assertion is a token of (6):

6. $\vdash$ <He^d, MAKING-A-MESS>

The semantic reference type in (6), He^d, is not a sub-type of I. Perry refers to himself in this token of He^d but wrongly thinks that he is referring to something else. For that reason, Perry's token of He^d is not a *de se* act of reference, and his assertion of (6) is not a *de se* assertion.

---

[5] This may have to be qualified in the light of cases of deferred utterance, e.g. Corazza et al.'s post-it note example, in which someone writes 'I am not here today' on a post-it note and sticks the note on a colleague's door. See (Corazza, Fish, and Gorvett, 2002) and (Stevens 2009) for discussion.

8.3 First-person Propositions and Communication

I can now give a definition of first-person propositions: a first-person proposition is any proposition that contains a *de se* semantic reference type, i.e., a semantic reference type that is a sub-type of I. This does not tie the nature of first-person propositions directly to the first-person pronoun. I want to at least allow room for the possibility of someone asserting a first-person proposition without using 'I', 'me', 'myself', or some other form of the first-person pronoun.

Despite their ability to solve the problem of *de se* belief, first-person propositions have been greeted with skepticism by most philosophers. This is often tied to skepticism about Frege's idea that "everyone is presented to himself in a special and primitive way, in which he is presented to no one else" (Frege 1918a, 333). Frege held that we often use 'I' to express these first-person modes of presentation, making the thoughts containing them inaccessible to others. Fregean first-person modes of presentation are widely regarded as mysterious or metaphysically suspect.[6] None of these concerns should arise for the present approach to first-person propositions. I have made no use of primitive properties or modes of presentation that are unique to me and which only I have access to, nor anything else in the vicinity, such as individual essences or haecceities. The underlying idea is that each of us has a way of referring to ourselves that is unavailable to others. I can refer to myself using the word 'I', but no one else can (at least not under ordinary circumstances—see footnote 5). That should not strike anyone as mysterious or psychologically dubious.

Another source of skepticism about first-person propositions has to do with the issue of communicability. It is widely thought that a first-person proposition would have to be inaccessible both in the sense that it cannot be asserted or believed by anyone else, but also in the sense that hearers would be incapable of grasping the proposition when someone else asserts it. This is the case for Fregean first-person thoughts. No one else can grasp the thought that Dr. Lauben thinks when he thinks the

[6] See (Chisholm 1981, 61), (Feit 2008, 13), (Kaplan 1989a, 533–4), (Perry 1977, 18–20), and (McGinn 1983, ch.5).

first-person Fregean thought that he was wounded, which means that he cannot communicate this thought to others.

On my account, propositions are types, and for a hearer to grasp the proposition a speaker asserted is for him to recognize that the speaker performed a token of that proposition. Let e be the context of interpretation for Dr. Lauben's assertion of 'I was wounded'. Here is the proposition that Dr. Lauben asserted:

7. $\vdash <\mathbf{I}^e,$ WOUNDED>

Leo Peter is incapable of performing a token of this type, and so he is incapable of believing or asserting this proposition. But there is no reason in principle why Leo Peter cannot recognize that Dr. Lauben performed a token of this type. On this view, grasping what a speaker asserted is a matter of categorizing the speaker's utterance under the appropriate type. To do this, the hearer himself need not be capable of performing a token of that type. Here is an analogy. I can recognize that someone is juggling five bowling pins (i.e. performing a token of that type of activity), but I myself am not capable of juggling five bowling pins. Grasping first-person propositions is similar. It is a matter of recognizing that someone has performed a token of a certain type that you yourself are not capable of performing.

In saying this I am drawing a distinction between grasping the proposition a speaker asserted and the Fregean concept of entertainment. Grasping, as I will henceforth use the term, is something hearers do in the course of interpreting the utterances of others. Entertainment is something a speaker is supposed to do prior to, or in the course of, judging or asserting a proposition. The Fregean picture runs these concepts together, treating them both as neutral, cognitive contact with a proposition. I think we should be skeptical about the Fregean concept of entertainment, but not the concept of grasping, as understood here.

The Fregean picture of propositional content lends itself to a transmission model of communication, on which contents are transmitted from one person to another through linguistic exchanges (Pagin 2008). The possibility of such transmission was fundamental to Frege's conception of sense:

The same sense is not always connected, even in the same man, with the same idea. The idea is subjective: one man's idea is not that of another. There result, as a matter of course, a variety of differences in the ideas associated with the same sense. A painter, a horseman, and a zoologist will probably connect different ideas with the name 'Bucephalus'. This constitutes an essential distinction between the idea and the sign's sense, which may be the common property of many people, and so is not a part or a mode of the individual mind. For one can hardly deny that mankind has a common store of thoughts which is transmitted from one generation to another. (Frege 1892a, 154)

Saying that contents can be transmitted from person to person is another way of expressing the shareability of content. Although a commitment to shareability does not on its own entail a theory of communication, it leads naturally to the view that communication succeeds when a content is transmitted, or shared, between speaker and hearer. Contents are transmitted in the sense that hearers are brought to grasp the propositions that speakers entertain in the course of making their utterances.

The transmission model of communication faces questions about the relation that must obtain between the propositions entertained by the speaker and those grasped by the hearer in order for communication to succeed. Perhaps this relation is identity, in which case the hearer would have to grasp exactly the same propositions as those entertained by the speaker. But this seems too demanding. We are often happy to count communicative exchanges as successful even though there are differences in how the hearer and speaker would report what the speaker said. And if the relation is not identity then what is it? Just invoking similarity gets us nowhere. Furthermore, any deviation from identity threatens to lead to the paradoxical result that communication can succeed even when the hearer grasps a proposition that the speaker neither entertained nor expressed.

The conception of content that I am defending leads to a much more fluid and open-ended model of communication. Let's call it the classificatory model of communication. Interpretation is a matter of hearers classifying utterances under types. Successful communication occurs when a hearer classifies a speaker's utterance under a type under which it actually falls. Flexibility in the account comes from the abundance of types. Any utterance falls under a huge and diverse range of types. I have sometimes spoken of "the" proposition a speaker asserts, but this is a loose way of speaking. An assertion has no unique propositional content. Any assertion falls under an enormous range of types, many of which deserve to be called propositions and many of which count as propositional contents of the speaker's assertion. Communication succeeds when a hearer classifies a speaker's utterance under one of the propositions in this range. But this allows for considerable contextual variation in the standards for success. We normally grant speakers authority over whether they have been understood. In some contexts a speaker might place specific demands on how her utterance is to be classified in order for it to be understood. In other cases, the speaker's requirements may be more open-ended.

Furthermore, it should be a truism that communication can come in degrees. This is something the transmission model of communication has trouble with, especially if identity of content is required for communicative success. Identity is all-or-nothing, but communication is not. Once again, the abundance of types helps clarify the sense in which communication comes in degrees. The more types a hearer accurately classifies a speaker's utterance under, the higher degree of success in communication. Furthermore, in measuring the degree of success it may not be that all types are treated equal. Depending on the speaker's or hearer's goals or interests, or any number of other conversational factors, certain types may count for more than others.

8.4 *De Se* Reports

Let's briefly review the account of propositional attitude reports from chapter 7. The account is a modified form of the standard relational analysis of attitude reports. For an attitude report of the form 'S v's that p':

    i. The attitude verb 'v' is used to express a binary relation between subjects and propositions.

    ii*. 'That p' is used to perform a token of the type p. Along with the subject S, this type (or a suitably related type) is the target of the speaker's act of predicating the v'ing relation.

    iii*. 'S v's that p' is true iff S bears the v'ing relation to a proposition suitably related to the proposition that p.

The propositions suitably related to p vary with context. In extra super- and super-standard contexts, the propositions suitably related to p are more coarsely grained super-types of p. In standard contexts p itself is the only proposition suitably related to p, and in sub-standard contexts the propositions suitably related to p are sub-types of p.

It is easy to extend this account to handle reports of *de se* assertions and beliefs. Compare the following two reports:

9a. Perry said that he himself is making a mess.
  b. Perry said that he is making a mess.

On its most natural reading, the truth of (9a) requires that Perry made a *de se* assertion about himself to the effect that he is making a mess. By contrast, (9b) can be true if Perry said 'He is making a mess' while pointing at himself in a mirror, or if he said 'Perry is making a mess'.

These kinds of examples show that we need to add another kind of context for attitude reports. Call these *de se* contexts. In a *de se* context the propositions suitably related to p are corresponding *de se* variants of p. Consider the proposition that Perry is a making a mess:

10. $\vdash$ <**Perry**, MAKING-A-MESS>

The semantic reference type **Perry** determines a corresponding *de se* reference type, the type of reference act in which someone makes *de se* reference to Perry. Call this I_{Perry}. I_{Perry} is a sub-type of **I** with Perry fixed as referent. Since only Perry can perform acts of *de se* reference to himself, only Perry himself can perform tokens of I_{Perry}. This type, I_{Perry}, is neither a super-type nor a sub-type of **Perry**, although it is uniquely determined by **Perry** by virtue of the fact that **Perry** uniquely determines its referent, Perry. In addition, like **I**, I_{Perry} is not a semantic reference type, although it can have semantic reference types as sub-types, e.g. I^a and I^b from our earlier examples. Substituting I_{Perry} into (10) gives (11):

11. $\vdash$ <I_{Perry}, MAKING-A-MESS>

Relative to a *de se* context, (11) is the proposition suitably related to (10). Now, consider an utterance of (9a). Assuming 'he' is anaphorically bound to 'Perry', the semantic content of 'he' is the same as that of 'Perry'. In other words, when a speaker utters 'Perry said that he himself is making a mess', she uses 'he' to perform a token of the semantic reference type **Perry**, the same type of reference act she performs with 'Perry'. The truth of (9a) therefore requires Perry to have asserted a proposition suitably related to (10). In a *de se* context, the proposition suitably related to (10) is (11). Consequently, relative to a *de se* context, the truth of (9a) requires Perry to have made a *de se* assertion about himself to the effect that he is making a mess.

184 FIRST-PERSON PROPOSITIONS

In an utterance of (9a) the speaker uses 'himself' to highlight her intention to make a *de se* report. In other words, the speaker uses the reflexive pronoun to flag the fact that the intended context is *de se*. Of course, a speaker does not have to use a reflexive pronoun to make a *de se* report. An utterance of (9b), 'Perry said that he is making a mess', could also be used to report a *de se* assertion. If so, the speaker's intention determines that the context is *de se*. In general, speakers' intentions determine whether the context for an attitude report is extra super, super, standard, sub-standard, or *de se*.

As I mentioned at the end of chapter 7, *de se* reports often involve infinitive complement clauses. Compare (12a–b):

12a. Obama believes himself to be eloquent.
  b. Obama believes that he is eloquent.

Unlike (12b), (12a) is naturally interpreted as a *de se* report. Imagine that Obama hears a recording of one of his own speeches but does not recognize his voice. Although either (12a) or (12b) could be used to report this belief, (12b) is preferable. Similarly, suppose Obama sees himself on TV participating in a debate, but for some reason does not recognize himself.[7] Impressed by the debating skills of the man on television, he comes to think that the man will win the election while remaining pessimistic about his own chances. In such a case, we could better report Obama's belief with (13b) instead of (13a):

13a. Obama expects to win the election.
  b. Obama expects that he will win the election.

The contrast here is similar to the one in (12a–b). We typically use infinitive clauses like the ones in (12a) and (13a) to report *de se* assertions and beliefs.

The infinitive clauses in (12a) and (13a) are the embedded versions of the imperative sentences (14a–b):

14a. Obama, be eloquent!
  b. Obama, win the election!

In English, these imperative sentences show up as infinitive complement clauses:

---

[7] This example is adapted from (Ninan 2010, 552).

15a. Obama wants to be eloquent.
  b. Obama intends to be eloquent.
  c. Obama promises to be eloquent.
  d. Obama ordered himself to be eloquent.
16a. Obama wants to win the election.
  b. Obama intends to win the election.
  c. Obama promises to win the election.
  d. Obama ordered himself to win the election.

On my account, speakers use these infinitive clauses to perform tokens of the following imperative propositions.

17a. ! <**Obama**, ELOQUENT>
  b. ! <**Obama**, WIN-THE-ELECTION>

In an utterance of (12a), a speaker uses the embedded infinitive clause 'himself to be eloquent' to perform a cancelled token of (17a). Now, (17a) determines the corresponding *de se* proposition, (18):

18. $\vdash$ <I_{Obama}, ELOQUENT>

Assuming the intended context for (12a) is *de se*, this report is true iff Obama is in a belief state formed via a token of (18). Similarly, assuming the intended context for (13a) is *de se*, this report is true iff Obama is in a state of expectation formed via a token of (19):

19. $\vdash$ <I_{Obama}, WIN-THE-ELECTION>

These examples fall into the category of attitude reports in which there is a mismatch between the type of content required by the attitude verb and the mood of the embedded clause, e.g. 'Obama knows whether Clinton is eloquent'. In these sorts of examples there is always a shift over to the appropriate kind of proposition. For example, the use of 'knows' forces a shift from the interrogative proposition to a corresponding predicative proposition. In (12a) and (13a), the use of 'believes' or 'expects' forces a shift from the imperative proposition over to the appropriate predicative propositions. In these latter cases, these predicative propositions contain *de se* reference types.

9

Asking and Ordering

To this point I have focused for the most part on predicative propositions—types of acts of predication. But these are only one of three different kinds of propositions. In this chapter I turn to the other two kinds of propositions, interrogative propositions and imperative propositions. The crucial difference between these kinds of propositions consists in the types of acts of combination whereby, in the simplest cases, subjects combine properties with objects. In an interrogative proposition a subject asks whether an object has a property. In an imperative proposition a subject tries to make it the case that an object has a property. This is to distinguish these kinds of propositions in terms of the combinatory acts out of which they are constituted. Another way to distinguish them is in terms of their satisfaction conditions. Only predicative propositions have truth conditions. Interrogative propositions have answer-hood conditions; they determine the predicative and anti-predicative propositions that count as their answers. Imperative propositions have fulfillment conditions; they determine the states of affairs under which they would be fulfilled. Another, related method of distinction is in terms of direction of fit. Predicative propositions have word-to-world, or mind-to-world, direction of fit. Interrogative propositions have what I will call word-to-word, or mind-to-mind, direction of fit. Imperative propositions have world-to-word, or world-to-mind, direction of fit. And there are other ways of distinguishing these propositions. In this chapter I clarify these distinctions and use them to draw some implications for the theory of speech acts.

9.1 Asking

Suppose Obama wonders or asks whether Clinton is eloquent. In doing so he does not predicate the property of eloquence of Clinton. We cannot evaluate these acts of wondering or asking for truth or falsity. By wondering or asking whether Clinton is eloquent Obama combines the property of eloquence with Clinton in a way other than predication. Let's call this *asking*, represented by the question mark. Here is the type of action Obama performs when he asks or wonders whether Clinton is eloquent:

1. ? <**Clinton**, ELOQUENT>

This is an interrogative proposition. Like predicative propositions, this type can have mental or spoken tokens. An act of wondering whether Clinton is eloquent is a mental token of (1). Uttering 'Is Clinton eloquent?' is a spoken token of (1). We report these actions using the same interrogative complement clause:

2a. Obama wondered whether Clinton is eloquent.
  b. Obama asked whether Clinton is eloquent.

This shows that we classify mental and spoken acts of asking under the same interrogative propositional contents.

What can we say about the act of asking? There is a long tradition in philosophy of treating questions as requests for information and therefore as a species of imperative. For example, according to Hare:

> It would seem, in fact, that questions can be translated without loss of meaning into commands; thus "Who is at the door?" can be translated "Name the person who is at the door" . . . and "Are you married?" can be translated "I am/am not* married, *Strike out whichever is inapplicable". (Hare 1949, 24)[1]

This suggests a way of understanding the act of asking. Perhaps asking whether an object has a property is to request someone to say whether the object has the property. In other words, an act of asking is a request for an act of predication on the part of the audience.

This isn't quite right. There are important differences between the satisfaction conditions for questions and requests. A request is fulfilled only if the audience for the request carries out the relevant action. A question is answered if the subject comes to have the relevant information, however that information is acquired. Suppose I request you to

---

[1] See also (Lewis 1969, 186), (Hintikka 1974), (Searle 1979, 14), and more recently (Fiengo 2007, 10).

tell me whether the door is open. You make no effort to satisfy my request, but someone else comes along and mentions that the door is open. In this case I got the information I wanted but my request was not fulfilled. The request was for *you* to tell me whether the door was open, and that request is not satisfied if someone else tells me that it is open. Now suppose I ask you whether the door is open. Again, you make no effort to answer my question, but someone else comes along and says that the door is open. In this case my question was answered even though you did not answer it. Requests can only be satisfied by the person to whom they are given. Questions can be answered by anyone.

This is closely related to a difference in the directions of fit for asking and requesting. Like all imperatives, requests have world-to-word direction of fit. The audience has to perform the requested action, and in that sense the world has to change in order for the request to be satisfied. By contrast, an act of asking has what we might call word-to-word, mind-to-mind, or more generally, representation-to-representation direction of fit. An act of asking is answered when the subject is provided with the appropriate representation, regardless of where that representation comes from. My act of wondering whether the door is open is satisfied if I hear someone assert that the door is open, or see that the door is open, or remember that the door is open, etc. Similarly, my spoken act of asking whether the door is open is satisfied if someone asserts that the door is open, or if I check and see that the door is open, or if I remember that the door is open, or in any other situation in which I am given or come to possess a representation to the effect that the door is open.

Another way to put this is that acts of asking are satisfied by acts of predication, but it does not matter who performs these acts of predication so long as the subject has the appropriate access to them. We might say that an act of asking is an *open* request for an act of predication, in the sense that the request places no restrictions on who can perform the act of predication. Ordinary requests are not open in this sense. This is why it isn't quite right to say that a question is a request for information.

To ask whether an object has a property, then, is to make an open request for an act of predication—but this shouldn't be viewed as an analysis or definition of the act of asking. Asking is one of the basic ways in which we combine objects with properties. Asking is on all fours with predication. Let's return to the analogy between predication and sorting. To predicate a property of an object is to sort that object with other objects according to a rule given by the property. But sorting would have no point in the absence of acts of asking. As Belnap observes, we "will not assert anything ever, nor profit from the assertions of others, without at least the traces of such interests as can be expressed by interrogatives" (Belnap 1990, 16).[2] The point of an act of predication is to resolve an issue about whether an object is a certain way, and the existence of that issue is due to an act of asking. In the total absence of acts of asking, predication would lose its point and the practice of predication would be unintelligible. Of course, the dependence also runs in the other direction. It is impossible to make sense of acts of asking independently of the acts of predication that would answer them. These two concepts, asking and predicating, are intertwined with one another, and neither is more basic than the other.

9.2 Wh-questions

I'm sure it hasn't escaped notice that I have focused on a small handful of interrogatives, all of which have been yes-no questions. Here I will give a brief sketch of a way to extend my account to wh-questions, i.e. questions expressed using the wh-expressions 'which', 'who', 'what', 'when', 'where', 'why', and 'how'. This is a vast and complex area. My aim is to show, in a very preliminary form, how to extend the account of contents as types to wh-questions, with the hope that this will allay concerns that my general approach to propositional content cannot be applied to such questions. The basic question I need to answer is about the actions we perform with wh-expressions. What type of action does a speaker perform when she uses a word like 'which' or 'who'?

As a start, let's review the approach to quantified propositions. Suppose Obama asserts that every politician is eloquent. In doing so, he performs a token of the following type:

3. $\vdash_2$ <<EVERY, POLITICIAN>, ELOQUENT>

EVERY is a type of action in which a subject expresses a function, $F_\forall$, from properties to second-level properties of properties. The act of expressing a function is different in an important respect from expressing a property

---

[2] Belnap credits the point to (Harrah 1963).

or relation. In expressing a function a subject identifies a certain function and applies it to an argument. This act of application is missing in cases of property expression. Acts of function expression are inherently applicative in a way that acts of property expression are not. In a token of (3), then, a subject expresses the function $F_\forall$, and applies it to the property of being a politician. This yields the second-level property of being a first-level property that holds of all politicians. In a token of (3), the subject predicates this second-level property of the property of being eloquent. This act of predication is second-order.

The contents of wh-interrogatives are similar in important respects, although of course not exactly the same. Suppose Obama asks which politicians are eloquent. In doing so he performs a token of the following type:

4.   ? <<WHICH, POLITICIAN>, ELOQUENT>

Like EVERY, WHICH is a type of act of expressing a function—call it $F_?$. This function maps a property to each of its instances (so technically $F_?$ is a relation, not a function, since it is one–many). In a token of <WHICH, POLITICIAN> a subject expresses and applies the relation $F_?$ to the property of being a politician, to yield as values all the individuals who are politicians. In a token of (4), then, a subject asks, of each of these individuals, whether he or she is eloquent. The kind of asking involved here is first-order. The targets of this act of asking are individuals. Compare this with asking whether every politician is eloquent:

5. $?_2$ <<EVERY, POLITICIAN>, ELOQUENT>

This is a second-order act of asking. In a token of (5) a subject asks, of the property of being eloquent, whether it has the second-level property of being instantiated by every politician. The target of this act of asking is a property, which makes it second-order. Even though the type of asking involved in (4) is first-order, there are no reference types in (4). In a token of (4) the subject does not refer to any of the politicians, nor does she need to know who any of them are or be acquainted with them in any sense. 'Which politician' enables us to ask something about each politician without referring to any of them or being able to identify them in any way.

This allows for the possibility of grasping the content of a question without having any idea what its potential answers are. One of my favorite examples of this is due to Jonathan Ginzburg:

Consider, for example, the following sentence:
(33) What is the word for "relaxation" in Chukotian?
uttered by someone who doesn't know what language family Chukotian belongs to, let alone possible word forms in the language. Clearly, I can ask or understand this question with little or no reference to or acquaintance with *any* singular proposition which instantiates an answer. (Ginzburg 1996, 400)

This shows that we cannot identify the content of an interrogative with its answers. It is possible to understand an interrogative—to know its content—without knowing any way to formulate a potential answer to that interrogative. The content of an interrogative has to be something that determines its answers but which is distinct from those answers. This is the type of view I am defending here.

In this respect, my approach is similar to leading theories of interrogatives in model-theoretic semantics, for example (Karttunen 1977) and (Groenendijk and Stokhof 1982, 1997). On Karttunen's theory, the intension of an interrogative clause is a function from possible worlds to sets of true answers. On Groenendijk and Stokhof's view, it is a function that maps a possible world to the true and exhaustive answer at that world. Consider the interrogative 'Which politicians are eloquent?' Suppose at w, Obama, Clinton, and Biden are the only politicians, and only Obama and Clinton are eloquent. On Karttunen's account, the extension of 'Which politicians are eloquent?' at w is the set containing the propositions <Obama is eloquent> and <Clinton is eloquent>. On Groenendijk and Stokhof's view, the extension of 'Which politicians are eloquent?' at w is the proposition <Obama and Clinton are eloquent, and Biden is not eloquent>. On both theories, the intension of an interrogative determines its answers with respect to a world, but is not identified with those answers. If intensions are contents, then, like my approach, on these views the content of an interrogative determines its answers but is not identified with those answers.

These theories are set in the framework of model-theoretic semantics, in which a proposition is identified with a set of possible worlds (or a function from possible worlds to truth-values). The problem for this account of propositions is familiar, and it carries over in a straightforward way to interrogatives. The possible worlds approach does not distinguish between the intensions of sentences that are necessarily true, e.g. '5 + 7 = 12', and 'First-order logic is undecidable'. Similarly, theories of interrogatives in possible worlds semantics cannot distinguish between the intensions of questions whose answers are necessarily true, e.g. 'Does 5 + 7 = 12?' and 'Is first-order logic undecidable?' Karttunen and Groenendijk and Stokhof have to assign the same intension to these interrogatives. Clearly, though, the contents of these interrogatives are distinct. Someone can ask whether first-order logic is undecidable without asking whether 5 + 7 = 12, or vice versa. We classify these as different questions, a fact which has to be reflected in our account of their contents. Now, in the case of declaratives, philosophers have drawn the conclusion that the propositional content of a declarative has to be more finely grained than a set of possible worlds. It has to be something with constituents and structure that mirrors the structure of the sentence that expresses it. We should draw exactly the same conclusion about interrogatives. The propositional content of an interrogative should be a structured entity that looks something like the interrogative sentence that expresses it. That is the kind of view I am proposing here. The propositional content of an interrogative sentence is a complex type of action, with a structure that mirrors the act of asking that someone performs in an utterance of that interrogative. Just as the propositional contents of declaratives are finely grained structured entities that determine, but are not identical to, truth conditions, the propositional contents of interrogatives should be identified with finely grained, structured entities that determine, but are not identical to, the truth-conditional propositions that are their answers. This is nothing more than a natural extension of the structured propositions framework to interrogatives.

Earlier I said that acts of asking are satisfied, or answered, by acts of predication. This was a bit oversimplified. In fact, acts of asking are satisfied by acts of predication *or* anti-predication. An answer to the question whether Clinton is eloquent can be an assertion that Clinton is eloquent, or a denial that Clinton is eloquent, where this denial is an act of anti-predication that can take several forms. Recall from chapter 7 that an act of anti-predicating eloquence of Clinton can consist in an utterance of any of the following:

6a. It is not the case that Clinton is eloquent.

 b. Clinton is not eloquent.

 c. Clinton isn't eloquent.

 d. No politician is eloquent.

 e. —Is Clinton eloquent?—No.

Utterances of any of these would count as an answer to 'Is Clinton eloquent?'. The yes–no interrogative proposition ?<**Clinton**, ELOQUENT> therefore determines the following predicative and anti-predicative propositions as its answers:

7a. ⊢ <**Clinton**, ELOQUENT>
 b. ⊣ <**Clinton**, ELOQUENT>

Now, in a token of ?<<WHICH, POLITICIAN>, ELOQUENT> a subject in effect asks, of each individual politician, whether he or she is eloquent. Roughly speaking, this determines the same answers that would have been determined had the subject performed separate yes–no questions for each of the various politicians. Suppose Obama, Clinton, and Biden are the only politicians. Then a token of (4) determines the following predicative and anti-predicative propositions as its answers:

8a. ⊢ <**Obama$_{obj}$**, ELOQUENT>
 b. ⊣ <**Obama$_{obj}$**, ELOQUENT>

9a. ⊢ <**Clinton$_{obj}$**, ELOQUENT>
 b. ⊣ <**Clinton$_{obj}$**, ELOQUENT>

10a. ⊢ <**Biden$_{obj}$**, ELOQUENT>
 b. ⊣ <**Biden$_{obj}$**, ELOQUENT>

Note that each of these propositions contains an object-dependent reference type. When someone asks 'Which politicians are eloquent?', she asks of each politician whether he or she is eloquent, but does not refer to any of these politicians. Since she has not referred to these politicians in any particular way, her question places no conditions on how they are to be referred to in its answers. What matters for an answer to (4) is that someone refers to each politician, in some way or other, and says of him or her that she is or isn't eloquent. An answer to (4) is *complete* if it combines one member from each of the pairs (8)–(10). So, in a token complete answer, someone performs tokens of one of the propositions from each of these pairs. A *partial* answer to (4) consists of at least one of the propositions in (8)–(10).

Let's see how this works for a relational wh-question. Suppose Obama asks which politicians admire Clinton. This falls under the type (11):

11.   ? <<WHICH, POLITICIAN>, <<∅, **Clinton**>, ADMIRES>>

In (11) a subject targets Clinton for the admiree role in the admiration relation, leaving the admirer role open. This yields the one place property of admiring Clinton. The subject also expresses and applies the relation $F_?$ to the property of being a politician, which determines all the politicians as values. To complete the question, the subject asks of each of these politicians whether he or she admires Clinton. This determines predicative propositions of the form ⊢ <<X_{obj}, **Clinton**>, ADMIRES> and their anti-predicative correlates as answers.

If we analyze other wh-expressions as which-phrases, we can extend this analysis in a straightforward way to other wh-questions. For example, we could analyze 'who' as 'which person', 'what' as 'which thing', 'when' as 'which time', 'where' as 'which location', 'why' as 'which reason' or 'which cause', and 'how' as 'which way' (cf. Groenendijk and Stokhof 1997, 1096). These are just preliminary proposals about how to analyze these wh-expressions. There is clearly contextual variation on the restrictions on 'which'. For example, 'what' in 'What did you buy?' means 'which thing', but not in 'What did you do this afternoon?'. Furthermore, just like quantifier domain restriction, the restriction on 'which' is usually narrowed even further in context. If I ask 'Who ate the last piece of cake?' I am not asking a question about everyone who ever lived, but about some contextually determined set of people. This is one of several semantic parallels between wh-expressions and quantificational determiners.

9.3 Ordering

This is the third type of combinatory act, represented by the exclamation mark '!'. I call this type 'ordering', but this is for lack of a better term. Tokens of this type can be orders, commands, and requests, but they can also be promises, desires, intentions, and hopes, along with many others. What unifies this category of actions and states is the possession of fulfillment conditions with world-to-word or world-to-mind direction of fit. All of these actions and states are reported using infinitive clauses:

12a. Obama ordered Clinton to be eloquent.
 b. Obama commanded Clinton to be eloquent.
 c. Obama asked Clinton to be eloquent.
 d. Clinton promised to be eloquent.
 e. Clinton wants to be eloquent.
 f. Clinton intends to be eloquent.
 g. Clinton hopes to be eloquent.

The form of the complement clause in each of these examples is the same. In each case there is a null pronoun, PRO, in the subject position of the infinitive clause that is coindexed to 'Clinton' (Chomsky 1981):

13a. Obama ordered/commanded/asked Clinton$_i$ PRO$_i$ to be eloquent.
 b. Clinton$_i$ promised/wants/intends/hopes PRO$_i$ to be eloquent.

The fact that we report these actions and states using the same infinitival complement clause shows that we classify them under the same propositional content. In (12a–g), we classify an order, command, request, promise, desire, intention, and hope under the proposition:

14. ! <**Clinton**, ELOQUENT>

This is the type of act of combining the property of eloquence with Clinton in the imperative mode.

The type of act of ordering an object to have a property, understood in the technical sense of 'ordering' as I am using it here, must therefore reside at a fairly high level of generality. It is a type of action that is general enough to encompass orders, commands, requests, promises, desires, intentions, wishes, hopes, and any other action or state with world-to-word/mind fulfillment conditions. Our scheme of classification according to content classifies all of these actions and states together under one general type. Of course, this allows for much finer distinctions within this category, e.g. a distinction corresponding to Searle's distinction between directives (e.g. orders) and commissives (e.g. promises) (Searle 1979). In my theory this distinction appears as a distinction between two sub-types of the type !. There are directive sub-types of ! and commissive sub-types of !. The difference between these sub-types appears to be largely a matter of whether the target of an act of type ! is the speaker herself (commissives) or someone else (directives).

In fact, all three of the types of combinatory acts, predication, asking, and ordering, should be viewed as residing at the same high level of generality. Each is sufficiently coarsely grained to cover a wide variety of sub-types. Acts of predication can be assertions, statements, affirmations, explanations, predictions, warnings, confessions, conjectures, guesses, or suggestions. Acts of asking can be, among other things, pointed, rhetorical, examination questions, choice questions,[3] mention-all or mention-some,[4] open or confirmation.[5] Fine-grained distinctions between types of speech acts appear, in this account, as distinctions between subtypes of the three major categories of propositional content.

Stepping back a bit, the idea is that we have three very high-level categories of content with which we sort our mental and spoken actions. This is reflected in our language, in the form of the three major sentence moods, declarative, interrogative, and imperative, and their corresponding embedded forms, that-clauses, whether- and wh-clauses, and infinitive clauses.[6] The three varieties of content also line up with the three-way distinction between directions of fit, word-to-world, word-to-word, and world-to-word, and their corresponding types of satisfaction conditions, truth conditions, answerhood conditions, and fulfillment conditions. All of this is summed up in the Table 9.1.

These are the three kinds of content with which we classify and individuate our attitudes and speech acts. Or rather, I should say that

---

[3] In a choice question (Belnap 1982), a speaker leaves it up to the hearer to make a choice between several candidate answers. Suppose I ask you 'What are two journals in which you have published papers?'. You can answer by mentioning any two journals in which you have published papers, and it is up to you to choose which journals.

[4] In a mention-all question, the speaker is asking for a complete list of all the things that satisfy a predicate. For example, if I ask who is coming to dinner, I am most likely asking for a complete list of dinner guests. By contrast, in a mention-some question, the speaker is asking just for some of the things that satisfy the predicate. Suppose a tourist is new in town and asks 'Where can I buy an Italian newspaper?' (Groenendijk and Stokhof 1997, 1111). The speaker is not looking for a complete list, but just some of the places where she can buy an Italian newspaper.

[5] The distinction between open and confirmation questions is due to (Fiengo 2007). In asking an open question a speaker displays ignorance about the answer to a wh- or yes–no question. In asking a confirmation question, by contrast, the speaker is in possession of an answer, but is looking for confirmation for that answer. For example, "if you walk in soaking wet, and I say to you *It's raining?* I present myself as wanting you to confirm my belief, based on your appearance, that it is raining" (Fiengo 2007, 11). The open/confirmation question distinction cross-cuts the distinction between wh- and yes–no questions.

[6] In fact, the three-way distinction between declarative, interrogative, and imperative sentences appears to be universal across all languages. See (König and Siemund 2007).

Table 9.1

Type	Satisfaction Conditions	Direction of fit	Sentence Mood	Embedded clauses
⊢	Truth conditions	Word-to-world	Declarative	That-clauses
?	Answerhood conditions	Word-to-word	Interrogative	Whether and Wh-clauses
!	Fulfillment conditions	World-to-word	Imperative	Infinitive clauses

these are the three kinds of content we use to classify our attitudes and speech acts that have propositional content. Greetings and exclamations do not have propositional content, and so do not fall under any of these types. In section 9.5 I discuss another important variety of non-propositional speech act, Searle's category of declarations. First, however, I would like to show how the account of propositional attitude reports from chapter 7 can be extended to attitude reports with embedded non-declaratives.

9.4 Non-declaratives in Attitude Reports

According to the account of propositional attitude reports in chapter 7, a speaker who utters an attitude report of the form 'S v's that p' uses the embedded sentence p to perform a cancelled token of the type expressed by p. Her utterance is true just in case S bears the v'ing relation to some type suitably related to p, where these suitably related types vary with context. Intuitively, the type p is surrounded by an array of less or more finely grained types. The truth-value of an attitude report in a context depends on whether the subject of the report bears the relevant attitude relation to one of the types in this array.

This account applies straightforwardly to embedded interrogatives and embedded imperatives, for example:

15.   Obama wonders whether Clinton is eloquent.

Utterances of (15) are tokens of the following proposition:

16.   ⊢ < <**Obama**, ~?<**Clinton**, ELOQUENT>>, WONDER>

In a token of (16) a speaker predicates the wondering relation of Obama and some proposition suitably related to the interrogative proposition

?<**Clinton**, ELOQUENT>. This interrogative proposition determines an array of types, and the truth of a token of (16) in context depends on whether Obama performed a mental token of one of the types in this array. For example, in a super-standard context, (15) is true just in case Obama is in a state of wondering that is a token of the object-dependent type ?<**Clinton**$_{obj}$, ELOQUENT>.

This applies *mutatis mutandis* to embedded imperatives:

17. Obama commanded Clinton to be eloquent.

An utterance of (17) is a token of the following type:

18. $\vdash$ < <**Obama**, ~!<**Clinton**, ELOQUENT>>, COMMAND>

A token of (18) is true just in case Obama performed a command that is a token of one of the types in the array surrounding the imperative proposition !<**Clinton**, ELOQUENT>. Note that in both (16) and (18) the internal non-predicative types, ? and !, have been cancelled. Attitude verbs like 'wonder' and 'command' create cancellation contexts for the acts of asking or ordering that take place in utterances of their embedded clauses.

The situation is only slightly more complicated when an interrogative or imperative is embedded under an attitude verb, like 'knows', that expresses a truth-conditional attitude. In chapter 7 I explained how this works for (19):

19. Obama knows whether Clinton is eloquent.

In an utterance of (19) a speaker performs a cancelled token of the interrogative proposition ?<**Clinton**, ELOQUENT>. This interrogative proposition determines the following predicative and anti-predicative types as answers:

20a. $\vdash$ <**Clinton**, ELOQUENT>
  b. $\dashv$ <**Clinton**, ELOQUENT>

The meaning of 'knows' forces a shift from the interrogative proposition over to whichever one of these two propositions is true. The truth of an utterance of (19) thus depends on whether Obama is in a state of knowing that is appropriately related to a judgment that is a token of one of the types in the arrays surrounding (20a) or (20b).

This extends in the way one might expect to cases in which a wh-interrogative is embedded under 'knows', for example:

21.   Obama knows which politicians are eloquent.

As before, let's assume that Obama, Clinton, and Biden are the only politicians, and let's suppose that Obama and Clinton are eloquent and Biden is not. Then, the interrogative proposition ?<<WHICH, POLITICIAN>, ELOQUENT> determines the following predicative and anti-predicative object-dependent propositions as answers:

22a. ⊢ <**Obama$_{obj}$**, ELOQUENT>
  b. ⊣ <**Obama$_{obj}$**, ELOQUENT>

23a. ⊢ <**Clinton$_{obj}$**, ELOQUENT>
  b. ⊣ <**Clinton$_{obj}$**, ELOQUENT>

24a. ⊢ <**Biden$_{obj}$**, ELOQUENT>
  b. ⊣ <**Biden$_{obj}$**, ELOQUENT>

The meaning of 'knows' forces a shift from the interrogative proposition to the true members of each of these pairs, which we are supposing to be (22a), (23a), and (24b). The truth of (21) in context requires Obama to possess knowledge-states that are the results of judgments that are tokens of these types. So, in order for Obama to know which politicians are eloquent, he has to know that Obama and Clinton are eloquent and that Biden is not eloquent.

9.5 Declarations and Other Non-propositional Speech Acts

Paradigmatic examples of declarations include utterances of sentences like 'I pronounce you man and wife', 'I christen this ship the S.S. Minnow', or 'I hereby terminate your employment'. As Searle explains, "declarations bring about some alteration in the status or condition of the referred to object or objects solely in virtue of the fact that the declaration has been successfully performed" (Searle 1979, 17). By saying 'I pronounce you man and wife' the celebrant brings it about that the man and woman are married; by saying 'I christen this ship the S.S. Minnow' the captain brings it about that this ship is named the S.S. Minnow. In most cases, the resulting status or condition depends on the existence of an extra-linguistic institution, and the success of the declaration depends on the speaker's occupying the appropriate position in this institution.

In Searle's theory, declarations submit to the same pattern of analysis that he applies to other varieties of speech acts, including assertives, directives, and commissives. This analysis is based upon the content–force distinction, codified in the form of Searle's '$F(p)$' schema. An illocutionary act is analyzed into a propositional content, p, with an illocutionary force, F. Searle fits declarations into this general pattern, with the consequence that declarations have propositional content. For example, if I christen this ship the S.S. Minnow then the propositional content of my declaration is that this ship is named the S.S. Minnow. If I pronounce you man and wife, the propositional content of my declaration is that you are man and wife. A declaration brings about a change in the institutional status of some target object or objects, and the propositional content of a declaration is that the target object or objects have this institutional status.

In addition, Searle holds that declarations have both word-to-world and world-to-word direction of fit. In a declaration a speaker says that certain things are thus-and-so, and thereby brings it about that they are thus-and-so. As Searle puts it:

> The reason there has to be a relation of fit arrow here at all is that declarations do attempt to get language to match the world. But they do not attempt to do it either by describing an existing state of affairs (as do assertives) nor by trying to get someone to bring about a future state of affairs (as do directives and commissives). (Searle 1979, 19)

Rather, in a declaration a speaker brings a state of affairs into existence by stating that that state of affairs is the case. This is why declarations have both directions of fit.

This analysis of declarations is wrong on all counts. Declarations do not have propositional content and they do not have direction of fit. Consider first the fact that there are no content clauses in the sentences used to report declarations:

    25a. She pronounced you man and wife.
       b. He christened the ship the S.S. Minnow.
       c. She fired you.

These sentences do not have the form of propositional attitude reports. There are no embedded clauses in these examples that would give their contents. The predicates in these sentences express actions that speakers perform on things like people and ships. They do not express relations to propositions.

Secondly, pace Searle, declarations have neither word-to-world nor world-to-word direction of fit. They have no direction of fit at all. If declarations had word-to-world direction of fit, then we should be able to evaluate them for truth and falsity. But declarations are not truth-evaluable.[7] It makes no sense to say that my act of marrying two people is true or false, or that my act of christening a ship is true or false. Similarly, if declarations had world-to-word direction of fit, then it would make sense to say that they are fulfilled or not fulfilled. But this does not make sense. My act of firing you cannot be fulfilled or not fulfilled. Of course, a declaration can be successful or unsuccessful. The success of a declaration typically depends on whether the speaker occupies the appropriate institutional position. For example, I cannot successfully fire you if I am not your boss. But the success conditions for a declaration are not satisfaction conditions. A declaration is successful iff the relevant state of affairs comes into existence, but it is not true or fulfilled under these conditions. The success conditions for a declaration are a form of felicity conditions, which must not be confused with satisfaction conditions.

Unlike Searle's categories of assertives, directives, and commissives, therefore, declarations do not have propositional contents and do not have satisfaction conditions. This is why declarations do not fall under any of the three types of propositions, $\vdash$, ?, or !. If we were to give a taxonomy of speech acts, the first distinction would be between propositional speech acts and non-propositional speech acts. Declarations would fall on the non-propositional side, along with greetings ('Hello') and exclamations ('Ouch'). Everything on the propositional side would fall under one of the three types $\vdash$, ?, or !. The following diagram captures this alternative taxonomy:

---

[7] Or rather, declarations *qua* declarations are not truth-evaluable. Some declarations take the form of assertions, e.g. 'You are out', 'You are guilty', 'The session is open'. Searle calls these "assertive declarations" (Searle 1979, 19–20). The distinctive feature of assertive declarations is that they take place in institutional settings in which an assertion that p by the appropriate speaker brings it about that p. These settings make it possible to do two things at once. *Qua* assertion an assertive declaration has a truth-value and propositional content, *qua* declaration it has neither. Note the different ways in which an assertive declaration can be reported, e.g. 'The chairman said that the session is open' versus 'The chairman opened the session'.

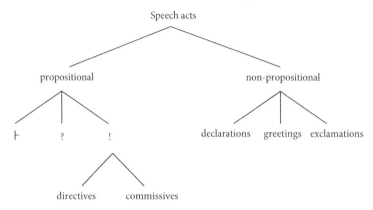

Note that Searle's categories of directives (orders, commands, requests) and commissives (promises) show up as sub-types of the category of speech acts with propositional content of the type !. In addition, this taxonomy has a separate category for interrogatives, which fall under the type ?. In Searle's taxonomy, interrogative speech acts are treated as a species of directives. Searle views interrogative speech acts as requests for information from the hearer. As I argued earlier (section 9.1), however, there are differences between the satisfaction conditions for requests and questions. The satisfaction conditions for questions are open in a way that those for requests are not. Furthermore, we have different sentence moods for questions and requests, and we report these speech acts with different kinds of embedded clauses—whether- and wh-clauses for questions, infinitive clauses for requests. These linguistic differences reflect differences in the ways we classify these speech acts.

What about Searle's category of expressives? Expressives include acts of apologizing, congratulating, or thanking. According to Searle, the propositional content of an expressive is that the speaker or hearer performed some action or has some property. If I apologize for stepping on your toe, the propositional content of my apology is that I stepped on your toe. If I thank you for being generous, the propositional content of my act of thanking is that you are generous. On Searle's account expressives have no direction of fit: "in performing an expressive, the speaker is neither trying to get the world to match the words nor the words to match the world, rather the truth of the expressed proposition is presupposed" (Searle 1979, 15). It follows that expressives have no

satisfaction conditions. Expressives can be defective or non-defective—
for example, an apology is defective if the speaker feels no remorse—but
not true or false, or fulfilled or unfulfilled.

Unlike declarations, the sentences we use to report expressives do
contain embedded clauses, which lends some credence to the idea that
expressives have propositional content. The verbs in these embedded
clauses are gerunds:

26a. He apologized for stepping on my toe.
   b. She congratulated me for finishing my dissertation.
   c. He thanked her for being generous.

Like infinitive clauses, gerundive clauses have a null element, PRO, in
subject position (Haegeman 1994, 275–6). So, for example, the form of
(25a) is 'He$_i$ apologized for PRO$_i$ stepping on my toe'. The gerundive
clause here, 'PRO stepping on my toe', expresses what Searle takes to be
the propositional content of his act of apologizing, in this case the
proposition that he stepped on my toe. But now compare these examples
with the following:

27a. They punished him for stepping on my toe.
   b. She paid me for finishing my dissertation.
   c. He hugged her for being generous.

These also have embedded gerundive clauses, but no one will conclude
on this basis that acts of punishing, paying, or hugging have propositional contents. The gerundive clauses in these examples do not give the
contents of these acts but rather specify states of affairs that explain or
provide reasons for the performance of the acts in question. For example,
(27a) tells us that they punished him *because* he stepped on my toe. The
gerundive clause explains why the act of punishment took place. On
reflection, this is what the gerundive clauses are doing in (26a–c). The
gerundive clause in (26a) does not express the propositional content of
his act of apologizing. It gives the state of affairs that explains why he
apologized. If I ask him why he apologized, he could say 'For stepping on
your toe'. The gerundive clause answers a why-question, which is a
distinctive mark of explanations. Expressives, then, do not have propositional content. That is why they lack direction of fit and lack satisfaction
conditions. Like declarations, expressives do not fall under any of the

three propositional types $\vdash$, ?, or !. They group with declarations, greetings, exclamations, and other non-propositional speech acts.

Stepping back a bit, it is clear that the source of the problems for Searle's analysis of declarations and expressives is his commitment to the content–force distinction. This distinction engenders a certain picture of the nature of speech acts, and Searle is in the grip of this picture. Crudely speaking, according to the content–force distinction, a speech act is something a speaker does with a proposition. The distinctions between varieties of speech acts amount to distinctions between what speakers do with propositions. These distinctions are distinctions in force. To give a theory of speech acts, then, is to catalog and describe the various kinds of forces. But this concept of force is inextricably tied up with the content–force distinction. To attribute force to a speech act, in this sense of force, requires finding propositional content in that speech act. This makes it virtually inevitable for Searle to find propositional content in speech acts where there is none. This illustrates the way in which the content–force distinction is an impediment to achieving an adequate philosophical theory of speech acts. The content–force distinction is a disaster both for the theory of content and for the theory of force.

Conclusion

Over the course of this book I have advanced an account of the semantic contents of proper names, a solution to Frege's puzzle about identity sentences, a theory of empty names and true negative existentials, a semantic analysis of propositional attitude reports, a solution to Kripke's puzzle about belief, an approach to the semantic contents of indexicals and demonstratives, a solution to the problem of *de se* belief, a proposal about the contents of interrogatives and imperatives, and, in outline, a new taxonomy of speech acts. This is rather a lot. It is a testament to the power of the general conception of content in which these views are framed that it lends itself so easily to solving these problems. But none of these views is as important to me as this general conception of content. The conception stands in contrast to a Fregean picture of propositional content that forms the backdrop for much contemporary theorizing in philosophy of language and mind. One of my hopes for this book is that it leads philosophers to become more cognizant of their commitment to this Fregean picture and that it comes to be seen as optional.

The Fregean picture is in large part the result of a reaction by Frege to a psychologistic conception of content that was prevalent among his predecessors. In response to psychologism Frege felt the need make contents as thoroughly objective as possible. The central features of the Fregean picture are reflexes of this striving for objectivity. Thus, on the Fregean picture, propositions are conceived as mind and language independent representations, which have their truth conditions prior to and independently of our thoughts and utterances. Their role is to serve as a source of truth conditions, and they endow our thoughts and utterances with the representational features that they have as a matter of their internal constitutions. To characterize the nature of propositions we must therefore leave out concepts of judgment and assertion, or any other concepts pertaining to mental or spoken actions. Propositions are out there, waiting to be entertained and judged and asserted, and judgments and assertions take on the truth conditions of the propositions that are entertained or expressed in their formation. This imposes a two-part structure on the nature of mental and spoken acts, in which these actions can be factored into neutral and non-neutral components. This structure is dictated by the Fregean conception of propositions as repositories of truth conditions that can be deployed in various ways in thought and speech.

I think that just articulating this picture of content goes some way towards destabilizing it. In many ways it is really quite bizarre. I hope to have shown that we can abandon all of the central aspects of the Fregean picture while preserving its commitment to the objectivity of content and without reverting to psychologism. The alternative I have defended finds its core motivation in the thought that we are the source of representation, not some abstract structures in the third realm. Representation originates with us, through our mental and spoken actions. When we form judgments or make assertions we perform acts of predication, which have truth conditions because they are acts of sorting or categorizing things according to rules. When we ask questions or give orders we perform different kinds of actions, which have their own distinctive kinds of satisfaction conditions. The role for propositions is to classify and individuate these actions, not to provide them with their truth or satisfaction conditions. Propositions are types of these actions, and they inherit their representational features from their tokens in the same way that types in general inherit features from their tokens. This solves, or perhaps dissolves, the problem of the unity of the proposition that plagues the Fregean picture.

I would like to conclude with some remarks about three ways in which the line of research in this book can be further developed. The first ventures into the territory surrounding Wittgenstein's rule-following considerations. The point of entry into these considerations is the concept of property expression—the idea that in performing an act of predication the subject expresses a property. What is it to express a property? What kind of act is that? It is natural to think of it along the lines of reference. There are properties out there, and to express one is to identify it, to single it out from the rest. I often talked this way when talking about acts of property expression, albeit with caveats. The problem is that this Platonistic conception of properties and property expression brings my account of representation uncomfortably close to the Fregean picture, and it raises its own metaphysical and epistemological problems. Properties are thought to have their satisfaction conditions as a matter of brute or primitive fact. When you perform an act of predication you latch onto one of these properties and apply it to an object. The correctness conditions for your act of predication would then flow directly from the satisfaction conditions of the property you latched onto. This is disturbingly reminiscent of the Fregean picture of abstract bearers of truth conditions, on which the truth conditions of our judgments and assertions flow from the truth conditions of propositions. Moreover, it exposes us to the Wittgensteinian problems about rule-following that have been forcefully brought to light in the writings of Kripke, Wright, and others. What facts about me, my past behavior, my dispositions, my overall mental state, determine that I have latched onto *this* property as opposed to one with divergent satisfaction conditions (Kripke 1982)? Furthermore, even if it is possible for me to successfully single out a property, how can I know what that property requires of me in a new application of it (Wright 2001)? How can I be guided by this property in making decisions about which objects to apply it to? The Platonic conception of property expression makes the metaphysics and epistemology of rule-following look utterly mysterious.

In the light of this, I would like to have a non-Platonic story to tell about property expression. I would like to have an account of how we fix the correctness conditions for our acts of predication that does not appeal to mind-independent, primitive bearers of satisfaction conditions. As of now I do not know how to tell this story. However, I don't think this poses a threat to the views I have been defending in this book. My explanatory strategy has been to explain the truth-conditions of (assertoric) propositions in terms of the truth-conditions of acts of predication. That explanation is not threatened by problems about rule-following. Rather, a non-Platonic theory of rule-following would extend the explanation in this book by giving a deeper account of how our acts of predication are capable of being true or false.

The second area for future research is about the relationship between mental and spoken acts of predication. Throughout the book I have been treating these on a level as different species of predication. But there is, I think, an important sense in which mental acts of predication are dependent on linguistic acts. Purely mental acts of predication, i.e.

mental acts of predication that are not instances of silent, internal language use, can be indeterminate in a way that linguistic acts of predication cannot, and when a mental act is not indeterminate it is because of a relationship it bears to a linguistic act of predication. Suppose you've been told to find out what is in an unfamiliar room. You go to the room and look around and acquire information about the furniture and other items in the room. Acquiring this information is partly a matter of performing mental acts of predication: you make judgments about what is in the room, you sort its contents into categories. But what exactly were these mental acts of predication? Did you judge that there was a chair in the room? A green chair? A green office chair? A chair next to a window? Remember that no language use took place. You were not silently saying to yourself 'There is a green office chair', or anything of the sort. There is an indeterminacy here in the contents of your mental acts of predication that can only be resolved through linguistic articulation. Later on you report back by saying 'There is a green office chair in the room'. Until that moment, though, you never thought this or any other sentence to yourself, although you were disposed to put your judgment into these words. Absent this disposition there is no fact of the matter about what you judged. The fact that you judged that it was a green office chair, and not merely that it was a chair, or a green chair, arises out of your disposition for expressing your judgment in the way you did.

If there is indeterminacy in your disposition, for example if you waver between different ways of expressing your judgment, then the same indeterminacy infects your judgment. Let me change examples. Suppose you are at the grocery store and you've just finished filling your shopping cart. You head to the front of the store and line up in one of the checkout lines. Why did you choose that checkout line? Because it was the fastest? The shortest? Both? Clearly you made a judgment of some kind about the line you choose, but perhaps you cannot say why you chose it, or you vacillate between different explanations. In that case your judgment failed to endow you with a definite disposition about how to express the judgment in an assertion. The judgment lacks a determinate content. You judged something about the line you chose, but there is no saying exactly what that was.

The potential for this kind of indeterminacy in the contents of our judgments seems to me to be undeniable. Think about the judgments that you make as you enter your house after being away, or as you choose what to have for lunch, or as you walk across campus, or while driving, or in countless other mundane situations. We guide our behavior on the basis of judgments about the world around us, and it cannot be that every one of these judgments consists in silent, internal speech. We perform mental acts of predication in these cases, but it is implausible to suppose that each and every one of these acts has a perfectly determinate content. This indeterminacy in mental acts of predication is a species of indeterminacy in actions more generally. The question 'What are you doing?' does not always have a clear answer, and when it does it is because the subject has a definite view about how to characterize her own action.

It is worth asking whether it is possible for this indeterminacy in the contents of our judgments to arise on the Fregean picture of content. For the Fregean, judgments have a two-part structure; first you single out a proposition by entertaining it and then you endorse that proposition. Any indeterminacy in the second stage, the act of endorsing a proposition, would be indeterminacy in the nature of the attitude taken toward the proposition, not in the propositional content itself. Locating indeterminacy in the first stage, the act of entertaining a proposition, would require making a dubious distinction between indeterminately identifying a proposition and failing to identify a proposition at all. Remember that the role for entertainment is to allow the subject to fix on a particular proposition so that she might endorse it in a judgment. If there is no fact of the matter about which proposition I have fixed my attention on then I have simply failed to identify a proposition, and without such identification no judgment can take place.

That leaves only two potential sources of indeterminacy for the Fregean, one metaphysical and the other epistemic. The metaphysical option is to hold that there are metaphysically indeterminate Fregean propositions; abstract objects that are like other Fregean propositions, but which do not have determinate truth conditions and are not determinately about any particular objects or properties. It is hard to make sense of this. The only remaining alternative is to go epistemic. The subject entertains and endorses a determinate propositional content, but does not know what that content is. Again, this failure of knowledge would have to apply to the act of entertainment, not to the attitude taken toward the proposition entertained. The idea would be that it is possible to entertain a proposition while failing to know which proposition has been entertained. Aside from the obvious challenges this possibility poses for self-knowledge, the problem is that this does not capture the indeterminacy we are after. That indeterminacy is metaphysical, not epistemic. It's not that sometimes we do not know the contents of our judgments, but that sometimes our judgments simply do not have determinate contents. Barring metaphysically indeterminate Fregean propositions, it looks as though there is no way to make sense of this on the Fregean picture. That draws out another contrast between the Fregean picture of content and the one I have been defending in this book, which I think is worth further investigation.

Finally, one topic that I haven't mentioned at all is how this approach to propositional content bears on issues about perceptual experience. Given that one of the main areas of recent debate in the philosophy of perception is about whether perceptual experiences have propositional contents I think a few preliminary remarks are called for.

As it is often framed, the debate is about whether perceptual experiences are *fundamentally* bearers of propositional content. According to Bill Brewer, for example, the issue is whether "the *most fundamental* [my emphasis] account of our perceptual relation with the physical world is to be given in terms of the complete representational *contents* of perceptual experience rather than in terms of our relation with any kind of *object*" (Brewer 2011, 55).[1] Now, it is not immediately clear how to understand this appeal to fundamentality. What would it be for perceptual experiences to *fundamentally* bear representational content? What would it be for them to be *non*-fundamental bearers of representational content? In a similar vein, Alex Byrne characterizes his position as the view that "perception *constitutively* [my emphasis] involves a propositional attitude rather like the *non*-factive attitude of believing" (Byrne 2009, 437). What is the significance of "constitutively"? A constitutive account of some fact F provides the facts that ground or constitute the fact that F obtains. For example, a constitutive account of the fact that a volume of gas has a certain temperature cites a fact about the kinetic energy of the gas molecules. To give a constitutive account of a

---

[1] See also Susanna Siegel on the Strong Content View: "all visual perceptual experiences consist *fundamentally* in the subject's bearing a propositional attitude toward the contents of her experience" (Siegel 2010, 73, my emphasis). It is not hard to discern the Fregean picture of propositional content lying behind this and many other presentations of the debate about the contents of perceptual experience.

perceptual experience, then, would be to provide the facts that ground or constitute the fact that the experience took place. Presumably, these are physical and biological facts about the subject and her environment. But that is clearly not the sort of thing that Byrne is after. So what does Byrne mean when he says that perceptual experience *constitutively* involves a propositional attitude?

The theory of propositional content in this book may give us some purchase on these questions. According to this view, for a mental episode to have a truth-evaluable propositional content in a fundamental or constitutive sense is for it to be an act of predication. Judgments, for example, are fundamentally bearers of propositional content because they are mental acts of predication. Pains are not fundamentally bearers of propositional content because they do not involve acts of predication. The question about perceptual experience, then, is a question about whether in having a perceptual experience the subject performs an act of predication. Of course, if this is the only way for a mental episode to have a propositional content then there is no point to adding the qualifiers 'fundamentally' or 'constitutively'. For these qualifiers to earn their keep there must be a non-fundamental or non-constitutive sense in which a mental event has a propositional content. The classificatory conception of content is helpful in this regard as well. Perhaps there is no predication involved in having a perceptual experience. Nevertheless, in order to bring our experiences into rational contact with judgments and assertions, we classify our experiences under the same types that we use for genuine acts of predication. This is what it would be for perceptual experiences to have propositional contents in a non-fundamental or non-constitutive sense. Perceptual experiences would be classifiable under types of acts of predication without being or containing acts of predication.

The debate about whether perceptual experiences have propositional contents, then, turns into a debate about whether having a perceptual experience involves performing an act of predication. The idea has a good historical pedigree, of course, in the form of Kant's view that there is spontaneity in perception. Perhaps, then, a return to Kant is in order.

References

Ackerman, Felicia 1979: "Proper Names, Propositional Attitudes, and Nondescriptive Connotations". *Philosophical Studies*, 35, pp. 55–69.

Ackerman, Felicia 1989: "Content, Character, and Nondescriptive Meaning". In Almog, Perry, and Wettstein 1989, pp. 5–21.

Almog, Joseph, John Perry, and Howard Wettstein (eds) 1989: *Themes From Kaplan*. New York: Oxford University Press.

Anderson, C.A. and Michael Zeleny (eds) 2001: *Logic, Meaning, and Computation: Essays in Memory of Alonzo Church*. Boston: Kluwer.

Austin, J. L. 1950: "Truth". *Proceedings of the Aristotelian Society, Supplementary Volume*, 24, pp. 111–29. Reprinted in Blackburn and Simmons 1999, pp. 149–61.

Austin, J.L. 1975: *How to Do Things with Words*. Second edition. Cambridge, MA: Harvard University Press.

Bach, Kent and Robert Harnish 1979: *Linguistic Communication and Speech Acts*. Cambridge, MA: MIT Press.

Bar-Hillel, Yehoshua 1973: "Primary Truth Bearers". *Dialectica*, 27, pp. 303–12.

Bealer, George 1993: "A Solution to Frege's Puzzle". In Tomberlin 1993, pp. 17–60.

Bealer, George 1998: "Propositions". *Mind*, 107, pp. 1–32.

Beaney, Michael (ed) 1997: *The Frege Reader*. Oxford: Blackwell.

Belnap, Nuel 1982: "Questions and Answers in Montague Grammar". In Peters and Saarinen 1982, pp. 165–98.

Belnap, Nuel 1990: "Declaratives are Not Enough". *Philosophical Studies*, 59, pp. 1–30.

Benacerraf, Paul 1965: "What Numbers Could Not Be". *Philosophical Review*, 74, pp. 47–73.

Blackburn, Simon and Keith Simmons (eds) 1999: *Truth*. Oxford: Oxford University Press.

Boghossian, Paul 2005: "Is Meaning Normative?". In Nimtz and Beckermann 2003, pp. 205–18.

Bonjour, Laurence 1978: "Can Empirical Knowledge Have a Foundation?" *American Philosophical Quarterly*, 15, pp. 1–13.

Brandom, Robert 1983: "Asserting". *Noûs* 17, pp. 637–50.

Brandom, Robert 1994: *Making it Explicit*. Cambridge, MA: Harvard University Press.

Branquinho, João 2003: "In Defense of Obstinacy". In Hawthorne and Zimmerman 2003, pp. 1–23.

Braun, David 1993: "Empty Names". *Noûs*, 27, pp. 449–69.

Braun, David 2005: "Empty Names, Fictional Names, Mythical Names". *Noûs*, 39, pp. 596–631.

Brewer, Bill 2011: *Perception and Its Objects*. Oxford: Oxford University Press.

Brown, Jessica and Herman Cappelen (eds) 2011: *Assertion: New Philosophical Essays*. Oxford: Oxford University Press.

Bruner, Jerome, Jacqueline Goodnow, and George Austin 1956: *A Study of Thinking*. New York: Wiley.

Burge, Tyler 1974: "Truth and Singular Terms". *Noûs* 8, pp. 309–25.

Burgess, John 2005: "Translating Names". *Analysis*, 65, pp. 196–205.

Byrne, Alex 2009: "Experience and Content". *Philosophical Quarterly* 59, pp. 429–51.

Caplan, Ben 2004: "Creatures of Fiction, Myth, and Imagination". *American Philosophical Quarterly*, 41, pp. 331–7.

Caplan, Ben and Chris Tillman 2013: "Benacerraf's Revenge". *Philosophical Studies*, 166, 111–29.

Cappelen, Herman 2011: "Against Assertion". In Brown and Cappelen 2011, pp. 21–48.

Cappelen, Herman and Josh Dever 2013: *The Inessential Indexical: On the Philosophical Insignificance of Perspective and the First Person*. Oxford: Oxford University Press.

Chierchia, Gennaro, Barbara Partee, and Raymond Turner (eds) 1989: *Properties, Types and Meaning, Volume II: Semantic Issues*. Dordrecht: Kluwer.

Chisholm, Roderick 1981: *The First Person: An Essay on Reference and Intentionality*. Minneapolis: University of Minnesota Press.

Chomsky, Noam 1981: *Lectures on Government and Binding*. Dordrecht: Foris.

Church, Alonzo 1950: "On Carnap's Analysis of Statements of Assertion and Belief". *Analysis*, 10, pp. 97–9.

Collins, John 2011: *The Unity of Linguistic Meaning*. Oxford: Oxford University Press.

Corazza, Eros, William Fish, and Jonathan Gorvett 2002: "Who is I?". *Philosophical Studies*, 107, pp. 1–21.

Crimmins, Mark 1998: "Hesperus and Phosphorus: Sense, Pretense, and Reference". *Philosophical Review*, 107, pp. 1–47.

Davidson, Donald 1968: "On Saying That". *Synthese*, 19, pp. 130–46. Reprinted in Davidson 1984, pp. 93–108.

Davidson, Donald 1975: "Thought and Talk". In Guttenplan 1975, pp. 7–24. Reprinted in Davidson 1984, pp. 155–70.

Davidson, Donald 1982: "Rational Animals". *Dialectica*, 36, pp. 317–27. Reprinted in Davidson 2001, pp. 95–106.

Davidson, Donald 1984: *Inquiries into Truth and Interpretation*. Oxford: Oxford University Press.

Davidson, Donald 1989: "What is Present to the Mind?" Reprinted in Davidson 2001, pp. 53–68.

Davidson, Donald 1997: "Indeterminism and Antirealism". Reprinted in Davidson 2001, pp. 69–84.

Davidson, Donald 2001: *Subjective, Intersubjective, Objective*. Oxford: Oxford University Press.

Davidson, Donald 2005: *Truth and Predication*. Cambridge, MA: Harvard University Press.

Devitt, Michael 1974: "Singular Terms". *Journal of Philosophy*, 71, pp. 183–205.

Devitt, Michael 1981: *Designation*. New York: Columbia University Press.

Devitt, Michael 1989: "Against Direct Reference". In French, Uehling, and Wettstein 1989, pp. 206–40.

Devitt, Michael 1996: *Coming to Our Senses*. Cambridge: Cambridge University Press.

Dowty, David 1989: "On the Semantic Content of the Notion of 'Thematic Roles'". In Chierchia, Partee, and Turner 1989, pp. 69–129.

Dummett, Michael 1981: *Frege: Philosophy of Language*. Cambridge, MA: Harvard University Press.

Evans, Gareth 1973: "The Causal Theory of Names". *Proceedings of the Aristotelian Society, Supplementary Volume*, 47, pp. 187–208.

Everett, Anthony 2000: "Referentialism and Empty Names". In Everett and Hofweber 2000, pp. 37–60.

Everett, Anthony and Thomas Hofweber (eds) 2000: *Empty Names, Fiction and the Puzzles of Non-Existence*. Stanford: CSLI.

Fara, Delia Graff and Gillian Russell (eds) 2012: *The Routledge Companion to Philosophy of Language*. London: Routledge.

Feit, Neil 2008: *Belief About the Self: A Defense of the Property Theory of Content*. Oxford: Oxford University Press.

Fiengo, Robert 2007: *Asking Questions: Using Meaningful Structures to Imply Ignorance*. Oxford: Oxford University Press.

Fine, Kit 2007: *Semantic Relationalism*. Oxford: Blackwell.

Frege, Gottlob 1884: *The Foundations of Arithmetic*. In Beaney 1997, pp. 84–129.

Frege, Gottlob 1891: "Function and Concept". In Beaney 1997, pp. 130–49.

Frege, Gottlob 1892a: "On *Sinn* and *Bedeutung*". In Beaney 1997, pp. 151–71.

Frege, Gottlob 1892b: "On Concept and Object". In Beaney 1997, pp. 181–94.

Frege, Gottlob 1918a: "Thought". In Beaney 1997, pp. 325–46.

Frege, Gottlob 1918b: "Negation". In Beaney 1997, pp. 346–62.

Frege, Gottlob 1918c: "Compound Thoughts". In Frege 1984, pp. 390–406.

Frege, Gottlob 1979: *Posthumous Writings*. Edited by Hans Kermes, Friedrich Kambartel, and Friedrich Kaulbach. Translated by Peter Long and Roger White. Chicago: University of Chicago Press.

Frege, Gottlob 1980: *Philosophical and Mathematical Correspondence*. Edited by Gottfried Gabriel, Hans Kermes, Friedrich Kambartel, Christian Thiel, and Albert Veraart. Translated by Hans Kaal. Chicago: Chicago University Press.

Frege, Gottlob 1984: *Collected Papers on Mathematics, Logic, and Philosophy*. Edited by Brian McGuinness. Translated by Max Black, V.H. Dudman, Peter Geach, Hans Kaal, E.H.W. Kluge, Brian McGuinness, and R. H. Stoothoff. Oxford: Blackwell Publishers.

French, Peter, Theodore Uehling, and Howard Wettstein (eds) 1994: *Midwest Studies in Philosophy 19, Philosophical Naturalism*. South Bend: University of Notre Dame Press.

Gaskin, Richard 2008: *The Unity of the Proposition*. Oxford: Oxford University Press.

Geach, P.T. 1965: "Assertion". *The Philosophical Review*, 74, pp. 449–65. Reprinted in Geach 1972, pp. 254–69.

Geach, P.T. 1972: *Logic Matters*. Berkeley: University of California Press.

Gelman, Susan 2003: *The Essential Child*. Oxford: Oxford University Press.

Gendler, Tamar 2008: "Alief and Belief". *The Journal of Philosophy*, 105, pp. 634–63.

Gertler, Brie 2011: "Self-Knowledge and the Transparency of Belief". In Hatzimoysis 2011, pp. 125–45.

Gibson, Martha 2004: *From Naming to Saying: The Unity of the Proposition*. Oxford: Blackwell.

Ginzburg, Jonathan 1996: "Interrogatives: Questions, Facts and Dialogue". In Lappin 1996, pp. 385–422.

Ginzburg, Jonathan and Ivan Sag 2000: *Interrogative Investigations*. Stanford: CSLI.

Groenendijk, Jeroen and Martin Stokhof 1982: "Semantic Analysis of WH-Complements". *Linguistics and Philosophy*, 5, pp. 175–233.

Groenendijk, Jeroen and Martin Stokhof 1997: "Questions". In van Benthem and ter Meulen 1997, pp. 1055–1124.

Guttenplan, Samuel (ed) 1975: *Mind and Language*. Oxford: Oxford University Press.

Haaparanta, Leila and Jaakko Hintikka (eds) 1986: *Frege Synthesized*. Dordrecht: D. Reidel Publishing Company.

Haegeman, Lilianne 1994: *Introduction to Government and Binding Theory*. Second edition. Oxford: Blackwell.

Hanks, Peter 2007: "How Wittgenstein Defeated Russell's Multiple Relation Theory of Judgment". *Synthese*, 154, pp. 121–46.

Hanks, Peter 2009: "Recent Work on Propositions". *Philosophy Compass*, 4, pp. 1–18.

Hanks, Peter 2011: "Structured Propositions as Types". *Mind*, 120, pp. 11–52.

Hanks, Peter 2013a: "First-Person Propositions". *Philosophy and Phenomenological Research*, 86, pp. 155–82.

Hanks, Peter 2013b: "What are the Primary Bearers of Truth?". *Canadian Journal of Philosophy*, 43, *Special Issue: Essays on the Nature of Propositions*, David Hunter and Gurpreet Rattan (eds), pp. 558–74.

Hare, R.M. 1949: "Imperative Sentences". *Mind*, 58, pp. 21–39.

Harrah, David 1963: *Communication: A Logical Model*. Cambridge, MA: MIT Press.

Hatzimoysis, Anthony (ed) 2011: *Self-Knowledge*. Oxford: Oxford University Press.

Hawthorne, John and David Manley 2012: *The Reference Book*. Oxford: Oxford University Press.

Hawthorne, John and Dean Zimmerman (eds) 2003: *Philosophical Perspectives 17: Language and Philosophical Linguistics*. Oxford: Blackwell.

Heck, Richard and Robert May 2006: "Frege's Contribution to Philosophy of Language". In Lepore and Smith 2000, pp. 3–39.

Heck, Richard and Robert May 2011: "The Composition of Thoughts". *Noûs*, 45, pp. 126–66.

Hintikka, Jaakko 1974: "Questions about Questions". In Munitz and Unger 1974, pp. 103–58.

Hom, Christopher and Jeremy Schwartz 2013: "Unity and the Frege–Geach Problem". *Philosophical Studies*, 163, pp. 15–24.

Horn, Laurence R. 2012: "Contradiction". *The Stanford Encyclopedia of Philosophy* (Spring 2012 Edition), Edward N. Zalta (ed). <http://plato.stanford.edu/archives/spr2012/entries/contradiction/>.

Kaplan, David 1989a: "Demonstratives". In Almog, Perry, and Wettstein 1989, pp. 481–563.

Kaplan, David 1989b: "Afterthoughts". In Almog, Perry, and Wettstein 1989, pp. 565–614.

Karttunen, Lauri 1977: "Syntax and Semantics of Questions". *Linguistics and Philosophy*, 1, pp. 3–44.

Keenan, Edward 1996: "The Semantics of Determiners". In Lappin 1996, pp. 39–63.

King, Jeffrey 1994: "Can Propositions be Naturalistically Acceptable?". In French, Uehling, and Wettstein 1994, pp. 53–75.

King, Jeffrey 1995: "Structured Propositions and Complex Predicates". *Noûs*, 29, pp. 516–35.

King, Jeffrey 1996: "Structured Propositions and Sentence Structure". *Journal of Philosophical Logic*, 25, pp. 495–521.

King, Jeffrey 2002: "Designating Propositions". *The Philosophical Review*, 111, pp. 341–71.

King, Jeffrey 2007: *The Nature and Structure of Content*. Oxford: Oxford University Press.

King, Jeffrey 2009: "Questions of Unity". *Proceedings of the Aristotelian Society*, 109, pp. 257–77.

King, Jeffrey 2013. "Propositional Unity: What's the Problem, Who Has it and Who Solves it?". *Philosophical Studies*, 165, pp. 71–93.

King, Jeffrey, Scott Soames, and Jeff Speaks 2014: *New Thinking About Propositions*. Oxford: Oxford University Press.

König, Ekkehard and Peter Siemund 2007: "Speech Act Distinctions in Grammar". In Shopen 2007, pp. 276–324.

Kremer, Michael 2000: "Judgement and Truth in Frege". *Journal of the History of Philosophy*, 38, pp. 549–81.

Kripke, Saul 1973: "Vacuous Names and Fictional Entities". In Kripke 2011, pp. 52–74.

Kripke, Saul 1979: "A Puzzle About Belief". In Margalit 1979, pp. 239–83. Reprinted in Salmon and Soames 1988, pp. 102–48.

Kripke, Saul 1980: *Naming and Necessity*. Cambridge, MA: Harvard University Press.

Kripke, Saul 1982: *Wittgenstein on Rules and Private Language*. Cambridge, MA: Harvard University Press.

Kripke, Saul 2011: *Philosophical Troubles, Collected Papers, Volume I*. Oxford: Oxford University Press.

Kroon, Frederick 2000: "'Disavowal Through Commitment' Theories of Negative Existentials". In Everett and Hofweber 2000, pp. 95–116.

Lappin, Shalom (ed) 1996: *The Handbook of Contemporary Semantic Theory*. Oxford: Blackwell.

Lepore, Ernest and Barry Smith (eds) 2000: *The Oxford Handbook of Philosophy of Language*. Oxford: Oxford University Press.

Lewis, David 1969: *Convention: A Philosophical Study*. Cambridge, MA: Harvard University Press.

Lewis, David 1973: *Counterfactuals.* Cambridge, MA: Harvard University Press.

Lewis, David 1979: "Attitudes *De Dicto* and *De Se*". *The Philosophical Review*, 88, pp. 513–43. Reprinted in Lewis 1983, pp. 133–56.

Lewis, David 1983: *Philosophical Papers, Volume I*. Oxford: Oxford University Press.

MacFarlane, John 2005: "Making Sense of Relative Truth". *Proceedings of the Aristotelian Society*, 105, pp. 321–39.

MacFarlane, John 2011: "What is Assertion?". In Brown and Cappelen 2011, pp. 79–96.

Margalit, Avishai (ed) 1979: *Meaning and Use*. Dordrecht: D. Reidel.

Markie, Peter 1988: "Multiple Propositions and 'De Se' Attitudes". *Philosophy and Phenomenological Research*, 48, pp. 573–600.

Matthews, Robert 2007: *The Measure of Mind*. Oxford: Oxford University Press.

McGinn, Colin 1983: *The Subjective View: Secondary Qualities and Indexical Thoughts*. Oxford: Oxford University Press.

McGlone, Michael 2012: "Propositional Structure and Truth Conditions". *Philosophical Studies*, 157, pp. 211–25.

McGuinness, Brian 1972: "Bertrand Russell and Ludwig Wittgenstein's 'Notes on Logic'". *Revue Internationale de Philosophie*, 102, pp. 444–69.

Merricks, Trenton 2015: *Propositions*. Oxford: Oxford University Press.

Munitz, Milton and Peter Unger (eds) 1974: *Semantics and Philosophy*. New York: New York University Press.

Neale, Stephen 2004: "This, That, and the Other". In Reimer and Bezuidenhout 2004, pp. 68–181.

Nelson, Michael 2012: "Existence". *The Stanford Encyclopedia of Philosophy* (Winter 2012 Edition), Edward N. Zalta (ed). <http://plato.stanford.edu/archives/win2012/entries/existence/>.

Nimtz, Christian and Ansgar Beckermann (eds) 2005: *Philosophy—Science—Scientific Philosophy*, Main Lectures and Colloquia of GAP.5, Fifth International Congress of the Society for Analytical Philosophy. Paderborn: Mentis.

Ninan, Dilip 2010: "*De Se* Attitudes: Ascription and Communication". *Philosophy Compass*, 5, pp. 551–67.

Ostertag, Gary 2013: "Two Aspects of Propositional Unity". *Canadian Journal of Philosophy*, 43, *Special Issue: Essays on the Nature of Propositions*, David Hunter and Gurpreet Rattan (eds.), pp. 518–33.

Pagin, Peter 2008: "What is Communicative Success?". *Canadian Journal of Philosophy*, 38, pp. 85–116.

Parsons, Terence 1990: *Events in the Semantics of English: A Study in Subatomic Semantics*. Cambridge, MA: MIT Press.

Parsons, Terence 1995: "Thematic Relations and Arguments". *Linguistic Inquiry*, 26, pp. 635–62.

Perry, John 1977: "Frege on Demonstratives". *The Philosophical Review*, 86, pp. 474–97. Reprinted in Perry 1993, pp. 3–32.

Perry, John 1979: "The Problem of the Essential Indexical". *Noûs*, 13, pp. 3–21. Reprinted in Perry 1993, pp. 33–52.

Perry, John 1993: *The Problem of the Essential Indexical and Other Essays*. Oxford: Oxford University Press.

Peters, Stanley and Esa Saarinen (eds) 1982: *Processes, Beliefs, and Questions,* Dordrecht: D. Reidel, 1982.

Pincock, Christopher 2008: "Russell's Last (and Best) Multiple Relation Theory of Judgement". *Mind,* 117, pp. 107–40.

Pinillos, N. Ángel 2011: "Coreference and Meaning," *Philosophical Studies,* 154, pp. 301–24.

Pustejovsky, James 1995: *The Generative Lexicon.* Cambridge, MA: MIT Press.

Quine, W.V.O. 1969a: "Natural Kinds". In Quine 1969b, pp. 114–38.

Quine, W.V.O. 1969b: *Ontological Relativity and Other Essays.* New York: Columbia University Press.

Recanati, François 1987: *Meaning and Force: The Pragmatics of Performative Utterances.* Cambridge: Cambridge University Press.

Recanati, François 2004: *Literal Meaning.* Cambridge: Cambridge University Press.

Recanati, François 2012: *Mental Files.* Oxford: Oxford University Press.

Recanati, François 2013: "Content, Mood, and Force". *Philosophy Compass,* 8/7, pp. 622–32.

Reiland, Indrek 2013: "Propositional Attitudes and Mental Acts". *Thought,* 1, pp. 239–45.

Reimer, Marga and Anne Bezuidenhout (eds.) 2004: *Descriptions and Beyond.* Oxford: Oxford University Press.

Ricketts, Thomas 1986: "Objectivity and Objecthood: Frege's Metaphysics of Judgment". In Haaparanta and Hintikka 1986, pp. 65–95.

Russell, Bertrand 1903: *Principles of Mathematics.* New York: Norton.

Russell, Bertrand 1904: "Meinong's Theory of Complexes and Assumptions (III)" *Mind,* 13, pp. 509–24.

Russell, Bertrand 1906: "On the Nature of Truth". *Proceedings of the Aristotelian Society,* 7, pp. 28–49.

Russell, Bertrand 1910: "On the Nature of Truth and Falsehood". In *Philosophical Essays.* New York: Simon and Schuster, pp. 147–59.

Russell, Bertrand 1912: *The Problems of Philosophy.* Oxford: Oxford University Press.

Russell, Bertrand 1913: *Theory of Knowledge, The Collected Papers of Bertrand Russell, Volume 7.* Edited by Elizabeth Eames. London: George Allen & Unwin.

Russell, Bertrand 1918: *The Philosophy of Logical Atomism.* La Salle: Open Court.

Sainsbury, Robert 2005: *Reference without Referents.* Oxford: Oxford University Press.

Salmon, Nathan 1981: *Reference and Essence.* Princeton: Princeton University Press.

Salmon, Nathan 1986: *Frege's Puzzle.* Cambridge, MA: MIT Press.

Salmon, Nathan 1998. "Nonexistence". *Noûs* 32, pp. 277–319.

Salmon, Nathan 2001: "The Very Possibility of Language: A Sermon on the Consequences of Missing Church". In Anderson and Zeleny 2001, pp. 573–95.

Salmon, Nathan and Scott Soames (eds) 1988: *Propositions and Attitudes*. Oxford: Oxford University Press.

Schiffer, Stephen 2003: *The Things We Mean*. Oxford: Oxford University Press.

Schwitzgebel, Eric 2010: "Acting Contrary to Our Professed Beliefs or the Gulf Between Occurrent Judgment and Dispositional Belief". *Pacific Philosophical Quarterly*, 91, pp. 531–53.

Searle, John 1968: "Austin on Locutionary and Illocutionary Acts". *The Philosophical Review*, 77, pp. 405–24.

Searle, John 1969: *Speech Acts*. Cambridge: Cambridge University Press.

Searle, John 1979: *Expression and Meaning*. Cambridge: Cambridge University Press.

Searle, John 2008a: "The Unity of the Proposition". In Searle 2008b, pp.181–96.

Searle, John 2008b: *Philosophy in a New Century: Selected Essays*. Cambridge: Cambridge University Press.

Shopen, Timothy (ed) 2007: *Language Typology and Syntactic Description, Volume I, Clause Structure*. Second edition. Cambridge: Cambridge University Press.

Siegel, Susanna 2010: *The Contents of Visual Experience*. Oxford: Oxford University Press.

Smith, Edward 1995: "Concepts and Categories". In Smith and Osherson 1995, pp. 3–33.

Smith, Edward and Daniel Osherson (eds) 1995: *Thinking*. Cambridge, MA: MIT Press.

Soames, Scott 2002: *Beyond Rigidity*. Oxford: Oxford University Press.

Soames, Scott 2010: *What is Meaning?*. Princeton: Princeton University Press.

Soames, Scott 2012: "Propositions". In Fara and Russell 2012, pp. 209–20.

Soames, Scott forthcoming: *Rethinking Language, Mind, and Meaning*. Princeton: Princeton University Press.

Sommers, Fred 2009: "Dissonant Beliefs". *Analysis*, 69, pp. 267–74.

Stalnaker, Robert 1987: *Inquiry*. Cambridge, MA: MIT Press.

Stalnaker, Robert 1999: *Context and Content*. Oxford: Oxford University Press.

Stanley, Jason 2005: "Review of François Recanati's *Literal Meaning*". *Notre Dame Philosophical Reviews*. September 2005.

Stevens, Graham 2009: "Utterance at a Distance". *Philosophical Studies*, 143, pp. 213–21.

Strawson, P.F. 1950: "Truth". *Proceedings of the Aristotelian Society, Supplementary Volume*, 24, pp. 129–56. Reprinted in Blackburn and Simmons 1999, pp. 162–182.

Textor, Mark 2010: "Frege on Judging as Acknowledging the Truth". *Mind*, 119, pp. 615–55.

Thomasson, Amie 1999: *Fiction and Metaphysics*. Cambridge: Cambridge University Press.

Tomberlin, James (ed) 1993: *Philosophical Perspectives 7: Logic and Language*. Atascadero: Ridgeview.

Tomberlin, James (ed) 2001: *Philosophical Perspectives 15: Metaphysics*. London: Blackwell.

Turner, Jason 2010: "Fitting Attitudes *De Dicto* and *De Se*". *Noûs*, 44, pp. 1–9.

Van Benthem, Johann and Alice ter Meulen (eds) 1997: *Handbook of Logic and Language*, Cambridge, MA: MIT Press.

Van Inwagen, Peter 1977: "Creatures of Fiction". *American Philosophical Quarterly*, 14, pp. 299–308.

Williamson, Timothy 1996: "Knowing and Asserting". *The Philosophical Review*, 105, pp. 489–523.

Wittgenstein, Ludwig 1913: "Notes on Logic". In Wittgenstein 1979, pp. 93–107.

Wittgenstein, Ludwig 1961a: *Tractatus Logico-Philosophicus*. Translated by David Pears and Brian McGuinness. London: Routledge.

Wittgenstein, Ludwig 1961b. *Notebooks 1914–16*: First edition. Translated by G.E.M. Anscombe. New York: Harper.

Wittgenstein, Ludwig 1975: *Philosophical Remarks*. Chicago: University of Chicago Press.

Wittgenstein, Ludwig 1979: *Notebooks 1914–16*. Second edition. Translated by G.E.M. Anscombe. Chicago: University of Chicago Press.

Wittgenstein, Ludwig 1995: *Ludwig Wittgenstein: Cambridge Letters*. Oxford: Blackwell.

Wollheim, Richard 1980: *Art and Its Objects*. Second edition. Cambridge: Cambridge University Press.

Wright, Crispin 2001: *Rails to Infinity: Essays on Themes from Wittgenstein's Philosophical Investigations*. Cambridge, MA: Harvard University Press.

Wynne, Clive 2004: *Do Animals Think?* Princeton: Princeton University Press.

Yagisawa, Takashi 2001: "Against Creationism in Fiction". In Tomberlin 2001, pp. 153–172.

Index

A

A-propositions 62
 truth conditions 62
Ackerman, Felicia 127
act/content distinction 26, 69, 71–2
act/product distinction 71–2
'actually*' operator (Soames) 146
adicity, concept of 49
admiration 84–6
AND 106–7
AND-D 107–8
answer-hood conditions 24, 186
anti-predication 102, 166–8, 193, 198
Aristotle 114–16, 121
ascription 56–61
asking 15, 20, 23–6, 24, 31, 46, 109–10,
 165, 186–204
assertions 12, 14, 17–20, 18n.1, 28–9,
 28n.5, 32, 34–5, 39, 42, 64, 70–1,
 70n.7, 79, 90–5, 98, 110–11, 161,
 170, 205–6
 truth conditions 44, 46, 61, 64, 68
Austin, George 64
Austin, J. L. 95–7

B

B-propositions 62
 truth conditions 62
Bach, Kent 95
Bar-Hillel, Yehoshua 67, 71
Bealer, George 44, 45n.2
belief 1, 164–6, 169
Belnap, Nuel 189, 189n.2, 196n.3
Benacerraf, Paul 85, 85n.12
Benacerraf problem 85, 85n.12
Bigfoot/Sasquatch example 131n.1
bilingual competence (Burgess) 128
Boghossian, Paul 66
Bonjour, Laurence 62–3
Brandom, Robert 18
Branquinho, João 145, 145n.10
Braun, David 144, 147, 147n.4
Brewer, Bill 210, 210n.1
Brigham, Daniel 121n.9

Bruner, Jerome 64
Burge, Tyler 135, 135n.5
Burgess, John 128
Byrne, Alex 210–11

C

cancellation 35
 actor 92–5
 chess analogy 32
 contexts 28, 90–8
 football analogy 94–5
Caplan, Ben 85n.12, 147, 147n.4
Cappelen, Herman 95
Carnap, Rudolf 143
categorization 64–5
Chisholm, Roderick 179n.6
Chomsky, Noam 195
Church, Alonzo 143–4
co-referential empty names 131
coercion 167, 167n.8
combination
 imperative mode of 24–6
 interrogative mode of 24, 26
commands 19
communication 179–82
complement clauses 5, 30–1
CONJ 105
conjunction 103–8
constitutive accounts 210–11
content–force distinction 9–10, 18–19,
 34–5, 34nn.6–7, 98, 112, 200, 204
 constitutive version 9, 19, 26, 90–2,
 104–5, 108
 taxonomic version 9, 19, 26, 90
contextualism 125
Corazza, Eros 178n.5
Cornwell, David John Moore 119, 121,
 126–7, 153–6, 160
Costello, H. T. 162–3n.5
Crimmins, Mark 142

D

Davidson, Donald 17, 138
de jure co-reference 124

de se assertions 183–4
de se beliefs 11, 170, 175–6, 179, 183–4
de se contexts 183
De Se reference 175–80, 185
De Se reports 182–5
 see also propositional attitude reports
declarations 199–204, 201n.7
demonstratives 11, 171
denial 166–70
denotation acts 114–15
Desdemona/Cassio example 81–2
Devitt, Michael 127
DISJ 105–6
disjunction 103–8
'dominant source' (Evans) 115
Dowty, David 86, 86n.13
Dr. Lauben/Leo Peter example 179–80
Dummett, Michael 14, 93, 95, 97, 110
Dürer's engraving of St. Anthony
 example 74–5

E
entertainment concept 14–18, 21, 33–6,
 40–1, 60–1, 97, 109–10, 170,
 180, 209
 yes–no questions 9, 16
evaluative properties 75–6
Evans, Gareth 115
Everett, Anthony 133, 133n.2
EVERY 88–9
existence 140–3, 141n.8, 146–8
expression 17–18, 23, 25–6, 32, 77, 87–8,
 100–3, 190, 206–7
expressives 202–3

F
falsity 13, 53, 67–9, 76
Fiengo, Robert 196n.5
first-order logic 192
first-relatum/second-relatum role 81–2
Fish, William 178n.5
Frege, Gottlob 3–4, 8–11, 9n.2, 12–19,
 27–8, 33–5, 48, 48n.4, 113–14, 118,
 120, 139–40, 170, 179–80, 205
Frege–Russell picture *see* Fregean
 picture
Fregean picture 12–20, 19–20, 25, 25n.3,
 28, 30, 32, 33–6, 40–1, 42–4, 46–7,
 51–2, 54–5, 59, 63–4, 91–3, 95,
 95–6n.3, 98, 108–9, 140–2, 170, 180,
 205–7, 209–10

Fregean picture alternative 20–32
function 49–50, 189–90

G
gas example 46
Geach, P. T. 91–2
Gelman, Susan 64–5
Gendler, Tamar 164, 164n.6
Gertler, Brie 164, 164n.6
gerundive clauses 203
Ginzburg, Jonathan 191
Goodnow, Jacqueline 64
Gorvett, Jonathan 178n.5
grasping concept 3, 10, 14–15, 170,
 180, 191
Groenendijk, Jeroen 19, 191–2, 194,
 196n.4

H
Haegeman, Lilianne 203
Hare, R. M. 187
Harnish, Robert 95
Harrah, David 189n.2
Hawthorne, John 123
Heck, Richard 50n.5
Heimson and Hume example 176

I
I 176–8
identity puzzle (Frege) 125–8
illocutionary/locutionary acts 95–7,
 95–6n.3
imperative mode of combination 24–6
indexicals 5, 8, 11, 118, 170–1, 174–5,
 205
indicative conditionals 108
indirect contexts (Frege) 137–8
interpretivist approach 62–3,
interrogative mode of combination 24, 26

J
judgments 1–8, 7–8, 12–17, 20–1, 29,
 34–6, 39–41, 42, 44, 46, 64, 79, 81–5,
 90, 110, 161–5, 170, 199, 205–11
 truth conditions 3, 13, 34–5, 44–6,
 61–2, 64, 97–8
Juliet example 165, 165n.7

K
Kaplan, David 145, 145n.10, 171, 179n.6
Karttunen, Lauri 191–2

Keenan, Edward 87
King, Jeffrey 42, 55–63, 55n.9, 59n.10,
    60n.11, 67–9
Kripke, Saul 11, 115, 115–16n.2, 120–5,
    141, 147–8, 147n.4, 207
Kroon, Fred 143
Kuster, Justin 94n.1

L
Le Carré, John 119–21, 126–7, 126n.11,
    153–6, 160
locutionary/illocutionary acts 95–7,
    95–6n.3
logical assertion (Russell) 53–4n.7
London/Londres example 143–6, 158

M
MacFarlane, John 18, 67–9
McGinn, Colin 179n.6
McGlone, Michael 44
McGuinness, Brian 162–3n.5
Manley, David 123
Markie, Peter 176
Mason, Michelle 71n.8
material properties 73–6
May, Robert 50n.5
measurement sentences 6–7
Meinongianism 52, 140
Merricks, Trenton 44
Mill, John Stuart 8–9, 113–14, 135
model-theoretic semantics 191
multiple relation theory of judgment
    (Russell) 52, 52n.6, 82, 161–3,
    162–3n.5
Murez, Michael 121n.9

N
n-tuples (Kaplan) 171, 171n.2
'Nadelhorn' 121–2
names
    descriptivist theory of 140
    empty 131–48, 131n.1
    and translation 128–30
negation 100, 103, 105, 163
negative existentials 8, 11, 131, 137–8,
    143–4
Negative Free Logic 135, 135n.5, 141,
    141n.8
Nelson, Michael 140
Ninan, Dilip 184, 184n.7
non-repeatability 170, 175

NOT 101
NOT-TRUE 100

O
object dependent types 116–17,
    116n.7, 193
object-and-name dependent reference
    types 117, 117n.5, 120
OR 107
OR-D 107–8
ordered sets 54
ordering 23–5, 25n.3, 31, 165–6, 186–204
Ostertag, Gary 46, 46–7n.3, 84, 84n.11
oxygen example 109–10

P
Pagin, Peter 180
Paderewski example (Kripke) 8, 120–5,
    120n.8, 156–60, 157–8n.4, 173n.3
Pagin, Peter 180
Parsons, Terence 68n.5
perceptual experience 210–11
Perry, John 175, 179n.6
Perry's *Enterprise* example 171–8, 183–4
Peter (Kripke) 120–1, 120n.8, 123–4,
    126, 157–60
Philby, Kim 119–20, 119n.7, 153–6
Pincock, Christopher 83
predication 4, 21–5, 23n.2, 25n.3, 28,
    34–8, 61, 66, 163
    acts of 64–73, 66n.2–3, 69n.6, 74–6,
        80, 83–6, 87, 94–8, 110, 135, 135n.5,
        193, 198, 206–7, 211
    anti- 102, 166–8, 193, 198
    behavioral acts of 65
    cancelled 32–3, 36, 39–40, 90–112,
        99n.4, 152
    existence 141–2
    linguistic acts of 65, 207–8
    mental acts of 207–9
    neutral 35–6, 40, 60
    second-order 87–9, 89n.15, 100
    sorted 85
    target-shifted 100, 105, 135–8, 149–52
    token acts of 36–9, 73–7, 173
    unsorted 85
primitive 43–7
Principles of Mathematics (Russell) 51,
    53–4n.7
Problems of Philosophy, The (Russell) 82
proper names 113–30, 170

propositional attitude relations 161–6
propositional attitude reports 32,
 149–69, 197–9
 see also De Se reports
propositions 1–3, 13–14, 20, 26–31,
 27n.4, 33–5, 72–3, 78–9, 78–9n.10,
 91, 110, 201, 205–6, 209–11
 anti-predicative 186
 assertive 9, 98
 compound 32
 first-person 170–85
 imperative 9, 15, 19, 186, 195
 interrogative 9, 168, 186, 191–2, 198
 monadic properties of 53
 predicative 168–9, 186, 194
 quantified 32, 86–90
 relational 32, 44, 80–7
 true/false 51–2, 54, 67
 truth conditions 3–4, 13, 28, 34–5,
 42–6, 51, 55–6, 58–63, 64, 79–80, 192
 unity problem 42–63, 42n.1
proto-intentional states 62–3

Q
quantification 87, 103, 107, 194
questions
 choice 196, 196n.3
 mention-all 196, 196n.3
 open and confirmation 196, 196n.5
 wh- 189–94
Quine, W. V. O. 65

R
R relation
 definition 118, 133
 ideal conditions 120–2
 R′ 133
 R* 171
 transitivity 129–30
Recanati, François 95, 95–6n.3, 124n.10
reference acts 113–20, 133, 135, 137–40,
 139n.6
 context sensitive 171–5, 173n.3
rigidity 113–6
rocks example 53
Russell, Bertrand 4, 12, 17, 33, 42, 51–5,
 81–3, 139–43

S
Sainsbury, Robert 135n.5

Salmon, Nathan 126, 143, 143n.9, 145,
 145n.10, 147, 147n.4
saturated/unsaturated
 distinction 48–51, 50n.5
saturation 49–51
Schiffer, Stephen 44
Schwitzgebel, Eric 164–5, 164n.6
Searle, John 67n.4, 95, 95n.2, 147,
 147n.4, 195, 199–204
second-relatum/first-relatum
 role 81–2
semantic competence 77, 118, 122
 names 122–5, 127
semantic innocence principle
 (Davidson) 138, 151
semantic reference types 8–9, 77–9,
 116–20, 121–5, 126–8, 129–30,
 131–5, 170, 174, 178–9, 183
semantic values 57
sense concept 180–1
senses
 name 49
 predicate 49
sentences
 non-finite clause 31
 that-clause 31
 truth conditions 56–7, 59
 whether-clause 31
sentential moods
 declarative 31
 imperative 31
 interrogative 31
 linguistic universal 196n.6
Siegel, Susanna 210, 210n.1
Smith, Edward 64
Soame's picture 33–41, 34n.6, 36n.8,
 37n.9, 59–61
Soames, Scott 12, 22, 38, 146–7, 147n.4
Sommers, Fred 164, 164n.6
sorting 22–3
Speaks, Jeff 54, 54n.8
speech acts 1–9, 11, 19, 24, 29–31, 44,
 46–7, 79, 90, 196–7
 alternative taxonomy 201–2
 interrogative 202
 non-propositional 201–2, 204
 propositional 201–2, 204
Stalnaker, Robert 6, 18, 46–7n.3
standard/super-standard
 contexts 152–5

Stevens, Graham 178n.5
Stokhof, Martin 19, 191–2, 194, 196n.4
Strawson, P. F. 66–7, 67n.4
sub-standard contexts 156–60
subsentential expressions 5
super-standard/standard
    contexts 152–5
Superman/Clark Kent example 132–4,
    133n.2
supposition 108–12
swimming example 56–60
syntactic relations 57–8, 124

T
T, property of 54
Taylor, David 111n.7
that-clauses 150–2
thematic roles 86–7, 86nn.13–14
Theory of Knowledge (Russell) 82
theory of propositions (Russell) 52
theory of propositions (Speaks) 54
Thomasson, Amie 147, 147n.4
thought 15, 49
    composition of 47–51
    truth conditions 49, 51
Tillman, Chris 85n.12
token/type distinction 69, 72, 180, 185,
    198–9
TRUE 99
truth 12–13, 16–19, 34, 39, 53, 68–9,
    76, 162–3
truth conditions 24, 26, 35, 37–8, 50–1,
    66–8, 71, 75–6, 100, 109, 115–16,
    186, 198, 207
    A-propositions 62

B-propositions 62
    judgments 3, 13, 34–5, 44–6, 61–2,
        64, 97–8
truth, correspondence theory of 53
truth-evaluable 36, 40, 61, 137, 201,
    201n.7
types 29–30

U
Union Jack example 74, 74n.9
unsaturated/saturated
    distinction 48–51, 50n.5

V
Van Inwagen, Peter 147, 147n.4

W
wasp example 65–6, 65–6n.1
wh-clauses 196, 196n.6
wh-expressions 11, 194
wh-interrogatives 32
Williamson, Timothy 18
Wittgenstein, Ludwig 2, 11, 161–3,
    162–3n.5, 206–7
Wollheim, Richard 74
wondering 24
Wright, Crispin 207

Y
Yagisawa, Takashi 147, 147n.4

Z
Zeus/Jupiter example 131–45, 133n.2,
    134n.3, 135n.4, 139n.7, 141n.8,
    147–8

Printed and bound by CPI Group (UK) Ltd, Croydon, CR0 4YY